MATCH 'EM UP! WIN BIG LAUGHS!

The Subject:
GOSSIPY WOMEN
WORK
CHILDREN
ROLLER SKATES
PARIS
BELUSHI

The Comment:
"If it's supposed to be so good for you, how come they have to pay you to do it?"

"Nasty little creatures who try to make life miserable for adults and one another."

"Ladies, please try to act like gentlemen!"

"If God wanted them out in the middle of the streets, He would have equipped their bodies with piston engines and a gas cap."

"Life isn't always fair. But it shouldn't cheat that much."

"I never go. You can't get real Velveeta from those barbarians."

MIKE ROYKO
LIKE I WAS
SAYIN'...

A JOVE BOOK

The columns in this book first appeared, in slightly different
form and often with different titles, in the *Chicago Daily News,*
the *Chicago Sun-Times,* or the *Chicago Tribune.*

This Jove book contains the complete
text of the original hardcover edition.
It has been completely reset in a typeface
designed for easy reading and was printed
from new film.

LIKE I WAS SAYIN' . . .

A Jove Book / published by arrangement with
E. P. Dutton, Inc.

PRINTING HISTORY
E. P. Dutton edition published 1984
Jove edition / December 1985
Second printing / March 1986

ISBN: 0-515-08416-6

Jove Books are published by The Berkley Publishing Group,
200 Madison Avenue, New York, N.Y. 10016.
The words "A JOVE BOOK" and the "J" with sunburst
are trademarks belonging to Jove Publications, Inc.

PRINTED IN THE UNITED STATES OF AMERICA

To Steve and Amy

Contents

II. 1979–1981, THE SUN-TIMES

III.   1981–1983, THE SUN-TIMES

IV. 1984 – , THE TRIBUNE

I.

1966–1977, THE DAILY NEWS

One Fan's Glory Romp

September 20, 1966

My favorite modern folk hero is the fan who runs on the field during the big game. He is even more wonderful than the dog that runs on the field during the big game.

Sometimes he just lopes around the bases, sliding into home plate. Sometimes he tries to hug Mickey Mantle. Sometimes he tries to punch a referee.

The cops always drag him away and the TV announcer makes some smart crack, like: "Well, that's the end of his game, ha, ha."

But nobody ever asks these wonderful free spirits who they are or why they must do it.

Last Friday, a skinny youth ran on the field during the tense final minutes of the Bears-Rams game in Los Angeles.

While more than 50,000 fans cheered and 8,000,000 people watched on TV, the youth sped down the field, his head held high, the wind in his face.

Then Mike Ditka stepped from the huddle and slammed him. The fans booed Ditka, but that was wrong. Ditka has been trained since high school to knock down anything that moves.

The young man flew in the air. He was limp when he landed and shaky when the police led him away.

More people saw that kid knocked down than saw all of Joe Louis' fights.

When the game is forgotten, that kid will be remembered.

This is a nation of people who are always asking each other questions. Where were you till 3 A.M.? Why did you go through a red light? How will you vote in November? Did you like your mother when you were three? What's up?

But nobody bothered to ask the young man who he was or why he did this daring thing: They just kicked him out of the stadium.

Well, let it be known that he is Felix Carbajal, nineteen, of Lomita, California. He is of Mexican ancestry and he is a laborer in a chemical factory.

He was sleeping when I called, having worked the Sunday night shift. His father, who has a broad accent, said he didn't know about what his son had done.

"I didn't even know he played football," Felix senior said.

Felix's mother said: "I know about it. I guess it was something he felt he had to do. Wait, I'll wake him up."

"Hello?"

Felix, I'm a reporter. Why did you do it?

"Gee. You're the first one to ask me that. The neighbors don't even know I did it."

Why did you do it?

"Somebody had to. Somebody does it nearly every game. So I figured I would do it. Me and my pal, Mike. He has relatives in Chicago and he was hoping they would see him."

What happened to Mike?

"I dunno, I guess he just sat there."

How did it feel?

"At first it felt weird. I thought: 'Gee, what am I doing?' Then when those thousands of people started cheering me, it felt pretty good.

"I was moving along pretty good. I thought I'd go all the way from one end zone to another. Those cops weren't even gaining on me.

"When I went by the Ram huddle, the players turned and looked at me and some of them smiled. I guess they were happy because they were winning.

"Just as I was getting to the Bears' huddle, one of the cops threw a nightstick. That's when I made my mistake. I turned my head to look at the nightstick and Ditka hit me with a blind-side block."

Did he punch you?

"No. If he had punched me, he would have killed me. I'm only 145 pounds. He just bumped me with his shoulder in my face."

Did it hurt?

"Yes. My nose still hurts. And my head. But he didn't knock me out. Just down."

Ditka says he is sorry.

"I'm not mad at him. I guess it was something he had to do. Just like me running."

Do you regret it?

"It was a good experience."

Will you do it again?

"I don't know. I'll have to give it some thought. Would you do me a favor?"

What?

"If you write something, would you send me a copy of the paper? I'm a glory hound at heart."

A Little Guy Wins a Skirmish

May 1, 1969

With protest movements getting more violent, raucous, and direct, it was refreshing to hear of the subtle methods used by Fred Branch.

Branch, an office manager, lives near a National Guard armory. Every Sunday, the guardsmen come to train and, because parking space is scarce, they park their cars on the sidewalks.

Branch couldn't walk on his sidewalk. His kids couldn't play on the sidewalk. This bugged him.

He called the police, but nothing changed. He called the National Guard, but nothing changed.

As any Joe College can tell you, when institutions become unresponsive the only alternative is to seek a confrontation and obtain meaningful concessions. But Branch knew he wouldn't have a chance if he tried to seize and occupy the armory and demand that the National Guard give in.

On a recent Sunday, Branch tried a different approach.

He got a clipboard and his Brownie camera, went outside and began writing down license numbers and photographing cars.

A guardsman spotted him and walked over.

"What are you doing?"

"That is my business," said Branch, mysteriously.

The guardsman went back to the armory. In a little while a police car showed up.

The policeman asked him what he was doing.

"That is my business," said Branch.

They took him into the squad car and asked more questions.

But Branch affected a stone face and the police gave up. There's no law against writing down license numbers or taking pictures of cars.

The following Sunday, Branch showed up again with his clipboard and camera.

Again a guardsman came over and asked: "What are you doing that for?"

"That is my business," said Branch.

The guardsman left but returned in a few minutes.

"The major wants to see you," he said.

"Where is the major?" Branch asked.

"In his office."

"Well, if he wants to see me, tell him I am right here."

The guardsman went back to the armory. In a few minutes the major appeared, followed by six other guardsmen.

"What are you doing that for?" the major asked.

"That is my business," said Branch, clicking his camera at cars.

The major pondered while Branch clicked and the enlisted men stood ready.

Finally he told Branch that he was also a policeman and, as a policeman, wanted to know what Branch was up to.

"That is my business," said Branch, busily scribbling license numbers.

"Do you want me to put you under arrest?"

"If that is your bag," said Branch, "OK."

A police car was going by so the major darted into the street and waved his arms. The police car slammed on its brakes.

Another car slammed into the rear of the police car.

The motorist and the policemen got out and glared at the damage, which was not minor.

The major tried to tell the policemen about Branch and the camera and clipboard, but the policemen waved their arms and stomped around their damaged vehicle.

Three more squad cars showed up to help the policemen with the damaged car and make out all the reports.

Branch stopped scribbling and clicking. He leaned against a building and laughed until his sides ached.

This angered the major and he tried to take Branch's clipboard from him. Branch jumped into a telephone booth and phoned a friend.

The major opened the door and asked him who he was phoning.

"That's my business," Branch said.

The major snatched the clipboard, pulled the license numbers off of it, and stomped back to the armory with his men.

In a few minutes, Branch's friend showed up. He is State Senator Richard Newhouse, a Democrat, who also lives in the neighborhood.

Together they went to the armory to demand Branch's list of license numbers.

They were met by the major's commander, Lt. Col. Earl Strayhorn. He is also a Democratic politician and vice president of the Sanitary District.

Strayhorn called the major in. They had a meaningful dialog. Then Strayhorn told the major to give Branch his piece of paper, and said he would issue an order that guardsmen can't park on Branch's side of the street any more.

Branch took his Brownie camera and his clipboard and went home, victorious, to watch a ball game.

Riverview Park:
A Coward's Tale

October 13, 1969

It was the red badge of courage, the moment of truth. It was put up or shut up.

There could be no conscientious objection—no draft card burning—when you faced the Parachute in Riverview Park.

This was it. You had what it took or you didn't.

And for those who didn't, the chance is gone forever. They will have to live with the knowledge that they couldn't do it.

Oh, you can say: "But I rode the Bobs, and the Bobs was really something."

I once rode the Bobs eight times without getting off.

Sure, it was rough, that first dip, and it took extraordinary courage.

But it wasn't the Parachute.

You couldn't see the Bobs from miles away. It didn't rise into the sky, warning you that soon you must look deep into your soul to see what, if anything, was there.

I'd start thinking about the Parachute even before I left the neighborhood. That's a lie. I thought about it the night before. Sometimes I'd pace the floor. That's what got me smoking at the age of twelve.

When we walked through the front gate, I'd try to stall. One of my tricks was to ride every ride. Sometimes, if I had the money, I'd ride them twice, or more.

I was the only kid in the neighborhood who rode the Tunnel of Love seven times straight—alone.

One time I stayed in the freak house so long that Slats Grobnik told everybody I had a crush on the reptile girl.

There used to be a thing called "The African Dip." You threw balls and if you hit the target a Negro fell from his perch into the water. They got rid of the thing when Negroes learned how to throw things back. But to delay the Parachute confrontation, I once knocked the same guy in the water twenty-three times. The effect of that on my youthful conscience contributed to my liberal tendencies, I'm sure.

My Parachute fears caused me to have my weight guessed by the same man four times. And he was right the first time.

Actually, that's the reason I stayed on the Bobs for eight straight rides. If Slats Grobnik hadn't got sick to his stomach, I'd still be on the Bobs, trying to duck the Parachute.

Then, finally, I'd be standing there. They would have to drag me away from the monkey races, off the merry-go-round, out of the Flying Turns. I'd ride the Shoot the Chutes so often that my clothes would be soaked.

And there it would be—fourteen miles high, the top of it up in the clouds. My mouth would hang open, my eyes would pop, and the only thing that would keep me from running was a temporary paralysis of the body.

But my nimble mind would be working.

ME: "I'm out of money."

SLATS: "I'll borrow you some."

ME: "I can't never pay you back."

SLATS: "I don't care."

ME: "I hear that thing is ready to keel over."

CHESTER: "No it ain't."

ME: "My foot hurts."

NORBERT: "You're chicken."

ME: "I rode that thing before with some other guys."

BIG RED: "Then you can ride it now with us."

ME: "No."

ALL: "You're chicken."

ME: Silence.

After that, even the darkness of Aladdin's Castle wasn't enough to hide the mocking smiles. Even looking bored on the Silver Streak couldn't remove the stain of cowardice.

On the way home, I'd be last on the crowded streetcar so I could stand on the platform step, dangling by one arm and a toe, hoping to regain some face.

Much later, I discovered the secret of riding the Parachute: Go there with a girl.

A boy has to suggest the Parachute to prove he is a dashing fellow. A girl has to say yes to prove she is a good sport. I'm told they still have this sort of arrangement, except now it is sex instead of the Parachute.

So I went there with a girl. We went to the Parachute. I bought two tickets. We got in line and waited. I looked cool. Our turn finally came and we walked toward the empty, dangling seats.

Then she screamed.

I can't really blame her for screaming, what with me falling over in a dead faint even before we got on.

So that's as close as I came. I've been back almost every summer to give it another try. But something always comes up. I run out of money, I have a sore foot, I'm chicken.

And now Riverview is closed forever. The Parachute gone, along with the old ladies who were experts at spotting counterfeit money and shortchanging people, the Bobs, the dumpy old beer garden and the rest.

Now I won't get another chance. But I know down deep that I would have made it.

It was just a matter of getting into the right frame of mind. I'm positive it would have been next summer.

I wish I could have another chance.

Never Ruffle a Virgo!

January 8, 1970

I sat down in a restaurant to have lunch, and there it was again.

On the place mat were printed those generalized horoscopes, the kind that reveals your personality and character traits.

I tried to avoid looking at it, because I knew what mine would say. They're always the same.

Finally I looked:

"You have a logical, analytical and precise mind, which causes you to hate disorder. You must guard against being cold, unemotional, and fault-finding."

That's the burden of being born between August 24 and September 23, a Virgo. Even if you are muddled, sloppy, sweet-tempered, compassionate, gentle, and kind—as I am—you are constantly told by the horoscopes that you are a cold-eyed, precise, logical nitpicker.

Not that I believe this nonsense. Logic tells me it is meaningless.

But it is irritating to be followed through life by it.

Had I been born a few weeks earlier, my horoscope on that place mat would have said I was a "born leader, bold, energetic, proud, and ambitious."

Almost any other sign is better than Virgo. Take Aquarius: "A trail-blazing mind . . . inventive . . . progressive . . . fair-minded, and tolerant."

Or Aries: "The pioneer type, with contempt for all difficulties and danger."

A few weeks' delay in birth and I would have read:

"Your shrewd business capacity would guide you to the very pinnacle of success. The magnetic personality which you possess has great glamor for the opposite sex."

All of it is silly, of course, but at least it would have been a bit more flattering. And accurate.

While sitting in the restaurant, I decided to conduct an experiment. I would ask the busboy, waitress, manager, and cook for their birth dates. We'd see how accurate the horoscope was.

The busboy came to the table, but before I could ask him his birth date, I noticed a speck on my fork, so I sent him off for a clean one, warning him against such slovenliness.

He mumbled something about the dishwasher, but I pointed out that he, as the bearer of the fork, bore the final responsibility for its condition. That had hardly been said when he put down the water glass hard, splashing the tablecloth, which I asked to be replaced.

The waitress came for my order. I had to repeat it twice. Then I had to send my drink back, because it had an olive instead of a twist of lemon.

I decided not to ask for her birth date because she probably wouldn't remember it. Besides, she was busy returning my food to the kitchen. It was underdone.

The owner, a woman, came out and asked what was wrong. Nothing was wrong, I told her, except that the entire meal had been miserably bungled.

She began to weep and talk about her problems as a widow, trying to run a business. I told her there was no need to get emotional about it. As an adult, she should be able to discuss her inadequacies rationally.

An example, I pointed out, was the salt shaker. Four of its eleven tiny holes were clogged. The ashtray contained an ash from a previous customer's cigar. And the salad had been placed on the wrong side.

I suggested that she study methods used by other, more efficient restaurants, and adapt them when applicable. Also, fire the cook.

The cook was her brother-in-law, she said, and desperately needed the job. I warned her against mixing sentiment with business but that, if she persisted in employing him, she could cut costs by lowering his pay.

Finally, I suggested she get rid of those place mats. She asked why, and I told her that I had come there to eat, not to be told I was unemotional, cold, fault-finding, and so on.

That was an insult, I added, and therefore my tip would be precisely ten percent, rather than the normal fifteen percent, or the more generous twenty percent.

With that, I departed. I never did get her birth date. She seemed to be upset, and was taking a tranquilizer. My final words were a warning to avoid getting emotional. And to turn down the music. It was much too loud.

A Nut to Pick with Mr. Nader

February 27, 1970

The consumer's revolt finally caught up with me last night and made me realize how it feels to be victimized by a shoddy, dishonest product.

Surprisingly, it didn't happen in the usual way.

From what I've read, the biggest single cause of the consumer's revolt is the automobile. Somebody who needs a $2,200 car, and can afford a $3,200 car, buys a $4,200 car and has a nervous breakdown when the door handle falls off with only 35 payments to go.

Others write to Washington when they discover that the jumbo-economy box of sugar-coated, air-filled, protein-packed crunchy-wunchies isn't full to the top. This deception means they have to get out of bed and fry eggs for the kids, but the Teflon pan sticks.

Or it is something like the electric toothbrush conking out between the uppers and lowers, or the TV going out between the first and second half.

None of these disasters has befallen me, so I did not really believe that there was such a thing as a consumer's revolt.

In fact, a revolt didn't seem possible because so many of the angry victims of shoddy merchandise are also the makers or sellers of shoddy merchandise, so who is there to fight with?

But I finally discovered what Ralph Nader is all about while I was eating a restaurant meal.

The main course was good. The chef's skill was such that you could not tell if the vegetable had been treated with nerve gas or the meat afflicted with tumors.

Then came the dessert. Being a gourmet, I ordered a double butter pecan ice cream.

Those who really like butter pecan ice cream know that you don't eat it the same way you eat vanilla or chocolate ice cream.

You swallow the ice cream, but you trap the pecans in your mouth, stashing them off to the side or tucking under the tongue.

Most people, after retaining the one or two pecans from an average-size spoon of ice cream, will chew or grind them, swallow them and go on to the next spoonful.

These people are only casually committed to butter pecans. They'd probably be just as happy with black walnut, or banana yogurt.

But there are those of us who just let the pecans pile up, spoonful after spoonful.

Then, after you've eaten all the ice cream, you have the extra bonus of a whole bunch of pecans to eat.

For statistic-conscious readers, it has been my observation that a person with a normal jaw can accumulate all the butter pecans in about a pint of ice cream before he has to start chewing.

Somebody with an exceptionally wide or long jaw, such as Slats Grobnik, can make it through a quart before chewing.

He did this only once, as I recall, and that was to win a bet in an ice cream parlor. When he finished, he smiled broadly, showing all of the pecans, which caused the Greek who owned the place to faint from disgust.

His brother, Fats Grobnik, almost matched that record, and would have done it because he never had any molars and had more room in his mouth for storing pecans. But he got the hiccups near the end and inhaled sharply. After that, when he took a free chest X-ray in City Hall, they would send him a card saying he had been dead for years.

I relate this historical data to show the dedication of true butter pecan eaters.

Last night, when the waiter brought dessert, I dug in. But after two spoonfuls, I didn't have a pecan anywhere in my mouth. Could I have swallowed it? I tried again. The results were the same.

It was a fraud. The ice cream was pecan *flavored* but there weren't any pecans in it.

I called the waiter and asked him what he was trying to get away with. He shrugged. So I called the manager. He looked at the ice cream, shook his head, and said, "I don't have anything to do with the ice cream."

"Who does?" I demanded.

"The owner," he said.

"Send him over," I demanded.

"He's gone for the night."

There it was—corporate institutional indifference. Everybody passing the pecan.

I could write a letter to the owner of the place, but you know what would happen. The hatcheck girl would probably answer it for him. And she'd just say that they have investigated my complaint, and there must be some mistake, because they don't serve buttered pidgeons.

Over and Out, Roger!

July 10, 1970

There were thirty minutes to go before the private screening of his first movie, so screenwriter Roger Ebert nervously asked the bartender for a shot and a beer chaser.

That was bold drinking for so young a man. Sure enough, he coughed on the shot.

Then he stuck me with the bar bill.

"Remember," he said, "I'm saving you three dollars by inviting you to my free screening."

"I have heard about your movie, and you aren't saving me a nickel."

He lapsed into a glum silence. Ebert, the popular, talented movie critic of *The Sun-Times*, had done something few critics would dare. He had written a screenplay—for the film *Beyond the Valley of the Dolls*. Even before it opened here, critics in other cities put aside any fraternal affection they may have felt for him.

"It is sure to disgust you!" raved a West Coast critic.

"Don't miss missing it," said New York.

Using Ebert's own movie rating system—five stars for great, and one star for terrible—he was averaging about one handful of crater dust per review.

The critics had generally agreed that it was dirty, violent, and not much fun.

I seldom see these kind of movies, since a normal day in Chicago can be dirty, violent, and not much fun, but Ebert had arranged for a private screening. He wanted his friends to see it.

We got there a few minutes late. A breast was already bounding across the screen.

"Did we miss the first act?" I asked.

"Yes," answered a voice from the darkness, "the first abnormal one."

It's not easy to read notes that were scribbled in darkness, but I can transcribe these from my note pad:

"Bare breasts . . . bottoms . . . naked couples . . . in bed . . . in bubble-bath . . . in Rolls-Royce . . . two young men, good grief . . . haystack . . . toe fetish . . . old man, young girl . . . young man, old girl . . . young man and old m . . . only half over . . ."

I can't report on my notes for the second half, which is when the violence came in, because it is difficult to write when you have both hands clapped over your eyes. It was something like the final cattle chute in the stock yards, except the movie used people.

When the lights went on, I was glad for Ebert that the room was filled with his friends. Strangers might have beaten him with the chairs.

My reaction, once I got outside and breathed the fresh polluted air, was one of puzzlement. I had always assumed, since I didn't know any, that creeps wrote all the dirty, violent movies. In fact, I had hoped they were written by creeps, because this would keep them busy and they wouldn't be climbing up my rose trellis and peeking in my bathroom window.

But Ebert is not a creep. Just the opposite. He is a peaceful, pleasant, thoughtful young man, only twenty-six or twenty-seven, with a cherubic face and a great writing talent. While still a student, he wrote a history of a university, and it was a clean book, which used to be possible when writing about universities.

Later, as we all leaned on a bar, Ebert asked his friends what they thought. We told him. This time, he ordered a double shot and a beer.

"Why did you write a dirty, violent movie?" I finally asked him.

"It was written as a parody of dirty, violent movies," he said.

"Did the producer and director know that?"

Although I am not a movie critic, I think I have figured out what went wrong, how so talented a writer and so decent a young man could be involved in that dog.

Ebert's problem is that he is not a dirty old man. If a dirty movie is going to be any good, it has to be written by a dirty old man. You wouldn't let an ROTC student write a war movie, or a Republican write a book about Chicago politics.

I believe that every young man is entitled to one big mistake, despite what the alimony court judges may say. And this movie is Ebert's, and I urge you to avoid it.

Someday he will write another movie, and I'm confident that it will be excellent. Even if it is dirty, it will be better. I'll be his technical adviser.

The Shoe Fit, But No Pinch

August 28, 1970

Somewhere on the West Side there is a young man who has to be one of the world's least competent purse snatchers.

A few days ago, he selected as his victim Mrs. Irene Newsome, who was walking on Damen near Madison in broad daylight.

I will give him credit for picking a likely victim. Little old ladies are the best people to snatch purses from and Mrs. Newsome is a genuine little old lady. She's almost seventy, stands four-eleven and weighs about a hundred pounds.

Mrs. Newsome, who had car trouble, was walking toward a service station to get help when the purse snatcher jumped out of an alley and grabbed her purse.

Then he started running back down the alley. But he couldn't run fast because Mrs. Newsome wouldn't let go of the purse.

"Leggo," he yelled.

"You let go," Mrs. Newsome screamed, hanging on with both hands.

Being a purse snatcher, he couldn't very well let go of a purse, so he just kept going, dragging the screaming Mrs. Newsome along the ground.

After they traveled half a block this way, Mrs. Newsome lost her grip on the purse, but then she grabbed him by one of his legs.

So they went on that way for several yards, the thief dragging the screaming Mrs. Newsome along by his leg.

Then Mrs. Newsome's grip slipped and she only had him by the ankle. But he kept going.

And suddenly, she was sitting there holding one empty shoe in her hand, while the purse snatcher limped around a bend in the alley and disappeared.

Her screams drew some people and they helped her to her feet and out of the alley.

"He got my purse," Mrs. Newsome said, "but I got his shoe."

Since there was only ten dollars in her purse, and the shoe was from a pair that cost at least that much, Mrs. Newsome had the satisfaction of knowing the thief had not profited.

As they waited for a police car, a young man came walking up the street in his stockinged feet, carrying the other shoe.

He went right up to Mrs. Newsome and said: "Give me my shoe."

She said: "I'll give you your shoe if you give me my purse."

"I didn't take your purse," the man said.

"If you didn't take my purse, how did I get your shoe?" Mrs. Newsome answered.

The young man then proved that he was an even worse storyteller than a purse snatcher.

He said he had loaned his shoes to a needy friend for the day, and that the friend returned only one shoe, saying that an old lady had stolen the other one.

"Do you expect me to believe that?" asked Mrs. Newsome, holding the shoe behind her back.

The young man started jumping around angrily, but several men from the neighborhood kept him away from Mrs. Newsome. And that was when the squad car arrived.

Police looked down the alley and found the purse, with most of her cards and papers intact, but the ten dollars gone.

They started to lead the man toward the squad car.

"Do you identify him as the person who took your purse?" they asked Mrs. Newsome.

She had to admit that she couldn't. "No, I never really saw his face. All I saw were his feet and legs."

That wasn't enough, the policemen said. A man can't be identified by his feet.

"But I have his shoe," Mrs. Newsome said.

That wasn't enough evidence, the policemen said, and they even made Mrs. Newsome give back the shoe.

As I said, he was remarkably incompetent. But he got away with it. In Chicago, you don't need much skill, just so long as you try hard and are crooked enough.

Principle vs. Principal

December 9, 1970

When the village dog warden came around to sell her a license, Mrs. Ann Shalla was ready to pay. She had her purse open.

Then the dog warden asked:

"Is your dog a male or female?"

"A female," Mrs. Shalla said, "but what difference does that make?"

"If it is a female, the license is three dollars. If it's a male, it's only two dollars," he said.

"Why?" Mrs. Shalla said.

"Because the females have the puppies," the dog warden explained.

Mrs. Shalla snapped shut her purse. The fervor of Women's Lib began coursing through her veins. Glaring at the dog warden, she said:

"Aren't you aware that puppies are sort of a joint venture?"

"That's the Franklin Park village ordinance," the dog warden said. "See, we want to discourage the dog population. But I'll tell you how you can save a dollar."

"How?"

"If you have her spayed, it'll only cost you two dollars."

Mrs. Shalla was outraged.

"What about male dogs? Do they have to be spayed to get a two dollar fee?"

The dog warden, unaccustomed to having his authority questioned, asked: "Are you going to pay or aren't you?"

"I'm not going to give you three dollars," Mrs. Shalla said. "I will give you two dollars. It is a matter of principle."

"Principal is what you earn interest on," the dog warden retorted, warming to the give and take of debate.

"My good man," Mrs. Shalla said, "not only don't you know anything about the reproductive inclinations of dogs, you do not know the difference between principle and principal."

"Then you are refusing to pay the fee?" the dog warden said.

"Yes, I am refusing."

"Then we will take you into court."

"Fine. Come and get me."

With that, the dog warden bellowed: "Principles ————!" and stalked away.

And Mrs. Shalla slammed her door, phoned a friend at the Chicago chapter of NOW (National Organization for Women) and prepared to fight.

Thus far, a legal battle hasn't developed because the Village of Franklin Park hasn't made the first move. But NOW has promised Mrs. Shalla the help of a lawyer should the need arise.

"My father always told me to do what I thought was right," Mrs. Shalla said.

I agree with her. The law is discriminatory in many ways, but primarily because it holds the female solely responsible for the birth of young.

As anyone who knows anything about dogs can tell you, males are more inclined to be more romantic most of the time than females.

"Males run around a lot more," is the way it was put by Dr. Kenneth Bone, who has offices on Elston Ave.

For that matter, simple mathematics establishes that male dogs have an even greater potential than females when it comes to increasing the population.

The average female dog can have only two litters of pups a year, with the typical litter being about five. This means that a female could account for about ten new dogs a year.

On the other paw, an exceptionally lascivious male could sire a litter a day. This means that one industrious male could cause the dog population to increase by some 1,750 dogs in only a year.

As with human males, it is only the lack of opportunity that prevents male dogs from carrying on in such a manner.

A survey of a dozen or so suburbs turned up only one other—Blue Island—that has a double-standard on its law books. It, too, provides a one dollar "bonus" for owners of a spayed female.

Yet, as Mrs. Shalla pointed out, there is no such inducement for the owners of male dogs to have this heinous alteration performed.

Mrs. Shalla can cite a personal experience as evidence of the unfairness of the Franklin Park law that arbitrarily points the finger of guilt at the female.

She has a female Irish setter that has won trophies in dog shows, and it is her intention to breed it.

But some time ago, a fence-leaping Dalmatian made a dramatic appearance in her back yard and forced his attentions on her Irish setter.

Had it not been for the quick action of a veterinarian, who aborted the affair, Mrs. Shalla would have been stuck with a litter of Dalmatian-Irish setters, unwanted, unloved and unprofitable.

"It was not my dog that was wandering around the streets, going in yards, seeking adventure," Mrs. Shalla said. "She was minding her own business."

So true. Yet, the female had to undergo the humiliation of the trip to the veterinarian's office, and Mrs. Shalla the expense, while the male dog loped off, independent and seeking his next conquest.

How like life. Male chauvinist dogs.

Helpful Hints for the Housewife

June 28, 1971

A truly strange letter has come to me from Mrs. George Pishko of Berwyn.

"I was listening to the radio," she writes, "and you were giving out a pancake recipe.

"My phone was ringing at the time, so I did not get it all. Could you be so kind and send it to me?

"And can you tell me why my ice cubes stick and never come out clear? What is my trouble?

"Also, my iron has a starch build. How can I get rid of that?

"Will be waiting to hear from you."

I can only assume that Mrs. Pishko has mistaken me for someone else, as I have never in my life gone on the radio to give a pancake recipe.

But since the letter was addressed to me, I feel obliged to help Mrs. Pishko with her kitchen problems, which appear to be considerable.

First, there is the matter of a pancake recipe.

Mrs. Pishko, I strongly urge you to forget about pancakes.

For one thing, if you can't stay off the phone long enough to jot down a radio recipe, you will surely be chattering away and they will just burn anyway, probably enraging Mr. Pishko, your husband. And if being confronted with burnt pancakes doesn't bother him, then don't bother with a new recipe—just fling the same old ones in front of him and he won't notice the difference.

Even if you don't burn them, what will you have? Do you realize that a plate of pancakes, covered with butter and jam or syrup, washed down with a glass of milk, will send about 1,000 calories coursing through your system? Is that what you want?

Take my advice, Mrs. Pishko, and poach an egg. Remember the old saying: "Men don't make passes at girls with big waistlines."

Now, for your ice cubes that stick and are not clear:

The sticking could be caused by several things, but the most common is water that is sticky.

You might call the water commissioner in Berwyn and demand to know if he is providing sticky water, and if so, why.

If he admits it, he might change his ways. If not, he'll be careful not to do it in the future, knowing you are watching him.

Of course, the reason for the sticking ice cubes could be something simple. You might be making your cubes too big, in which case it would be natural for them to stick. If so, just try making them smaller and they will drop from the tray ever so easily.

If this doesn't work, then you'll just have to use the old-fashioned method of rapping the tray against something to pop the cubes loose. The edge of a sink or the brow of an unruly child works fine.

Foggy ice cubes: I suspect that your ice cubes aren't clear because somebody is creeping into your kitchen and pouring goodness knows what into your ice cube trays. This can easily be avoided by keeping your back door bolted and maintaining a sharp eye for furtive strangers lurking in your back yard or your kitchen.

On the other hand, it might be that you are getting foggy water. If so, call the Berwyn water commissioner and tell him you object to foggy water as vigorously as you do to sticky water.

Starch build on your iron: Frankly, I don't know what a "starch build" is, since I've never been troubled by one on my iron or anywhere else. And I'm not going to go around asking my friends about it, as they'd probably laugh and point at me.

But it seems to me that if your iron has one, and you don't want it, the quickest way to rid yourself of the problem is to shout "Look out" and toss it out the window. If you are lucky, it will land on whoever has been putting a foreign substance in your ice cube trays, thus solving two pesky problems with one iron.

To avoid the problem of starch build in the future, I'd recommend that you stop using starch.

I assume that you have been starching your husband's shirts. Believe me, if you keep shoving those butter-soaked pancakes into that man, and then force him to wear a shirt with a stiff, starch collar, you are going to have a husband with a purple face, bulging eyes and protruding tongue, and that is not the most pleasant kind of creature to have around the house.

I hope these household hints are helpful, Mrs. Pishko. And if you, or anyone else, has kitchen prob-

lems that puzzle you, just drop me a card or letter and
I'll try to help you along the road to total confusion.

A Pickin'-Packin' School Memo

March 27, 1974

Fellow bureaucratic memo collectors, have your scissors
ready. Here is another for the scrapbook.

It comes from the Chicago Board of Education,
which consistently puts out the highest quality bureaucratic memos in the city.

This one originated in the school system's purchasing
department.

It is called:

"Proposed Changes in Packaging at the Division of
Supplies:

"At the present time all high schools and other organ-
izational units with unit numbers under 2000 have the
privilege of ordering specific items for specific teachers.

"The system is set up so that a separate picking/pack-
ing slip is originated for each individual room and the
items are picked separately, as a privilege to these or-
ganizations. (Primarily high schools.)

"At the present time the Division of Supplies is filling
picking/packing slips based on the chronological is-
suance of these picking/packing slips, wherever possible.

"A number of temporary measures will be taken in
the Division of Supplies and Transportation Services in
order to eliminate the backlog of the delivery of supplies
to the schools.

"In order to increase the efficiency of the picking and

packing operation, thereby enabling the Division of Supplies to handle a greater volume of commodities in the same time frame, the Division of Supplies will eliminate the practice of handling each picking/packing slip separately and will combine as many as possible in one shipment.

"This will mean that the schools will have to check the items, packed loosely in a carton with the accompanying picking/packing slips for the same category of commodities in one package, rather than having them picked separately by the picking/packing slip."

A teacher who saw this memo, passed it along to me with this observation:

"I interpret this as being a tongue-twisting riddle, but I think it would be phrased differently:

"If a picker/packer packs a package, does the picking/packing slip show how big a package the picker/packer packed?"

On the other hand, it could mean:

"A picker/packer packed a package for a picking/packing slip. How many items did the picker/packer pack in the package with the picking/packing slip?"

To see which of us was right, I called the school headquarters and asked for the purchasing department.

Somebody answered the phone and I said I wanted to know about the tongue twister in the general bulletin.

"The what?"

"The one about how many items a picker/packer packs in a package, rather than having them picked separately by the picking/packing slip."

There was a long pause. Then the voice said: "Which department did you want?"

Purchasing, I said.

"Oh," she said, sounding relieved. "They switched you to the wrong office."

I was switched to purchasing, but they had gone to lunch. So I showed the document to Tom Sellers, who covers School Board matters for this paper. He is adept at decoding the secret message often found in educational documents. He has also become fluent in the strange language known as "educatorese," which is spoken by professional educators.

He studied it, then said:

"Yes, I think I know what it means. Translated from educatorese, it means:

"From now on, supplies won't be sent to individual teachers. They'll be sent to the school in one package, and the teachers will have to sort them out."

That made it completely clear. And it meant that the tongue twister in the bulletin should probably be:

"If a picker/packer packs a package, can a teacher pluck the item the picker/packer packed?"

"Exactly," Sellers said.

Peter Piper lives. And he's educating our children.

Can Tiny Tim Tiptoe Back?

September 25, 1974

Of all the freaks, weirdos, and whackos who pranced across the American landscape during the 1960s, my favorite was Tiny Tim of the ukulele, falsetto voice and old songs.

I liked him because he was the only freak, weirdo, or whacko who wasn't trying to establish his own government. His goal was making "Tiptoe Through the Tulips" a hit again.

He came out of nowhere in early 1968, went on the Carson show, and the nation's jaw dropped. He giggled, gushed, and fluttered his hands, his complexion was sickly pale, his hair was like a witch's. He dressed as if some Maxwell Street store had draped its worst stuff on him.

You could understand why, when he once tried to

enlist in the Army at a time men were being drafted, the
recruiter said: "We're all filled up."

But he was a sensation. Overnight, he was talked
about, written about, deep thinkers pondered the meaning of it all, serious musical critics analyzed his singing.

It was best summed up by Dick Christiansen, of
Panorama, who wrote:

"It is, in its way, the great American dream—the possibility that a noodnik can suddenly be a rich and
quoted celebrity, whose whole life had counted for
nothing until suddenly a mystical moment arrived and
all the doors that had been closed were opened and fame
and fortune came flooding in."

Or, as someone else said: "He is one of the great
dingalings of our time."

The Tiny Tim madness peaked on December 18,
1969, when he married Miss Vicki, a teen-ager, on the
Johnny Carson Show. One of the biggest TV audiences
in history gaped and declared their disgust. But they
watched.

The wedding was a perfect ending to America's nut-
tiest decade.

The honeymoon was front page. So was the birth of
their child, Tulip. "I can't believe he actually did it,"
people gasped. And the sad separation of Tim and Vicki
was reported at length.

Then, as suddenly as it began, it ended. Like so many
other strange creatures of the decade, Tiny Tim was
gone.

The other day, I was looking through some old papers
and saw one of the early Tiny Tim stories. I began
wondering what had become of him. Had he bought a
Robert Hall suit, a crewcut, and started selling life insurance?

A few long distance phone calls later, we were talking. Surprisingly, for all his bizarre mannerisms in
public, he talks sensibly and straight.

Yes, he said, he had gone into "a slump."

"It was a fantastic slump. But when it happened, it

didn't surprise me. Life is a series of streaks and slumps, just like in sports."

It began in 1969, when he discovered he didn't have much money, despite the enormous sums he had earned. It seemed that his agent at that time had sort of spent it, or invested it, or something. Anyway, when he went to the bank, he found that he didn't have enough to get a free clock radio.

"By the time the wedding came, I knew I was on financially shaky ground. Tiffany, the diamond store in New York, was threatening to sue if I didn't pay the $2,000 balance on Miss Vicki's wedding ring.

"I felt the slump coming, and it is a feeling that hits you in the pit of the stomach when it comes. I was at least prepared for it, but Miss Vicki wasn't, and her parents weren't.

"They started murmuring: 'What did he do with all that money? Look at all the things he wasted money on, all those creams and lotions for his skin.' "

Suddenly his novelty was gone. How many times will audiences pay to hear someone who can sing like Rudy Vallee, or Jeanette MacDonald, even if he can do 1,000 oldies? No more concerts, Lake Tahoe, Las Vegas. No more network TV appearances.

"No, after he moved to California, Mr. Carson didn't call again. I didn't get a lot of calls. But I would never have asked Mr. Carson to go on. This is a business, when you're hot you're hot. And I wasn't hot.

"So at the beginning of 1970, I started doing clubs. I guess you could call them dives.

"I'd call it the has-been circuit.

"I did more little clubs in middle-class neighborhoods than when I was first coming up. I was really in the nation's marshlands."

There were hecklers along the way. But, then, Tiny Tim is the kind of person who has always been heckled. There is always a kid in every high school who is strange, and the normal kids never let him forget it.

"I guess it's basically human nature. You've seen

those movies about guys who made it big then fell. It's the same thing in life.

"I was playing a club in the Catskills and I was walking across the lobby of the hotel when a man came up to me and said: 'Tell me how it feels to be on your way down.' I said: 'Thank you very much,' and kept walking.

"In an airport terminal, some people noticed me and one of them said very loud: 'Him? Who'd want HIS autograph?'

"But, you know, I found it a challenge, spiritually and physically, and I found it very rewarding. I did meet good people. I think if I ever got big again, I'd insist on playing those places. Most entertainers, when they make it, want to spend the rest of their lives in Las Vegas. Maybe it would be good for them to go to places like Carterville, Illinois, to play police and firemen benefits like I've been doing. Those people love to see talent. They can be appreciative."

In the grand tradition of show biz stories, there should now be the big comeback. Tiny Tim is trying.

"We've been rehearsing since June. The act is a little different now. I've got a four-piece band, and two girl dancers. They're called the Tulips. I still sing old songs, but now we do more nostalgia from the 'fifties and 'sixties. It's gone over well on our last trip. We just finished one-night stands in places like Carterville, Illinois, and Dearborn, Michigan.

"But our big opening is in New York, at the end of October. We're going to do ten days at Jimmy's. It's the hottest place in New York. This is the first time I'll be working in New York City in a long time."

And what of Miss Vicki? Show biz tradition includes the big reunion, à la Dan Dailey and Betty Grable.

"No, we tried last year again. But she left me. I think she's just tired of marriage, at least with me, and wants to be on her own and have a good time."

And what if the comeback flops? What if it is back to the dives, the heckling?

"I was $25,000 in debt when the slump came, and I still am. Even more. My new managers have shelled out $10,000 to put this new show together.

"But I'll never have anything to complain about. So many people have it worse. Look at the people in hospitals, people with problems. I'm fortunate.

"And a lot of much better talent never have made it. So I have nothing to complain about."

Hey, Frank Sinatra, with your goon-bodyguards and your foul mouth. Listen to Tiny Tim. You can learn something.

Music to Get Pregnant By?

December 2, 1975

Because of my interest in rock music, the following news item out of Tallahassee, Florida, caught my eye:
TALLAHASSEE—Damning rock music for its "appeal to the flesh," a Baptist church has begun a campaign to put the torch to records by Elton John, the Rolling Stones and other rock stars.

Some $2,200 worth of records were tossed into a bonfire this week after church officials labeled the music immoral.

The Rev. Charles Boykin, associate pastor and youth director at the Lakewood Baptist Church, said he had seen statistics which showed "of 1,000 girls who became pregnant out of wedlock, 986 committed fornication while rock music was being played."

It was the last part—the amazing statistic—that intrigued me. I considered getting a portable radio and blasting rock music at the first 1,000 women I met.

But first I decided to get further details from Mr.
Boykin. I phoned him and we had the following interview:

Where did that statistic come from, the one about all
those girls getting pregnant while listening to rock
music?

"I want to be accurate, so let me correct you. They
didn't all listen to it DURING the sex act. I was speaking of listening to it as a prelude to fornication, as well
as during."

I see. But rock music was involved in all but 14 pregnancies out of 1,000 cases?

"That's right. It was sort of like a Gallup Poll of un-
wed mothers."

And who provided the statistics?

"This man. He's from West Virginia. Or maybe
Virginia. He stopped in our church one day and gave us
the statistics."

He's a professional poll taker?

"Uh, no. He's an evangelist. He travels all the time."

And you believe his statistics?

"Oh, yes. There's a definite relationship between il-
licit sex and any music with a syncopated beat. That
covers rock and country music and even some Gospel
music."

Goodness, a decent girl has got to walk around with
earmuffs on. Tell me more.

"Well, the low bass tones of the bass drum and the
bass guitar make people respond sexually."

(They make me put my fingers in my ears. Am I
strange?)

But the syncopated beat has been around a lot longer
than rock music, hasn't it?

"That's right. And the debauchery began when
Benny Goodman introduced swing music."

Benny Goodman caused debauchery?

"That's right. His music had a syncopated beat."

Then why weren't lots of girls getting pregnant
because of his music?

"They were, but it was covered up. When Goodman

had a concert in Los Angeles in 1938, there was open sex.''

In 1938?

"That's right. The syncopated beat did it."

How about Glenn Miller, Lawrence Welk?

"When they use the syncopated beat, yes."

Remarkable. I wouldn't have thought Lawrence Welk capable of such rascality. It makes me wonder what really goes on in all of those nursing homes.

"It doesn't matter whether a song is slow or fast. It is the syncopated beat. You can trace it all the way to the jungle, where the beat was introduced. It is primitive, pulsating, hypnotic."

How alarming! Then what kind of music should a nice girl listen to if she doesn't want to be swept up by a jungle, animal instinct?

"Well, the syncopated beat is not predominant in patriotic songs or in most Gospel music."

How about classical music?

"I'm not advocating all classical music. In his later music, Bach introduced some syncopated beats."

Aha! I suspected as much of Bach. The old hipster fathered twenty children.

Have you conducted any other scientific research, besides the Traveling Evangelist Poll?

"Well, we made some tests with plants. We played classical music for one group of plants, and rock music for another group, and we didn't play any music for a third group.

"The plants that were exposed to classical music grew in the direction of the speakers.

"The plants that weren't exposed to any music grew straight up."

And—let me guess—the plants that listened to rock music fornicated and all but fourteen of the plants became pregnant, right?

"No, the plants that were exposed to rock music just grew away from the speakers. Then they died."

Well, that's better than breaking your daddy's heart.

Panama—the Ideal Enemy

May 7, 1976

Ronald Reagan's remarkable surge at the polls is partly the result of his having struck a responsive chord in millions of Americans—their anger at Panama.

This is also a tribute to Reagan's leadership qualities, since most Americans weren't even aware that they were mad at Panama until Reagan told them they were. Many still don't know why they are angry, but it is enough that they are.

Of all the candidates, Reagan is the only one to recognize the significance of the Panama issue. In fact, he might be the only person in the country to recognize it.

President Ford has taken the position that normal diplomatic methods will be used to negotiate a new treaty for the Panama Canal. Ford also has indicated that he believes Reagan might be getting a little soft in the head.

But Reagan has made it clear that if elected, he would be willing to respond militarily to any further pushing around by Panama.

He hammered at the Panama issue in Texas, and voters responded with enthusiasm. It may be that Texans, who remember the Alamo, are aware that Spanish is spoken in Panama.

Reagan feels so strongly that he has encouraged his wife, Nancy, normally a mild sort of lady, to go on Texas TV and radio to denounce the "tinhorn dictator" of Panama.

In contrast, Mrs. Betty Ford has not even conceded

that she knows who the tinhorn dictator of Panama is, or even indicated that she disapproves of him.

Nor has the wife of the tinhorn dictator of Panama responded to Mrs. Reagan's allegations that he is a tinhorn dictator.

Reagan's emphasis of the Panama issue is more than a political masterstroke. It also is a sound military decision.

It was obvious that this country needed somebody to be mad at. After Vietnam, it appeared that it might be a long time before we got mad at anybody again.

It was feared that not being mad at anybody could make us weak, pliable, listless, and irregular.

As former President Richard Nixon pointed out in a magazine article not long ago, when a country has the blahs, it sometimes takes something exciting, like a war, to get everybody together again, hup-hupping along. And that is very true. Germany is an example. After World War I, everybody sat around cabarets getting drunk and perverted. When they got mad at Poland, they all felt better.

But it's not enough to want to get mad at another country. Finding the right country is what's important.

The world is covered with all kinds of countries, but most of them must be disqualified for one reason or another.

There are China and Russia and their satellites. But we've been mad at them for so long, on and off, that there's nothing novel about it. Besides, they have the bomb, and nobody really wants to get that mad.

Then there are smaller countries that it would be safe to be mad at. But many of them are our friends and dependents. We'll probably get mad at them eventually, but there's no reason to rush things.

Then there are the little countries we don't particularly like, but we don't have a specific reason to be mad at them either. We could probably find a reason when the heat is off the CIA, but we need something now.

So you can see that selecting a country to be mad at isn't as easy as it might appear. Which is why Reagan's choice of Panama is so astute. He couldn't have made a better choice.

It's not a Russian satellite. It doesn't have nuclear capability. In fact, it doesn't even have a regular army. Panama's military strength consists of a 7,000-man militia. We haven't had an adversary like that since William Randolph Hearst cried "Remember the Maine."

Best of all, most of the 1.6 million citizens of Panama are at least part Indian. Fighting them would be like old times.

By golly, this might give Reagan the chance to be the first American President in the century to lead a cavalry charge.

The Coroner Marches Out

December 7, 1976

A retired detective remembers going to the County Morgue late one night, after a well known gangster had been killed.

"I saw all these people lined up to see the body. I thought the guy must have more next of kin that Moses.

"Then I realized what was going on. A deputy coroner was charging people five dollars to take a peek at the stiff."

The same detective recalled when he was working on a paddy wagon and was sent to a hotel room where a body had been found by the night clerk.

When he got there, somebody already was in the room—a stocky man, wearing pointy shoes, a gray fedora, with a big cigar in his mouth.

"He was yanking on the stiff's ring finger. He had

one foot under the armpit to brace himself, and he was pulling and tugging, trying to get the ring off.

"I said: 'Who the hell are you?'

"He keeps pulling and says: 'Coroner's office.'

"I said: 'Whadya think you're doing?'

"He didn't even blink. He says: 'OK you can have the wristwatch.' "

Then there was the case of the movie actor who dropped dead while passing through O'Hare Airport a few years ago.

The coroner's office bundled his personal effects in a box and shipped them to the widow in California.

The widow was surprised to find that her husband's personal effects included three Chicago telephone directories.

She was even more surprised to find that the personal effects didn't include his ring, cuff links and silver bracelet.

Ah, Chicago history. This particular chapter ended a few days ago when the political office of the Cook County coroner ceased to exist. It was abolished and has been replaced by a professional medical examiner.

We are told this will make the investigation of deaths more efficient and scientific. Compared with the coroner's office, even Dr. Frankenstein and Igor were more scientific.

"Gentlemen," a coroner once declared when a head was found in a city sewer, "this is the work of a murderer."

In recent years, the office has been rather subdued. But in its heyday, when coroners were political wildmen, they loved to get all the publicity any way they could.

So their main job was to rush to the scene of big murders and pose for pictures, pointing a finger or cigar at the body.

They also liked grisly crimes, in which the victims were put in oil drums, garbage cans, and other receptacles. The coroner would pose with his head in the can, peering about for a clue. Or even the killer.

One coroner especially relished the slayings of gang-sters who had been shot through the hat, as well as the head. He would then pose for a picture with his fore-finger sticking out of the hole in the hat.

Not that they weren't scientific. A reporter once asked a coroner how deep the wound was in a corpse.

"Lemme check," said the coroner, using his ballpoint pen to measure.

"Hmmmm," he said, looking at the pen. "About three inches." Then he popped the pen back in his vest pocket.

The coroner also held inquests, which had little legal standing, but they provided a few hours' work for elderly men who always sat on the jury.

It was always a poignant scene when the bereaved relatives of the deceased sat and listened to the terrible testimony, while a jury of old geezers in yellow shirts and purple ties and straw hats sat there loudly snoring.

But the real stars of the coroner's office were the deputy coroners—a small army of ace investigators who could walk into a room and in thirty seconds give you an accurate appraisal of every piece of jewelry on the corpse.

To qualify as a deputy coroner, you had to possess the following: a letter from your ward boss, a wide-brimmed gray fedora, a diamond pinky ring, and a cigar.

When somebody died of anything but natural causes, a deputy coroner rushed to the scene. They always rushed, because they were afraid the wagon men might grab a locket.

Once there, it was the responsibility of the deputy cor-oner to have the body sent to the nearest funeral home owned by his brother-in-law.

Then he would gather the facts. It was done this way:

He would get the name of the dead person. If the name was "James Doe," he would go to the phone and call his downtown office and say: "James Roe" is dead. The downtown coroner would say "Got it." He would write "James Sloan" on his list of dead people. Then he

would call a newsman and say: "Blain Cohen is dead."
And the next day, Blain Cohen would read it in the
paper and have a heart attack.

Then the deputy coroner would go to Blain Cohen's
house and write down: "James Roe."

Progress is good, I suppose, but dying won't be the
same without a coroner's office.

I doubt if a scientifc medical examiner will ever match
the legendary coroner who was there when a politician
named Dingbat Oberta was found with a bullet in his
head and a can of aspirins in his pocket. The coroner
held up the aspirins and said:

"He died of a headache."

No Lust Lost
on Fawcett-Majors

February 22, 1977

Every time I see picture of Farrah Fawcett-Majors, the
nation's new sex symbol, nothing happens.

I don't have any unspeakable thoughts, or pant, or
say boy-oh-boy-oh-boy, or otherwise express my admiration.

The first time nothing happened, I thought it might
be the cold weather. The next time, I got a little worried.
The third time, I conducted a test on myself.

I looked up some pictures of Sophia Loren, Marilyn
Monroe, and Raquel Welch.

Within moments, I had at least six unspeakable
thoughts.

So I can't accept the blame for my indifference to Ms.
Fawcett-Majors. The fault is with her.

I've always been willing to leer and say wow and let my eyes bulge and make all the other appropriate signs of respect due a national sex symbol.

But it is the responsibility, even the duty, of a national sex symbol to inspire me.

So the question is, where and why has Ms. Fawcett-Majors failed?

In the past, successful national sex symbols tried to present a consistent image.

Rita Hayworth, for example, was almost always shown wearing a loosely clinging negligee while sprawling cat-like on a large bed. The bed appeared too soft for proper support, which could lead to a backache, but that seemed irrelevant.

Whenever I saw one of Miss Hayworth's pictures, I knew what she had in mind.

Or at least I knew what she had in mind for me to have in mind. Because that was what I immediately had in mind.

But the last time I saw Ms. Fawcett-Majors she was on TV doing a commercial for a health club. She was all over the screen, straining at one machine, kicking another, tugging, bending, twisting, and working up a heck of a sweat.

So I'm not sure what Ms. Fawcett-Majors has in mind. Whatever it is, a man might develop a hernia before he got around to it.

The very first time I saw Ms. Fawcett-Majors on TV, she was doing an automobile commercial.

When somebody tries to sell me a car, I experience many emotions—fear, distrust, loathing. But never lust.

Another time I saw Ms. Fawcett-Majors, she was on TV selling shaving cream.

If that's what it took to arouse my passions, long ago I would have leaped over the counter and into the arms of Mr. Solomon, my druggist.

When the past sex symbols appeared in movies, they played the part of glamorous women, fallen women, betrayed women. They were mysterious, passionate, romantic, elusive. Men were always pursuing them.

In her TV series, Ms. Fawcett-Majors plays some kind of cop. How can you pursue someone who might put the cuffs on you when you catch her?

While riding in my car (which I bought from a short, fat man with a mustache, who aroused only heartburn in my heart) I heard a woman on the radio explaining why Ms. Fawcett-Majors had become so popular.

"She's the ultimate in good nutrition. She has lots of protein in her hair and calcium in her teeth. Her hair and teeth are wonderful."

My dog Ole has great teeth and hair, too. And he can kill rats. But there's more to lust than that.

I don't know how a female person gets to be the national sex symbol, and in the past I didn't care as long as she caused me to breathe erratically. But now I'm suspicious about the whole process.

Being the national sex symbol is a responsible position. The person who achieves it gets on the cover of *People* magazine, appears on the Dinah Shore show, is quoted in all the better gossip columns, and Johnny Carson might even make up a dirty joke about her. So it is no small honor.

I would like to show just how Farrah Fawcett-Majors achieved this status.

Early sex symbols could sing, dance, act, or something. But all Ms. Fawcett-Majors has done is go on TV and be a female version of the Polk brothers.

Maybe that's the answer. She might be the inevitable choice in our additive-filled, micro-wave, Astro-turf, pre-packaged, health club-conditioned times.

Miss Plasti-sex.

Ralph Nader should study her. If he does, and he doesn't blush, I'm right.

Super Agent O'Brien Reporting

March 31, 1977

I really hope O'Brien made it home all right. Under-cover work can be risky.

But let me start at the beginning.

The phone rang at about 5 P.M. The operator said it was a collect call from O'Brien.

I wasn't expecting a call from anybody named O'Brien. So I asked her where the call was being placed.

"In Chicago," she said. I accepted.

"My name's O'Brien," he said. "You want a big story?"

I'll take a little story. What is it about?

"Bribes. Corruption. Payoffs."

Who, what, where, how?

"Awright, take this down. I just got off work. I'm sitting in a bar. And I just saw a cop take a payoff. I don't like it. So I got his badge number. It's ——. Got that?"

Got it. How big was the payoff, could you see?

"Yeah. What happened was this. He came in here, and told the bartender he wanted two packs of Win-stons. The bartender gave him the Winstons, but the cop didn't give him any money. I was watching. Not a cent."

Cigarets?

"Yeah, two packs."

Well, look O'Malley.

"It's O'Brien."

Sorry. But two packs of smokes isn't really that shocking.

"What'ya mean? I pay for my smokes, let him pay for his. Are you condoning it?"

Absolutely not. Thank you for the information.

"Don't mention it."

The phone rang a half hour later. The operator said it was another collect call from O'Brien.

"I forget to tell you where the tavern was," he said. "And I got the bartender's name. It's Eddie. I heard a guy call him that."

Eddie.

"Right. I'll call you again later."

An hour later the operator called collect again.

"Lishen," O'Brien said, "it happened again. I jus' saw it. Except it was worsh."

More cigarets?

"An' cigars. Thish time it was two packs Kools and one pack Luckies, and two cigars. He din pay anything. The dirty crook. I got his badge number. It's——."

Thanks, O'Brien. But why don't you call it a night? Go home to your wife.

"To hell with the wife. I'm on to this thing now. I'm not going to quit jus' when it's gettin' good."

But you sound tired, O'Brien. Your speech is even slurred.

"Don't worry 'bout me. Jus' you sit tight. I'm on these guys."

Another hour went by before the next call.

"O'Brien here. G'nother one."

Another cop?

"Right."

More cigarets?

"Nhh-nhh. A drink. Din' pay."

A drink?

"Uh-huh."

What kind of drink?

"Ornjuice."

Orange juice?

"Glass ornjuice."

Are you all right, O'Brien?

"Din get badge nummer. Too dark. But I can tell you what he looks like."

What does he look like?

"Big. He's big."

Call it a night, O'Brien.

"Ne'r mind. I'll get more."

The last call came a half hour later. O'Brien was shouting.

"Take down these badge numbers!"

More orange juice?

"No. They threw me out. I called 'em chiselers, and they threw me out. Two of 'em."

O'Brien, go home. It's late.

"No, sir. I'm goin' back in there. I'm not takin' this from chiselers. I'll call you back when I'm done with 'em."

That was the last I heard of O'Brien.

So I'm writing this because I want Mrs. O'Brien to know why he was out late. She should know that he was trying to root out corruption.

I mean, in case she thought he was just goofing around.

II.

1979–1981,
THE SUN-TIMES

End of a Dream

January 30, 1979

Unlike many men who pretend otherwise, I've never bought a car for any practical reasons.

Every new car I've ever owned has fulfilled a fantasy. I don't ask salesmen about the gas mileage, peer at the engine, kick the tires, or measure the seating space for passengers. I don't care about these things.

All I care about is whether the car makes me feel suave and dashing and romantic.

To put it bluntly, almost every car I've owned has been a phallic symbol.

I see nothing wrong with admitting it. The auto makers spend millions on advertising to promote this concept. In those TV commercials, it's obvious the beautiful models aren't lusting all over the cars because of the warranties. So it would be un-American of me to resist.

The first new car I bought was a red convertible. I had wanted one since I was twelve because it was believed by my peers that anyone with a red convertible could pick up girls.

By the time I bought my red convertible, girls were not impressed, since I usually had my two kids in the back seat.

When that car wore out, I traded it in for a low, sleek, flaming orange Datsun 240-Z sports car. I bought it during a period of my life in which I preferred to think of myself as James Bond. I would glide up Milwaukee Avenue, glancing in the rearview mirror to see if I was being tailed by agents from the evil SMERSH.

In most cases, I was being tailed by a CTA bus. But, then, the agents of SMERSH would do anything to disguise their presence, as Bond could tell you.

When the low, sleek 240-Z aged, I traded it in for a low, sleek Camaro, which had a four-speed stick shift and a huge Corvette engine. It could have a trail of rubber a block long.

A friend of mine looked at the Camaro the day I got it and said:

"You must be crazy."

"Why?"

"This is a hot rod, a bomb. You are a balding, near-sighted, middle-aged man. You are not the Fonz. You should be driving a sedate sedan, not a teen-ager's dream."

I told him: "When I was a teen-ager, the only thing I rode was the Logan Square L. This was the kind of car I dreamed about. Now I have it. I am fulfilling a fantasy. I am going to be James Dean for a while."

"You're crazy."

"Maybe. But do you dare challenge me to a drag race?"

He refused, of course. And while driving his sensible sedan, his arteries hardened and he entered premature senility. Meanwhile, I was leaving teen-agers popeyed as I joyously peeled away from them at stoplights.

When I attended his wake, I leaned down and whispered to his waxen remains: "You should have had a four-speed stick shift, you old coot. At least you would have gone out with mufflers roaring."

But now that is all behind me. No more stick shifts, convertibles and sleek sports cars. No more James Bond. No more being a dashing, romantic figure. There seems little point in owning a phallic symbol if you have to keep asking bystanders to help push it out of a snowbank.

Like most Chicagoans who drive, I have spent the last two weeks spinning my wheels in side-street ruts.

So a few days ago, I skidded to a car agency and asked the salesman if he had something that would drive through snow.

He went outside and pointed at a vehicle. "That will go anywhere," he said. "It has four-wheel drive."

"It looks like a truck," I said.

"It is a Bronco," he said. "It is more than a truck. It is a four-wheel-drive recreational vehicle."

Maybe so. But it looked like the kind of thing you'd use to pick up and deliver dry cleaning.

We took it for a test drive and he was right. We zipped through the worst side streets without difficulty. We aimed it at snowdrifts and drove in and out with ease.

"What do you think?" he said.

"I like the way it goes through the snow, but don't you have something suave that also goes through snow? A four-wheel-drive phallic symbol?"

"I'm sorry," he said, "but there is no such thing as a suave, functional, four-wheel-drive phallic symbol. Any psychiatrist would tell you that."

So ended an era in my life. After years in bucket seats only a few inches above the road, I found myself in a practical, square vehicle, sitting so high I could look down on the roofs of ordinary cars.

I suppose life is full of trade-offs. Now I can handle any blizzard or icy ruts.

But when I pull up in front of a restaurant, which is a joy to do in a low, sleek sports car, the doorman will probably tell me to deliver the vegetables at the back door.

I'll have to revise all my automotive fantasies. No more sleek, bejewelled women with foreign accents sliding in and out of my suave sports cars, with just a flash of leg for the envious pedestrians.

Now, in my squat, functional, four-wheel-drive Bronco—with optional plow attachment—I'll have to fantasize about a truck stop waitress named Pearl who has a heart of gold and varicose veins.

In my sports cars, I was James Bond. Or, on a slow day, Rex Harrison.

Now in my truck, who am I? Willie Mike? Mikey Bob? Billy Carter?

"Breaker, breaker, ol' buddy, tell Pearl to put on a clean apron and to set me up a cup of java and a bowl of beans, cuz ol' Willie Mike is highballin' round the bend."

I'll get used to it, I guess.

And heck, Pearl ain't half bad, especially when she's wearin' her teeth.

Rigging Up the Bronco

February 4, 1979

When I recently bought a four-wheel-drive truck to cope with the snow, I wasn't aware of the many extras needed to make the truck presentable.

Since writing about it, I've been bombarded with advice, especially from several acquaintances from Texas, Mississippi, and other Southern states, where trucks outnumber station wagons and are a greater status symbol.

"First thing you have to do," said the Texans, "is git a CB."

I hate the jabber of CB.

"Don't matter. You can't have a proper truck 'less you have a CB."

What else?

"You should get some decals an' put your CB handle on the back of your truck. That dresses it up."

I don't have a CB call handle.

"We'll think of one. How about the Milwaukee Avenue Cowboy?"

I can live with that.

"You'll need some bumper stickers," said the Mississippian. "Maybe one that says? 'Honk If You Love Jesus.' That's popular on trucks."

I don't want people honking at me.

"OK, then git one that says: 'Goat Ropers Need Love, Too.' "

I like that.

"Now, you'll need a rifle rack in the cab," the Texan said.

I don't have any rifles. I'm not a hunter.

"You don't have to hunt. You can shoot at billboards and traffic signs. In my part of Texas, every road sign has a hunnert bullet holes in it."

"You'll need a sack of feed in the back," said the Mississippian.

"Right," said the Texan. "And you have to get some Pearl Beer in cans from Texas."

I don't like Pearl Beer.

"You don't have to drink it," the Texan said. "Pour it all out. It's the cans that are important."

What do I need the cans for?

"For throwin' out the window while you're wheeling along. You can't be a real truckin' man unless you throw Pearl Beer cans out the window."

"You'll have to get a new dog," said the Mississippian.

I already have a dog.

"Yeah, but not a coon dog."

But I don't hunt raccoons.

"Don't matter. Got to have a coon dog. It'll look great back there."

"You'll have to get a bass boat and a trailer," said the Texan.

I have a little aluminum boat.

"Not good enough. You have to hook up a real bassin' rig. A 16-foot Fiberglas, with a speckled metallic finish and built-in sonar, and a 150-horse motor."

But I don't need that powerful a boat.

"Nobody needs one, but nothin' looks as pretty as a bass boat hooked up to a good truck."

"Where's your tire iron?" the Mississippian said.

It's stored under the hood.

"No good," said the Texan. "You have to keep the tire iron under the front seat."

Why?

"So it's handy in case you have to whup someone."

With a tire iron?

"Why, sure. What'ya think they're for? And you'll have to get some different clothes."

What kind?

"Some bib overalls would look good. With some STP patches on them. And some kind of long-billed cap, with a truck company name on it. Is your wife gonna ride with you?"

Sometimes.

"Tell her to wear her hair in curlers when she's ridin' in the truck. And when you stop at a honky tonk, tell her to wait in the truck for you. And after you been inside a while, if she comes in the honky tonk, you holler: "Woman, I told you to wait in the truck!"

I'm not sure that will work out.

"Are you a truckin' man or a mouse?"

I'll have to think about that.

"What about your sons, what are their names?"

David and Robert.

"No good. Have to give them new names."

Such as?

"Name one Bubba, and the other Junior."

I don't think they'll like that.

"Then name one Junior and the other one Bubba."

Yeah, that might work.

"Now, can you get hold of a dead deer?"

What for?

"For layin' across the hood. It's not required, but it sure dresses up a truck, havin' a deer on the hood."

"I prefer a dead boar or a bear," said the Mississippian.

"They're nice, too," the Texan said. "And don't forget to pick up some Red Man."

What's that?

"Chewin' tobacco."

Can't I substitute some bubble gum?

"I don't think you have the makin's of a truckin' man."

And maybe I can substitute a plastic flamingo for the deer?

The Lowdown on High-rises

March 25, 1979

While walking down Lake Shore Drive the other day, I noticed a few drops of water splattering on the sidewalk near me.

I looked up to see if it was raining. Instead, I saw a man standing on the ledge of a building. He was looking down and large tears were dripping from his nose.

Even at that distance, I recognized him as an acquaintance named Hy Rise. As always, he was wearing a multi-colored jogging suit and Adidas shoes. In one hand, he had a racquetball wand and in the other a ski pole. On his head was his rumpled Irish tweed walking hat.

A crowd quickly gathered and he began swaying.

"Don't jump, Hy!" I shouted, and I rushed to his tenth-floor, two-room apartment.

Leaning out the window, I said: "Hy, why are you standing on the ledge?"

"I'm going to end it all," he said in a sorrowful voice.

"But why?"

"Because I have just been condoed out."

"That's no reason to do this. Come inside and let's talk about it."

"No. It's too late. I, Hy Rise, the high-rise man, am going to punch the Big Down Button. Then I'm going to the Great Penthouse of the Big High-rise in the Sky."

"That's no solution."

"Well, at least they won't be able to condo me out of heaven. After I'm gone, give my stereo system to the girl I was living with. How I loved her!"

"What's her name?"

"I don't know. I haven't lived with her that long."

"C'mon off the ledge, Hy. There are other nice places to live besides in a high-rise on the lake."

"That's a lie."

"No, it's the truth. Just look in the for-rent ads. There are lots of apartments that aren't condo."

"Where?"

"Jefferson Park, Edison Park, Six Corners, just to name a few."

"I've never heard of those high-rises."

"Those aren't high-rises—they're neighborhoods."

"Where are they?"

"They're west of Ashland Avenue."

"Now I know you're lying to me. There's nothing west of Ashland Avenue. That's where the world ends. If you go there, you just fall off the edge into space."

"That's not true. There are people, apartment buildings, houses, two-flats, three-flats, twelve-flats. You can find terrific apartments."

"Really?"

"Sure. C'mon back in. We'll look at the for-rent ads together."

"Not yet. These places you're talking about—do they have a view of the lake?"

"I'm afraid not."

"Then I'll jump. I can't live without a view of the lake."

"But you hardly ever look at the lake."

"I know. But when I entertain, I like to show my view of the lake to my friends who don't have a view of the lake. These places you're talking about—what do they have a view of?"

"That depends. Maybe a tree or two. Or a lamppost. A dog. Or the building across the street. I mean, views aren't that important."

"Well, I guess I could do without the view. Just as long as I can walk to my jogging path."

"I'm afraid there aren't a lot of jogging paths there."

"No jogging paths? Where do the people jog?"

"You can always jog on the sidewalk. Or in the school yard."

"On the sidewalk? School yard? Do you think I got this multicolored jogging outfit to jog on a sidewalk? Do airlines stewardesses live in those buildings?"

"I don't think so. But the landlord usually does."

"What do I care about the landlord? I'm not attracted to landlords. Do you think I jog and stay lean and get my hair styled for a landlord? These neighborhoods you mentioned—will I be able to walk to Faces?"

"I don't think so."

"What about R. J. Grunts? Or Jonathan Livingston Seafood?"

"Probably not."

"Or Lawrence of Oregano or the Great Gritsbe's Flying Food Show?"

"No, I think they're too far. You'd be miles away."

"That's insane. How can anyone live miles away from Faces and R. J. Grunts? Where do they disco? Where do they eat?"

"Well, there are a few disco places out there."

"Name one."

"Ziggy's Disco. It's on Milwaukee Avenue."

"Do you actually expect a member of Faces to go to a place called Ziggy's?"

"I'm sorry. Try to stay calm."

"What about French restaurants? Which ones will I be able to walk to?"

"To tell the truth, there aren't many. But we have some good pizza joints."

"The thin or deep dish?"

"Both."

"Aha! I knew it, you idiot. *Everybody* is eating *stuffed* pizza."

"But there are some good bars."

"Such as? Butch McGuire's? The Rookery?"

"No. But places like Stan and Mary's and the Stagger Rite Inn."

"Do they have a lot of swinging singles?"

"No, but they have jukeboxes and shuffleboards."

"This is madness. What kind of life-style do you think I lead?"

"Life-style? But I thought you needed a decent place to live."

"Do you consider that living! What's the nearest racquetball club to those places?"

"There aren't too many of those, but there are a lot of bowling alleys."

"That's it, I'm jumping. Sell my cassettes, my leather racquetball bag, my skis and my fur coat. They should bring enough to pay for my funeral. And remember to destroy my credit cards—all thirty of them. Good-by."

And he jumped.

Fortunately, he landed on his head and is recovering nicely. But the girl he loved took his stereo anyway.

A Pitch for Opening Day

April 5, 1979

It's always one of the best events of the year, the real beginning of Chicago's spring, and I remember the first time I took part.

The old man had hit on the daily double, and to celebrate we were going to opening day at Wrigley Field and sit in the grandstand. There were four of us in the group—the old man, Dutch Louie, Shakey Tony, and me.

It was a cold, blustery day, so everyone dressed accordingly—long underwear, wool pants, heavy jackets, and a pint of Jim Beam. Except me. I didn't get to wear Jim Beam because it was 1939 and I was six. The old man wasn't permissive.

That was not only my first opening day, but it was the first Cubs game I ever saw, and the first time I saw Wrigley Field.

Today it is considered tiny, the smallest ball park in major league baseball. But when we got off the streetcar and there it stood, I couldn't believe anything could be that big and magnificent. To this day, I still have a trace of that awe whenever I see it. Of course the awe dissipates when I see the players.

As we walked toward the ticket gate that afternoon, a cop pointed at me and sternly said: "Shouldn't that kid be in school?"

Dutch Louie said: "He stayed home sick."

"What's wrong with him?" the cop asked.

"Pneumonia," said Louie.

The Cub leadoff man—the first Cub I ever saw bat—
was Stan Hack. And on the first pitch, he ripped a
screaming, hissing, rocket down the foul line toward
right field. It bounced once and banged into the wall.
Hack's feet barely touched the ground as he raced
around the bases, ending up at third base with a theat-
rical slide.

I was hooked. From that moment on I was a Cub fan.
I felt great. I was too young to realize it was a curse.

The next inning Phil Cavaretta came up. Shakey
Tony went crazy. He was on his feet waving his arms,
whistling between his teeth, yelling, "Hey, Phil, Phil,
it's me. Tony."

He sat down and explained that he and Cavaretta had
both gone to Lane Tech, both were Italian, and he had
once met Cavaretta's uncle in a tavern. So Cavaretta
was his friend and hero.

When Cavaretta flied out, a man in the next box
shouted an insult. Shakey Tony stood up and snarled at
the man: "Hey, you want to die? Huh? You want to
die?" The man didn't say anything for the rest of the
ball game. Even when he ordered peanuts, he used hand
motions.

I don't remember much about the rest of the game,
except that the Cubs easily won. That was expected
then. They were the defending National League cham-
pions.

Ten years passed before I went to another opener. By
then I had been to countless games and knew every
statistic in Cub history. I flunked algebra, but I knew
Hack Wilson's lifetime batting average.

But in April 1949, the Cubs were no longer defending
champs. They could barely defend themselves against
ground balls. This may have been the most pitiful era in
Cub history, and I think I know why.

In 1945, with World War II still raging, the Cubs won
a pennant with a team made up of some 4-Fs.

When the war ended, P. K. Wrigley, the Cub owner,
apparently reasoned that the way to win a championship
was with 4-Fs. So while other teams began putting

healthy athletes on the field, Wrigley continued hiring players who walked funny and had strange physical infirmities.

I remember two things about that 1949 opening game. The Cub pitcher, Dutch Leonard, a sly old man, threw the knuckle ball, and he had the Pittsburgh hitters so confused and helpless that they looked almost like the Cubs.

In nine innings, they had just two or three dinky hits. But in the ninth inning, one of them hit an easy grounder to Roy Smalley, the Cub shortstop. He was the only shortstop in baseball who had a deformed hand. I guess Wrigley figured that if another war ever broke out, he'd be set at that position.

Smalley pawed at it, slapped it, finally picked it up and stared at it. Someone hit a pop-up and the Cub catcher and the third baseman collided at their foreheads and fell down. The run scored and we lost one-nothing. I was learning that some Cub fans carried Jim Beam for more than the cold.

I didn't make another opener until 1960, and by then Wrigley had abandoned his 4-F program. He had decided to stock his team with people who had big biceps, like George Altman and Frank Thomas and Ernie Banks and Moose Moryn. They could really hit home runs. The trouble was, most of them had big biceps in their arches, too, and the old ladies behind the concession counter could run faster.

But it was a good opener. Altman hit a long.homer, Thomas hit an even longer one, Moryn knocked some mortar out of the right field wall, the Cubs scored eight runs, and the Giants scored only ten.

I stayed away from any more openers until 1969. And that may have been the greatest of them all. There were almost 41,000 of us there that day.

Ernie hit a homer in the first. Then he hit a homer in the third, and we all jumped up and down and screamed and acted like crazy people. Then the other team tied it, and the suspense mounted until a fine hulk named Willie Smith pinch-hit a homer in the eleventh inning.

Jack Brickhouse screamed himself into a hernia, some fans didn't fall out of the nearby saloons until closing time, and the city was gripped with season-long pennant fever.

We all remember what happened that season. It was the best Cub team in thirty years. No 4-Fs. No strange mutants. For the first time in three decades, the players were better athletes than the grounds crew.

It didn't help. When the crunch came, the Cubs swallowed their tongues, and New York, in its greed, had another championship. Since that season I have made a point of seeing the movie *Fail Safe* every time it is on TV because the movie ends with New York being nuked.

I haven't been to an opener since, partly because I'm mad at the Cub management for trading Jose Cardenal, the only player I saw who could sleep between innings. In fact, Jose could sleep between pitches. With his potential, I had hoped he would remain in Chicago and someday become a distinguished alderman.

But when the day arrives, it's hard to resist. So if I can scrounge a ticket, I might be there.

Just look for a guy wearing long underwear and Jim Beam. My old man has become permissive.

The Rites of Citizenship

May 18, 1979

Alfred Wojdyla had finished work and was waiting under a streetlight for a bus at Ashland and Milwaukee. That's when Angel Gonzalez and a couple of pals came sauntering down the street, looking for something to do and someone to do it to.

They looked Alfred over and he seemed a likely prospect—not very big, about 5 feet 5 inches and 130 pounds, and neatly dressed, which meant he might have a few dollars in his pocket.

They glided up to him and stood one on each side and Angel in front.

"Hey, man," said Angel. "How about some money?"

Alfred hasn't been in this country very long, about two or three years, and he hasn't picked up much English.

So he responded in Polish. Loosely translated, he said: "Go away."

Angel and his pals bridged the communications gap by grabbing Alfred's arms and lifting his wallet from his pocket. Then they took off running, two of them going north and Angel going south.

Alfred is about forty, but his wind and legs are in good shape, so he hoofed after Angel and caught him about a block away, grabbing a handful of Angel's flowing hair.

They wrestled around a bit, then Angel broke away and took off again. And again Alfred caught him.

This time, Alfred started throwing punches, mostly wild left and right roundhouses. Angel responded with fast footwork and quick jabs. Neither man landed any punches, but they stirred up the air pretty good.

Just then, a police car happened by. The cops got out and said:

"Awright, what's going on here?"

Angel, looking indignant, said: "Hey, this guy's causin' trouble."

The cops turned to Alfred and asked him for an explanation.

Alfred, calling on his limited English, said: "He chasem me, he catchem me."

The police put both men in the squad car and went to the Wood Street station where they questioned them further.

Again, Alfred said: "He chasem me, he catchem me." And he added: "Wantem portfolio," referring to his wallet.

"What portfolio?" the cops asked.

"He chasem. He catchem me," said Alfred.

So the police wrote up their reports and filled out some forms. They gave Alfred a piece of paper and said he could leave.

A few days later, Alfred stopped to see a neighborhood lawyer, Ray Rysztogi, who speaks Polish.

He told the lawyer what happened, then showed him the piece of paper the police had given him.

"You dummy," said the lawyer. "They charged YOU with disorderly conduct. What did you tell them happened—in English."

"He chasem and he catchem me."

"You dummy, you told them he was chasing you."

"No, no, no," said Alfred.

"Yes," said the lawyer. "You got it backwards."

The lawyer called one of the cops and asked if any charges had been brought against Angel.

"No," the cop said. "Angel said this guy did something to him so he chased him."

"What about his wallet?"

"He didn't say anything about a wallet. He said something about a portfolio—not a wallet. We didn't see any portfolio."

"Didn't you have anybody who could translate Polish?" the lawyer asked.

"No, but his English was OK," said the cop.

On the court date, Alfred showed up. But Angel didn't. Angel is no dummy. He already had the wallet, so why should he bother trying to put Alfred in jail.

Later, Alfred's lawyer asked him about the personal papers and ID cards in the missing wallet.

Alfred is an efficient person. And he proudly explained that immediately after the robbery, he went to the various agencies and got duplicates of his missing papers.

Among the places he went was the immigration office

to report his green card being missing. He is not yet a citizen, but he was hoping to be sworn in soon.

He gave the lawyer the paper he had shown the immigration people.

"You showed them this?" the lawyer asked.

Alfred nodded.

"Oh, no! What did you show them this for? This is the arrest report. It shows that you got in trouble with the police. This could foul up your citizenship."

The lawyer contacted the immigration authorities, and they told him that a question had arisen about Alfred's worthiness. He had been arrested.

The lawyer explained that Alfred was the victim, even though he had been arrested, and that Angel was the criminal, even though he had not been arrested.

Fortunately, the immigration people are familiar with the Chicago legal process and that made sense to them.

So Alfred probably will become a citizen soon, assuming he doesn't figure out what actually happened to him and decide to go back to Poland.

If Alfred is going to become a citizen, he had better start working on his English. And for starters, I would suggest he memorize this sentence, which any sensible Chicagoan learns at an early age, if he is to survive.

So repeat after me, Alfred:

"Honest, the OTHER guy did it."

School of Hard Knocks

June 19, 1979

The boy is only 13, but big for his age: about 6 feet 1 inch and 175 pounds. He's also matured beyond childish games. His leisure-time activity is stealing.

"Yeah, I'll be honest about it," said the boy's uncle. "The kid's a thief. He runs with a bad crowd. He's on the streets all the time and this is a rough neighborhood.

"But even if he's a thief, and even if he's in the wrong, is there any excuse for a cop to do *this* to him?"

By "this," the uncle was referring to the condition of the boy's face.

Normally, it would be a nice-looking face, despite the fashionable teen-age pout.

But now it could make a person wince. The eyes were blackened. The upper lip was swollen and cut. The rest of his features were puffy and the color of Concord grapes. It was obvious somebody had worked him over.

A cop did this?

"Yeah," said the uncle, speaking for the nephew, who was not the talkative type. "A cop."

In the police station? During questioning?

"Uh, no. It was on the street. He was breaking into a car. Yeah, he admits it. He was busting into it. He does that. He steals from cars.

"And the owner of the car came up on him. And the owner's brother was there. The brother is a cop and he was off duty.

"So they grabbed him, and he tried to get away, and that's when they pounded him. They really teed off on him, you know what I mean? Just look at his face."

The uncle's voice rose as he became more and more indignant.

"Now is that necessary, to beat him up? Why couldn't they just arrest him. That's all they're supposed to do, right? Beating him up like this, that violates his rights, don't it?

"So something ought to be done about this. This ought to be publicized so that cop gets what's coming to him. A guy like that shouldn't be on the police force. This ought to be written up so people know about it and that cop gets in trouble. This is just brutality."

That was one way to look at it, I suppose. And if you strip it down to the basic facts, it does sound unfair:

Two grown men, one of them a cop, beating up a thir-teen-year-old boy.

And, as a rule, I'm against police brutality and have written about more cases of it than I can remember.

But on the other hand, I'm in favor of appropriate punishment, which is something that is rarely applied.

The fact is, the amount of crime in this country greatly exceeds the supply of punishment. And the im-balance is growing all the time.

Even if the courts wanted to jail every person caught breaking into a car, there aren't enough cells in this country to accommodate them.

We're like a city that is hosting a huge convention, but has only a few hotels.

Because of the shortage of jail space, the courts have established certain priorities. Cells are reserved for people who murder, rob, stab, and shoot, although not all of them are accepted.

Then they accept a limited number of people who rape, burglarize, sell dope, mug, maul, and maim, al-though most of these are turned away.

By the time you drop down to people who pop car trunks, lift wallets, snatch purses, shoplift, and run off with another man's snowblower, there's hardly an inch of jail space available.

Thus, the judges have to become actors and pretend they are punishing them. They listen to the testimony, find them guilty, glower, warn them not to do it again, and make a lot of ominous notations on the court docu-ments. But it's all an act, because they then put them on probation, which is a greater hardship for the over-worked probation officer than it is on the small-time thief.

The shortage of punishment becomes even more acute when dealing with someone like the big thirteen-year-old with the bruised face.

There aren't enough juvenile homes in America to hold all the teen-aged thieves and vandals. There prob-ably aren't enough hotels in America to hold them all.

So about the worst that will happen to most of them is that they visit Juvenile Court with their parents. It's rough on the parents. Mothers become unnerved and cry. Fathers feel ashamed and drink. But the kid usually feels pretty good. He'll return to the neighborhood with a minor juvenile record, which will give him special status in the eyes of his contemporaries.

Because most people who commit crimes in America go unpunished, there is a big increase in frustration for those who are the victims.

Every morning, thousands of people awake to find that their car window has been smashed and their favorite cassettes are gone. Or their garage door has been popped and their lawn mower is missing. Or they come home from a weekend trip and find that some kids have not only broken into their house and taken their stereo, but thrown a party while doing it.

That's frustrating. But they're lucky if nobody is caught, because then they would have to go to the police station, then to court, and see nothing come of it, and that's even more frustrating.

So the question is, what can be done? And the answer is, not much. It's probably cheaper in the long run to just write off our losses than to expand the justice and penal system to provide punishment.

And that brings us back to the big thirteen-year-old thief who was punched around by the off-duty cop, and the question of whether he was the victim of police brutality.

My feeling about this case is one of envy. I have to be honest—I wish I had caught him so I could have given him a few punches.

After being on the receiving end of three burglaries, four car break-ins, and a variety of window-smashings and paint-splatterings, it has become a favorite dream of mine to catch just one of the nasty boogers. I wouldn't want to cause any permanent damage. No scars or broken bones. I'm no sadist. But it would feel good to punch and kick him a bit. Just a few satisfying shrieks of agony is all I ask.

The car owner and his brother the cop are among the few lucky victims. Now, when they go to Juvenile Court and see the kid sent home, they'll at least have the sweet memory of his welts and bruises.

And that boy is lucky, too, although he might not realize it. At only thirteen, he now knows that being caught stealing someone else's hard-earned property might carry with it something more than a tired judge trying to look stern, a mother looking distraught, and an uncle being indignant.

It might also involve a hard smash in the mouth.

That, I think, is educational. And I just wish more of us had the chance to be the teachers.

A New Overture, Boys!

June 28, 1979

The Fourth of July is this country's most significant holiday. And this city's biggest gathering will probably occur the night before at the Grant Park band shell, where a free concert will be held.

If it proves as popular as last year's concert, more than 100,000 people will attend.

And once again, the highlight of the concert will be a rousing piece of music composed by a Russian.

Granted, there will also be music by American composers, such as George Gershwin and John Philip Sousa.

But the big number, the show stopper, the mind-blowing grand finale will be the *1812* Overture, composed by Peter Ilich Tchaikovsky.

I'm against it.

No, I have not become a cold warrior or slid to the political far right.

And I have nothing against the *1812* Overture as a piece of music. I like it. It's wonderfully noisy, and it has cannons and bells and when I play it loud, my stereo woofers have convulsions and my tweeters go berserk; my cats run up the drapes, my dogs howl and foam at the mouth and nails pop out of the walls of my house. It is my kind of classical music.

Nor does my objection have anything to do with Tchaikovsky himself. From what I have read about him, he was a nice guy and a perfect example of what a great musical genius should be. Especially in temperament.

He started having nervous breakdowns when he was about nine years old, and he had them regularly for the rest of his life. Even though he was homosexual and fell madly in love with his nephew, Bob, he married a woman. He didn't want to marry her, of course, but she was a little crazy and threatened to kill herself if he didn't. So he decided to be Mr. Nice Guy. (Musical geniuses always seem to find themselves in these kinds of nerve-wracking situations.) Even worse, his wife turned out to be a nymphomaniac, which didn't help his sexual self-confidence any.

Besides his romantic problems, every time he wrote something good, which was most of the time, he thought it was awful, so he would go into a funk, or get drunk, or brood about jumping into the Volga. He finally got fed up with all of his woes and drank some polluted water and caught the fever and died, which probably gave him the first good night's sleep he'd had in years.

Considering everything, he probably should have taken his father's advice in the first place and become a lawyer.

On the other hand, if he had become a lawyer and had kept having nervous breakdowns and falling in love with his nephew Bob, his clients would have probably taken their business across the street to Borscht, Borscht, and Blackbread.

But to get back to my reasons for objecting to Tchaikovsky's *1812* Overture being played as the showpiece of our big July Fourth Grant Park concert:

This country has been in existence for 230 years. It was already 66 years old when Tchaikovsky was born. (He was a very depressed baby, incidentally. He would cry *while* eating.)

You would think that after all this time, some American composer would have written a piece of music big enough and dramatic and exciting enough to be the finale at something like our Grant Park concert.

And more importantly, a piece of music that would have as its theme something American, not Russian.

The theme of the *1812* Overture is the defeat of Napoleon's army by the Russians. And while I can understand Tchaikovsky and other Russians being proud of that, I'm not sure it was a good thing. Sure, Napoleon was probably the most arrogant short guy in history, but it might have been better in the long run if he had won. Then France would have taken over Russia, and by now the Russians would be content to sit around eating pâté de foie gras and garlicky snails, sipping Burgundy and sneaking off for nooners with their skinny mistresses as the French do, and they wouldn't be looking for ways to cause us headaches.

Now, the main reason the *1812* Overture is played in our concert is the use of cannons. The music is good, yes, but there are many greater musical compositions. The music is dramatic and exciting, but there are other works more dramatic and exciting. Ah, but the cannons! Even stereo owners who don't like classical music own the record just to hear the cannons in their left speakers blasting at the cannons in their right speakers.

So I propose that the City of Chicago commission a Chicago composer to write a piece of music to replace the *1812* Overture in future July Fourth concerts.

I further propose that it be called the *1979* Overture.

As I envision this piece of music, it would not be uniquely American, but it would be uniquely Chicagoan.

The *1979* Overture would also feature the use of cannons. But remember, in much of Chicago, the word cannon has a different meaning than in other places. An example of this difference would be a cop saying: "So I'm walkin' down this dark gangway when out of the basement jumps this guy and he whips out his cannon."

He is referring, of course, to something along the lines of a .45.

So, in the *1979* Overture, as the music reaches its dramatic conclusion, we will suddenly hear from the left the roar of a thousand Chicago cannons being fired by members of the Insane Idiots street gang, recruited for this performance.

And from the right we will hear the thunderous response of a thousand more Chicago cannons fired by members of the Deranged Disciples street gang.

In a classic performance of the *1812* Overture, when the cannon fire ends, the glorious ringing of great cathedral bells is heard.

And in the *1979* Overture, we'd have bells, too. But we'd go beyond bells. We'd have police sirens, fire sirens, ambulance sirens, burglar alarms, the 10:30 Tuesday air-raid whistle, and a chorus of 1,000 women blowing the kinds of little whistles worn on chains around the neck to scare off rapists.

Finally, there would be the fireworks during the closing bars of music. But in addition to fireworks, in front of the band shell, between the Insane Idiots and the Deranged Disciples, there would be exploding cars, their hoods being blown sky-high by dynamite charges—a display known in some circles as The Old Chicago Ignition Trick.

And that would be a concert to remember.

Now I must go off to brood or have a breakdown. The creative process ain't easy.

Big Shots in Small Cars

July 3, 1979

We pulled up to the same red light. He and his female companion were in a small economy car. It looked shiny and new. I was in my four-wheel-drive truck.

I happened to glance at them and saw that they were studying my truck with what appeared to be contempt. Then she looked at me and her lips began forming words.

I rolled my window down and asked: "Did you say something to me?"

"Yes, what kind of gas mileage does that *thing* get?" she asked. The way she said "that thing" made me feel as if I was driving something obscene.

"Uh, the mileage is not very good," I answered.

"Well, do you think it's fair for someone to drive a *thing* like that in these kinds of times, with the fuel crisis and all the other problems, and when people have to make sacrifices?"

"There was no crisis except a snow crisis when I got it," I said, wondering why I was sitting there answering questions like a criminal suspect.

"That may be so," she said, "but do you think that you have the right . . . ?" That was as much as I heard. I rolled my window up. She sneered. He leaned over and sneered, too.

When the light changed, I made a right turn, although I wasn't going that way. But I was afraid that they would get at me again at the next light and at the one after that. By the time I got home, I'd be filled with so much guilt that I might slash my own oversized tires.

So it is starting. The people with the fashionably frugal EPA ratings are going to be giving disdainful looks to those of us who are stuck with the disgusting EPA ratings. The status symbols have been reversed.

Only a few short months ago, my four-wheel-drive was a great status symbol. I bought it at the height of the great blizzard in order to get to work. I bulled it through snowdrifts, easily drove up and down snow-clogged side streets while looking down at the little snow-covered lumps that lined the curbs—small economy cars that couldn't go anywhere.

In snowy January, the owners of the snow-covered lumps looked envious as I went by. Now, in gasless July, all those little lumps are the status symbols. And their owners are filled with self-righteousness.

A friend of mine who drives a big black Cadillac said he is beginning to notice it.

"Just the other day, I got sneered at on the toll road by a family in a VW Rabbit," he said. "There I was, driving along, and they went by me and the wife sneered at me. So did the little kids in the back seat. The kids pointed at me like I was some kind of pervert. They had a tiny dog and even the dog looked unfriendly.

"They made me feel so ashamed that I slowed down and got behind a truck to sort of hide.

"Then the next time I went to the gas station to fill up, there was a guy at the next pump, and he had a little Japanese car. He watched the gauges to see how many gallons I was getting, and he kept shaking his head. Why should I have to put up with that kind of humiliating treatment from a guy with a Japanese car?

"I never thought I would see the day come in America when a man driving a big black Cadillac would be looked down at by people in a tiny VW. Don't they know how hard I had to work and connive to own it?

"The way I had been taught, people in little cars were supposed to look at people in big expensive cars with admiration and envy. That's what I did when I owned a little car.

"But now that isn't the way it is. Instead of taking their turn and looking envious, they are looking at me with contempt.

"Now I see car commercials where people pull up in front of restaurants in tiny cars and *they* act like big shots.

"Everything has been turned upside down. After all those years of work, I finally get my Caddy, and now they are making me feel ashamed. Is that right? Is that the American way?"

I didn't know how to answer him. I guess it is the new American way, and we'll just have to live with it, and try to avoid making eye contact with people who have little cars.

But if it will make him feel any better, he might consider this: Before the summer is over, all those people on roller skates will probably be sneering at people in small cars.

Up from the Pig Farm

July 11, 1979

At 3:35 P.M., Thursday, July 12, 1979, a three-inch piece of Skylab fell on a pig farm near Bumpkin, Illinois, lodging in the head of one Jasper Banal, twenty-seven, a hired hand.

Mr. Banal said, "Owwweee," and slumped to the ground. The farmer and his wife, after first scolding him for loafing, saw the wound and loaded him in the back of their pickup truck and drove him to the clinic in Bumpkin.

Not having the facilities to treat the wound, the clinic rushed Banal to a hospital in Chicago.

There, doctors X-rayed his head and decided it would be dangerous, possibly fatal, for them to remove the Skylab fragment.

"He can lead a full and normal life," the chief neurosurgeon said, "so long as no one tries to dislodge the fragment. We have created a protective hat for him to wear to prevent someone from accidentally doing so."

Mr. Banal then was brought into the hospital auditorium to meet the world's press, which was eager to see a man who had actually been struck by Skylab.

He was wearing a small, cone-shaped, metal hat with a chin strap, resembling those worn by New Year's Eve revelers. He also wore a simpleminded grin.

"Mr. Banal," a reporter asked, "how do you feel about this?"

" 'Bout what?" said Jasper, scratching his new hat.

"About Skylab falling on your head?"

"Heck, my ol' daddy uster hit me harder than 'at when he got mad."

"Well how do you feel about having to wear that cone-shaped metal hat the rest of your life?"

"Ah don't mind that, neither. Ah think it looks kinder nice. Ah seed a soldier wear a hat like that on TV once."

"Doctor, has this injury affected Mr. Banal's mind? He sounds sort of . . ."

"No, we are told by those who know him that this is the way Mr. Banal has always sounded."

"That's right," said the farmer. "Ah've known Jasper since he was a boy, and the fact is, he's always been kind of simple."

"Stupid is what he is," said the farmer's wife.

"That's right," said Banal, with a huge grin, "I'm simpleminded. Everybody knows that."

"Mr. Banal, you will be receiving a substantial amount of money from the government to compensate you for your injury. What will you do with it?"

"I'm gonna buy me some whisky. I sure like whisky. And I'm gonna buy a yeller leisure suit like President

Billy Carter wears. And I'm gonna ask Pearl the truck stop waitress if she'll marry me, and if she will, I'll buy her some new teeth. And I'm gonna give a gift to Nelly."

"Is Nelly a girl friend?"

"No, Nelly's my favorite pig."

After several days of appearing on talk shows, during which he giggled a lot, Jasper returned to the farm and to the obscurity of tending pigs.

One morning, four weeks later, the farmer found him reading a newspaper.

"Stop foolin' 'round, Jasper," he said, "you can't read."

"Yes I can," said Jasper, quickly reading stories aloud.

"When did you learn that?" said the amazed farmer.

"I don't know," said Jasper. "I just started doing it."

They took Jasper back to the hospital where he was given intelligence tests. They found that his IQ had risen 100 points, from 80 to 180. A week later, it had climbed beyond 200.

By then, Jasper was speed-reading pages of books in a single glance. In only days, he absorbed a complete encyclopedia, the collected Great Books of Western Man and the Durants' *Story of Civilization*.

The government, reasoning that the head injury had turned Banal from an idiot into a genius, refused to pay him compensation. It considered billing him for services rendered.

But that didn't matter. Within two years, he had not only completed college, but had four advanced degrees and was practicing corporate law and making a fortune on the stock exchange. He then used his wealth to write, produce, and direct several films, which swept most of the Oscars and made box-office history.

To improve his appearance, he personally designed a curly hairpiece that covered the pointed Skylab fragment in the top of his skull. That, combined with glistening caps on his teeth, and his powerful farmboy physique, gave him a ruggedly handsome look, and he starred in several of his own films.

He lived in a vast oceanfront estate and had apartments in New York and Paris, as well as a ranch in Wyoming. He married Haut Brion Hemingway, the beautiful and bright young model and actress.

Then he became bored. "I believe that I can save mankind from itself," he told his wife. "I'm going to go into politics and run for President."

His speeches, which he wrote himself, were brilliant. They explored in great detail the many great problems of our time and he proposed lengthy, specific solutions.

People either fell asleep, walked out, or booed. In the polls, he was running far behind "no choice," as well as the other candidates.

"I don't understand it," he told his political advisers.

"You've got to streamline," they told him. "You need slogans and buzzwords. We'll use your good looks in TV commercials. Get you in *People* magazine. We'll make you a populist-conservative-liberal-labor-management candidate."

"Never," vowed Jasper, and he campaigned his way, until the polls showed him falling behind even the "don't vote" category.

The day before the key New Hampshire primary campaign began, a depressed Jasper sat talking to his wife.

"I've failed," he said.

"You did your best," she said, absentmindedly running her fingers through his hair to console him.

In doing so, she dislodged the piece of Skylab in his skull.

A simpleminded grin suddenly creased Jasper's face, and he said: "Hey, yer prettier than Pearl the waitress. Even prettier than Nelly, my pet pig. Got any whisky, sweetie?"

That night, while his wife wept, his advisers taught him a short and simple speech with some buzzwords and slogans. They quickly cut a commercial, showing his fine teeth and profile, and using an announcer's voice for the brief message.

He became a sensation, sweeping through the primaries, receiving the nomination and winning by a landslide.

After being sworn in, he would sit in the Oval Office and watch TV, while his advisers ran things and planned his next campaign.

At night, when he was alone, he would wear his old metal, cone-shaped beanie.

"It looks kinder nice," he would say with a happy grin.

Moral: In politics, sometimes no head is better than one.

Crisis in a Cool High-rise

July 19, 1979

After President Carter unveiled his plans to conserve energy, I happened to talk to a modern young High-rise Man, and he was nervous.

"I don't know if I can face that kind of future," he said.

You mean not having enough gas for your car?

"No, I can live with that. I have a tiny car. And my High-rise job is not that far from my High-rise home. And the high-rise that my High-rise girl friend lives in is not that far from my high-rise. Besides, I may sell my car and switch to roller skates."

Then what is bothering you?

"Sweating. They are going to turn down the air conditioning in my office. In the restaurants I go to. In the discos. In the swingles bars. Where I get my hair styled. Everywhere I go, I will sweat."

Well, you've sweated before, haven't you?

"Occasionally, but only under certain conditions that are appropriate for sweating. When I play racquetball, I sweat. When I jog, I sweat. And when I roller-skate, I sweat."

So you're accustomed to sweating.

"But only when I'm supposed to sweat. As soon as I'm done, I stop sweating and I immediately shower and apply a deodorant that keeps me dry and gives me twenty-four-hour protection against sweating. But it can't protect me if the air conditioning is going to be turned down. I will be sweating everywhere I go."

There's nothing wrong with that.

"You can't be serious. It is unnatural."

To sweat? But people have sweated throughout history. They have sweated since they began walking upright.

"Did they have energy shortages back then, too?"

I mean before there was air conditioning.

"You mean there once was no air conditioning?"

Why, of course, there wasn't. It didn't really become common until after World War II. Didn't you know that?

"Why, no. I thought there had always been air conditioning. I've always had it. How could people live and work without it?"

We just sweated.

"You actually did without air conditioning?"

Sure. We all did.

"In your homes? Your jobs? Your discos? Your restaurants? You sweated in all these places? How awful for you."

Oh, it wasn't that bad.

"It sounds barbaric. When you discoed, you must have been dripping with sweat. Your clothes must have looked awful."

Well, we didn't disco, but we danced. And, sure, we sweated.

"You must have had to take showers every few hours."

No. Most homes didn't have showers. But we took a bath every Saturday.

"Once a week? Everybody must have . . . you know . . ."

Must have what?

"You know. Smelled."

Toward the end of the week, yes.

"But how could someone go up to a girl in a swingles bar if he was sweating and she was sweating. I mean, what a turnoff. You'd both be all wet. What kind of deodorant did you use—the stick or spray?"

I don't think we used any kind. I guess some ladies used them.

"You sweated and you did not use a deodorant? Didn't you . . . offend?"

Well, you sort of learned to keep your arms close to your sides. If you didn't flap your arms too much, you were all right.

"And when you slept on hot nights, didn't you sweat?"

Sure. But a person can sweat and sleep at the same time—even Spiro Agnew could do that.

"But what about people who were married or living together. You mean they would be in bed and both would be sweating?"

Why, yes.

"How uncool. Didn't your hair spray get gummy?"

We didn't use hair spray.

"How could you keep your hair in place?"

Brilliantine.

"But that's greasy. And you were sweaty. You were greasy and sweaty."

I guess so. And sometimes gritty.

"Greasy and sweaty. And gritty?"

Yeah. And grimy, too.

"Greasy and sweaty and gritty and grimy?"

Except on Saturdays when we took baths.

"It sounds like a nightmare. I'm starting to feel sick."

It won't be that bad. Stay calm. Why, you're starting to sweat.

"See, it's starting. Why did my parents bring me into this kind of world?"

Hogging the Jogging Path

August 3, 1979

A heated battle has broken out between the joggers and the people who want to ride horses in Lincoln Park.

The joggers do not want to share their jogging path with horses because they do not want their high-priced Adidas shoes landing in horsey-do.

Those who want to ride horses say the joggers have no right to hog the jogging path. And a woman who wants to open a stable has even offered to put the horses in plastic diapers.

The dispute will have to be settled by the city's aldermen, who must decide whether to allow Mary Supera, the horse diaper lady, to open her proposed riding academy.

It's my policy never to let any controversy pass without taking sides.

And in this case, I am on the side of the horse people. I have two reasons: First, I like horses. Second, I do not like joggers.

I'll begin with my second reason:

Joggers, in their quest for strong lungs, hearts, libido, and an eternally youthful appearance, have become overbearing. Especially the High-rise Men and High-rise Women who make up a big part of Lincoln Park's jogging population.

Anyone who works with joggers knows what I mean. They are smug and boastful as they recite how many miles they run a day, a week, a month, a year.

When they aren't telling us how many miles they run, they tell us about their weight, blood pressure, and pulse rate. Joggers really love talking about their pulse rate. One day at lunch, a jogger, picking at his health-food salad, told me: "My pulse rate in repose is forty beats a minute." Right out of the blue, he told me that. Then he asked: "What's yours?"

"In repose?" I asked, picking at my martini and spaghetti with chicken liver sauce.

"Yes."

"In repose, my pulse rate is 150 to 180 beats a minute. It constantly fluctuates."

He put down his fork and looked horrified.

"Why that's terrible. You're in dangerously bad shape."

"Really?" I said, holding my breath until my face turned purple, rolling my eyes back into my head, and sliding out of my chair while making a death rattle sound.

He almost fainted, and it was the last time he ever mentioned his pulse rate to me.

When joggers began proliferating, they made dogs their enemies and started picking on them. They screeched to the authorities and the press about the indignity of stepping in doggy-do. Then they claimed that while they jogged, dogs were constantly trying to bite their ankles, calves, and parts of their bodies too embarrassing to mention.

They ran to City Hall and demanded that all dogs in the parks be on leashes, even nice old dogs that couldn't gum a jogger's foot.

One paranoid jogger even began carrying a baseball bat and broke the leg of some tiny mutt that yapped at him.

It never occurred to them that jogging is the most simple-minded of sports and that being chased by dogs could make it exciting. Then they could brag about the bite scars on their legs instead of their damned pulse rates in repose. But they don't have enough competitive spirit for that.

Now, having lowered their pulse rates, squeezed their tiny behinds into designer blue jeans, and made countless dogs miserable, they want to prevent people from riding horses on what was a bridle path long before joggers appeared.

They forget that fact. But back when the only people who ran in public were thieves and the coppers chasing them, horses galloped along what now is the jogging path.

And the horsemen and women were never the pains in the neck that the joggers are. They didn't complain about dogs. If a dog bothered a horse, the horse just stepped on him. Muggers, too. Squish. Boy, that's the way to handle a mugger.

I have to admit that I'm biased toward the riding of horses because I grew up in what some people refer to as "the horsey set." My uncle Bruno owned his own horse, named Thunderbolt, which pulled my Uncle Bruno's junk wagon. Uncle Bruno, incidentally, never jogged a step in his life, and he lived to be ninety-one. His horse never ran either, and he made it to sixty-four.

This country did not become great by jogging. Men on horses pioneered it. Name me one movie in which John Wayne was shown in a tailored jogging suit and Adidas shoes. Or Randolph Scott. Or the Cisco Kid. You can't.

How would it have looked if the Lone Ranger had slapped himself on the hip and gone jogging across the plain shouting, "Hi ho, Adidas, awayyy." They would have locked him up as a crazy.

So I say let the horses into the park. The joggers can learn to leap over the horsey-do. It will add another dimension to their sport.

Or, as Marie Antoinette might have said: "Let them wear boots."

A Leery Survey

August 28, 1979

Thousands of female state employees are being surveyed to determine if they are being leered at by male state employees.

The study is being done as part of the growing awareness of "sexual harassment" of women by the men with whom they work.

This has become one of the hottest social issues in the country. Judging from what women are revealing on talk shows and in TV documentaries, a working female cannot get through an eight-hour day without being chased 'round and 'round the water cooler.

Since the results are so predictable, the state study probably is a waste of time and money. Of course women will say that men leer. Even women who never are leered at will say they are. Pride.

But, in truth, most men don't really leer, even those who try, because genuine leering isn't easy to do.

My dictionary defines the word "leer" as "a side glance, especially of sly or insulting suggestion or malicious significance."

Just try it. Get a mirror and see if you can whip off a side glance of sly or insulting suggestion or malicious significance. It is not easy. In fact, it is very difficult.

Rather than leering, you'll find yourself looking simple-minded.

Groucho Marx could leer, probably better than anyone in the world. So could Slats Grobnik, who was born with a natural leer that was his only expression. Slats even leered in church, which always puzzled the priest.

But when most of us try to leer, the result usually is a smirk or a gawk, and there is a big difference.

A smirk is defined this way: "To smile in an affected, would-be-agreeable, or offensively familiar way."

Smirking is what Clark Gable usually did. Smirking is much easier than leering. All you have to do is let your eyelids droop and curl your lips in a small, mirthless smile.

As for gawking, it means "to stare stupidly." And that is what many men wind up doing when they think they are leering or even smirking.

So I have to question the validity of a survey that doesn't distinguish among leering, smirking, gawking, or even gaping. (Gaping is similar to gawking, except the jaw hangs open.)

These distinctions are important since the survey is intended to stamp out the leering at females by males.

Those who are making the survey say that if they find that leering and other forms of sexual harassment are widespread, corrective action will be taken.

They didn't say what kind of corrective action this would be, and I can't imagine how the state could legislate against leering, smirking, and so on.

For one thing, there always exists the possibility of an innocent person being accused of leering when he really isn't. Hay fever can cause a pseudo-leer. So can the morning sun shining through an office window. Near-sightedness is another common cause of what appears to be a leer. After Rudolph Valentino died, it was revealed that this world-renowned romantic leer was caused by weak eyes. Rather than leering at women, he was just trying to see them.

Then there is the question of motive. Some female

persons will become angry at me for saying this, but there are times when a male person can be provoked into leering, as well as smirking, gawking, and gaping.

Some time ago, I wrote about the effect of slit skirts. By boldly flashing their limbs in public, female persons were causing male persons to leer, smirk, gawk, gape, or just happily beam.

Dozens of angry female persons wrote or called to say that men who leered at their slit skirts lacked couth and were only one step removed from being barnyard creatures.

Since then, I have refrained from leering at slit skirts. When I'm in the company of someone wearing one, I keep my eyes elevated and look at her ear or nostril or some other nonprovocative part of her anatomy. Sometimes I merely yawn and close my eyes, giving the impression that a flashing thigh is putting me to sleep.

But not all men have my strong character, and if women persist in wearing slit skirts, skin-tight jeans, see-through blouses, and other immodest garments, there are bound to be men who are too weak to fight off the urge to leer, smirk, gawk, etc.

Therefore, the state survey should be broadened to include men and the question of why they leer. Did someone bat a flirtatious eyelash? Or wiggle a hip? Or flash a limb?

I'm not saying men are blameless. There are some who would leer at the most modestly dressed granny, or even a department store dummy. Why, I heard a song about a man in Chicago who even leered at his own wife.

But if government is going to step in and outlaw leering, it must also take a stand on swiveling, slinking, wriggling, and waggling.

Or maybe we should just have a survey to determine who thinks up these kinds of surveys, and how fast they can be fired.

Technology and the Bull

October 28, 1979

It is said that there is an R&D crisis in this country. That means Research and Development: inventing new products, creating, devising, improving. And our leaders say we are lagging behind other eager-beaver countries.

To them, I say bull!

At least that is what I'm saying since becoming aware of an American company called International Biologics Inc.

This small firm, showing the kind of original thinking that has made this country the world's leading producer of almost any kind of thingumajig imaginable, has now found a way to successfully make commercial use of an, uh, of, uh, a uh. . . .

I'm not sure just how to say it. So why don't I just go ahead and print the advertisement, exactly as it appeared recently in a magazine called *Potentials in Marketing*.

The ad, accompanied by a picture of a pretty model holding a golf putter, said:

A GOLD PUTTER MADE FROM WHAT?
You may not believe it, but the golf putter this young lady is holding is made from the pizzle of a bull.

That's right. The entire intact male reproductive organ of a grown bull . . . and this beautifully finished, full sized, functional putter would make a unique gift for your colleagues, employees, or some of your best customers.

Also available are walking sticks, billiard cues,

gavels, ashtrays, backscratchers, pointers, etc., all made from the same raw material.

Send for your brochure and prices today!

I've always been intrigued by the workings of the inventine mind, by the ability to see the same things others see, but in a creative way.

For some great minds, the ideas came in an instant revelation, as was said to be the case of Newton with his apple. For others, such as Edison, it could be a long hit-and-miss process.

So, after seeing the ad, I became curious. Under what circumstances does a person look at, as the ad put it, "the pizzle of a bull" and envision it as a golf putter, walking stick, billiard cue, back scratcher, etc.

A few phone calls led me to Walt Mackey, a rural veterinarian in New Brighton, Minnesota, and head of International Biologics, which is located there.

Dr. Mackey, a cheerful, outgoing man of fifty-five, was eager to talk about his creations, of which he is quite proud.

"I'll tell you how the idea came to me. It was many years ago, when I was a youth. I saw a farmer had hung this deceased bull's appendage on a fence to dry. I asked him why he did that, and he said that they used them as the handles for bullwhips.

"So I always remembered that. And a few years ago, I was thinking about it and it occurred to me that they can be used in other ways, too.

"I began experimenting. You see, as a veterinarian I specialized in large-animal medicine, so I knew a lot about all parts of bulls.

"I found I could make all kinds of products with the pizzle, so that's how the business got started.

"It fits in with the ecology movement. People today are conserving or recycling cans and cardboard. Well, we can recycle that part of the bull."

How does one go about obtaining that portion of a bull's anatomy?

"Well, when a bull gets old, and he's not able to do what bulls are well known for doing, then he is retired from his earthly domain. He ends up in a packing plant.

"Now, these plants claim they use every part except the squeal. But that's not true. They don't use that part. They throw it away.

"So we make their claim come true. We buy our pizzles from the packing plants."

Is it possible for you to explain, I would hope in delicate terms, how one goes about converting a bull's pizzle to a golf club grip, or a cane or billiard cue?

"I'll try. When the pizzles arrive from the packing plant, naturally they are kind of, uh, uh, limp."

Naturally.

"Fortunately, mother nature has provided us with a solution to that problem. We insert an aluminum rod in order to make them firm and functional. Then we dry it until it is as dry as a potato chip. Then there is sanding and cleaning and finishing and the result is a very beautiful, shiny, lustrous, sturdy, functional item."

When you speak of using them as a walking stick or a billiard cue, I assume you are referring to only the handle.

"Not at all. For some items, such as the putter, it is only the handle, which would come from a modestly endowed bull. But for walking sticks, canes and pool cues, the entire item is the pizzle."

There are pizzles that long?

"Definitely. Believe me, there are some impressive old bulls in this land of ours. Obviously, a pool cue would take a well endowed beast."

I'll say. Now, the word "pizzle" itself. Did you make that word up?

"No. When we first began advertising, we had a problem. Most publications would not accept our ads using the more clinical word. Then somebody told me that the word pizzle meant the same thing. It wasn't in my dictionary, so I called the St. Paul public library and asked the lady there if she could look in some of the real big old dictionaries for the word pizzle.

"She asked me what it meant. I said I'd rather not say what I thought it meant. So she went and looked it up and when she came back she said: 'Well! It means what you probably think it means! And I'm glad you did not tell me what you thought it meant!' I guess she was kind of shocked."

How is business?

"Great. It started slow but now that we have the word pizzle, and can advertise, it's really going. One man in Texas ordered seventy putters to give to his friends. And the putters sell for eighty dollars. That's our most expensive item."

Do you anticipate that the mortality rate of old bulls will be high enough to keep you in pizzles?

"I think so. And I'll tell you the joke that's going around. Folks are saying that we've got every bull in Minnesota nervous. Ha!"

That's a real thigh slapper.

"I'll send you our brochure. You might want to think about something we've got for your Christmas list."

Do that. One never knows when he will meet a cow.

Bottoms Up, L.A.!

December 6, 1979

The phone rang and the caller said he was a writer on a Los Angeles newspaper. He was calling some Chicagoans to get our opinions on Mayor Byrne's new appearance.

As he put it: "What do you think of her face-lift?"

The questions startled me. "First of all, a gentleman does not discuss such matters. Second, it is not called a face-lift."

"What is it called?" he said.

"It is called 'cosmetic surgery,' " I said. "And I'm surprised you, of all people, would make that mistake."

"Why should that surprise you?"

"Because you are in California, and there is more plastic surgery done per square inch of human skin in your scatterbrained state than anywhere else in America, or possibly the world."

Which is true. Californians, with their obsession for a youthful, sun-kissed appearance, are constantly getting the wrinkles, and bags in their faces ironed out.

They also lead the nation in having their breasts lifted, expanded, and pointed in the proper direction (straight ahead, rather than at their toes).

And Californians—male and female—are big on having their behinds lifted—"a fanny tuck" they call it.

I'm not sure how a fanny tuck works, and I'd rather now know, but the idea is for the man or woman to have a tiny, perky behind, suitable for display on a beach or in tight jeans. The shape and youthfulness of their behinds is very important to Californians.

Recycling sagging bods is a big business in California. There are high-priced resorts that specialize in squeezing off weight, snipping out sags, injecting magic potions into the flesh, reshaping noses and chins, capping teeth, and having the hair from their armpits transplanted to their bald domes.

They even have knee-lifts. That's right. Some Californians are so concerned about the appearance of their knees they have cosmetic surgery done on them.

They spend so much time getting their skin stretched tight that if you checked the backs of Californians, you would probably find that many of them have a ridge running along their spines, like a Rhodesian Ridgeback.

And with all that body-processing going on under his nose, a California writer makes an eight-dollar phone call to ask about our mayor's face.

"But how do Chicagoans feel about her cosmetic surgery?" he persisted.

"Never mind her," I said. "What about your Governor Moonbeam? What about his surgery?"

He sounded surprised. "I didn't know Jerry Brown had cosmetic surgery."

"Then he should."

"Why? He looks youthful."

"I don't mean for the way he looks. He should have a brainlift."

"What's that?"

"I don't know. But the way he jabbers, he should have some kind of cosmetic surgery on his brain. It couldn't hurt."

"Look, could we talk about your Mayor Byrne? Aren't Chicagoans more accustomed to politicians who have sagging jowls?"

What a dumb question. Of course we are accustomed to politicians with sagging jowls. And sagging bellies. And sagging behinds. And sagging wallets, from the weight of them.

But those are male politicians. Because our male politicians sag, that doesn't mean that we want our female politicians to have sagging jowls.

"Are you suggesting," I asked, "that in Chicago we prefer our women to have sagging jowls?"

"No, I didn't mean to suggest that."

"Well, I should hope not. Just because we don't get our fannies tucked doesn't mean that we don't have an eye for a pretty face. And we no more prefer sagging jowls on females than you do."

"I didn't mean to offend . . ."

"Then why are you asking about our mayor's cosmetic surgery?"

"Well, it is newsworthy, don't you think?"

"As a matter of fact, no, I don't think it is newsworthy. Especially not in California, where men get their fannies tucked. I think males having their behinds reshaped is far more newsworthy. In fact, I find it shameful and alarming. I think it is a definite indication of the decline of this country's virility and moral standards. In a crisis, how could we put together a real army with men who are concerned about the pert shape of their rear ends?''

"I don't understand how we got on that subject."

"I'll tell you how. Can you name me one Chicago politician, one alderman, one ward committeeman, one state senator, who has had his fanny tucked?''

"Well, no."

"Of course you can't. But California is crawling with them and that is what you should concern yourself with. Frankly, I'm suspicious of your Governor Moonbeam. Have you ever noticed how he looks in tight jeans?''

"He's pretty slender."

"Ahah! So can you say for certain that he hasn't had a fanny tuck?''

"I have no idea."

"Then why don't you check on that before sticking your nose into Chicago's business?''

"Wait a minute. A minute ago you said Jerry Brown may have had a brain-lift. Now you are saying you suspect he had his behind lifted. Do you think he had both?''

"With him, my good man, I don't see how you could tell the difference between his brain and his bottom.''

Write on, Barbarians

December 12, 1979

Robert Maszak, an English teacher at Bloom Township High School in Chicago Heights, has sent me a stack of angry letters written by his students as a classroom assignment.

The students were reacting to a column I wrote last

week about eleven people being trampled to death at a rock concert in Cincinnati.

In that column, I said those who would climb over people's broken bodies to reach a seat in an auditorium could be called "the new barbarians."

The dictionary definition of barbarian that I used is "the opposite of civilized." And I think anyone who tramples someone to death can wear that definition.

In sending me the letters, teacher Maszak, apparently proud of his students' efforts, wrote: "Some 'barbarians' do write."

Yes, they do. But frankly, if I were an English teacher and they were my students, I'd lock the letters away where no one could see them.

I'd be embarrassed if this many juniors and seniors not only wrote incoherently, but also apparently have not been taught to read or to think. I'd also be alarmed by their tribe mentality.

Almost every letter said something like: "Why are you picking on us teen-agers?" and "What have you got against rock music?"

The fact is, I did not use the word "teen-ager" anywhere in that column.

Nor did I say that new barbarians are found only at rock concerts. I wrote: "Rock concerts aren't the only mass-gathering place for the new barbarians. They've become visible at sports events, too." And I described the sometimes violent conduct of sports fans of all ages.

The point of the column was that in many places we now see more and more mindless mob violence and mob mentality. This behavior isn't limited to teen-agers or rock fans, although there's probably less of it in your average nursing home.

I shouldn't be surprised that these students didn't notice that. Any kid who gets to be a high school junior or senior and writes like Mr. Maszak's students isn't going to absorb details. An example, exactly as written:

"Dear Tenage hater

"I was disappointed by you writen on the Who concert. From what you said I can see you have know so called barbarism. You used some strong words in there with very little fact, you say everyone was numbed in the brain. I will say from concert experience maybe half or three forths were high on something or nether but I allso know that theres not one forth to half that weren't. You say everyone was pushing and throwing elbows, did you ever think that some of the thrown elbows were from people who didn't like getting pushed. You said something about when you were a kid, well times have change since then.''

Mr. Maszak, is that the best you can do? If so, have you thought of another line of work?

Another sample:

"In Tuesday Dec. 5th addition of Mike Royko you clearly stated that all teenagers and people who go to rock concerts are barbarians."

I clearly stated nothing of the kind. You really should try to teach them to read, Mr. Maszak.

Or this: "For one think there were no real big popular bands when you were a kid."

If you are going to let them babble about music, Mr. Maszak, spend a few minutes giving them a little musical background. Or maybe you haven't heard of the big band era, either.

Then we have this gem. Mind you, it is written by a young man who has spent almost twelve years attending school:

"When you talked us in your paper you called us barbarians. It is even more rude than when you call us delinquents. You cant compare us to 50 years ago because we don't wear knickers' and deliver newspapers. All you Old Farts are the same. At Cominskey Park we were just expressing our feelings about disco, because disco sucks. If you write another column like that you will have to answer to me in person."

And there was the lad who denied being a barbarian. But he spelled it "barbian."

I can't go on. It's too depressing, and not only because most of them can't write, read, spell, or think— and it's getting a little late for them to learn.

It's depressing because almost none even mentioned the fact that eleven human beings were trampled to death. And none sounded concerned about that grotesque fact.

They became highly indignant that someone would be less than worshipful about rock music. They became emotional—even menacing like the above writer—in their hatred for disco music. Some became obscene over imagined slights against teen-agers.

But that eleven people were trampled by a music-hungry mob?

One of the few who mentioned the deaths saw it this way:

"If there were someone yer looked up to and yer went to see them in person and thier were thousands of people just like you and wanted to see him up close would you fight yer way in?"

And as another breezily put it:

"People die every three second. What would you do if you paid $15 for a ticket?"

You're no barbarian, kid. But try zombie.

No "Selective" Service

January 25, 1980

If this country has to start the military draft again, I hope that this time we do it right.

Please, no more professional athletes and sons of politicians being magically jumped to the top of the list for stay-home service in the reserves.

There was nothing as ludicrous during the Vietnam War as the sight of magnificent physical specimens throwing seventy-five-yard passes while being cheered by people whose own spindly legged sons were slogging through rice paddies.

And please, no more loopholes that permit someone whose parents can afford the tuition to stay in college until he's over the draft age or can get a deferment for teaching in an inner-city school.

The draft during the Vietnam mess involved as much clout as job hunting in City Hall.

The result was that the war was fought primarily by working-class white and ghetto blacks; farm boys and factory workers; hillbillies and second generation city ethnics.

But side-door exits of all sorts were provided for the off-spring of families with money or connections or both. More of them cashed in from drug overdoses than Viet Cong bullets.

Those who couldn't find a loophole developed instant social consciences that evaporated just as quickly when the war ended.

So if Carter thinks that he must take the first step toward a draft by asking Congress for registration, then I have a few suggestions.

First of all, a draft should be run as a hundred-percent lottery system. No exemptions for going to college. Why should someone spend his time squeezing coeds' bottoms because he happened to be born into a family that could pay his tuition.

No exemptions for working in do-good activities. Once the Vietnam War ended, those young men who had taught in inner-city schools went looking for jobs on the stock exchange.

No exemptions for being married. If she loves you, lad, she will be true. If not, tell your relatives to keep an eye on her.

Any doctor caught providing medical excuses that aren't valid—and thousands of men got out of Vietnam that way—should be drafted as an enlisted man himself.

The lottery should also apply to the reserves. Let luck decide who will be a weekend warrior. That way a punch-press operator will have as much a chance to sit it out at home as a star quarterback or the sons of a Chicago mayor.

Let the lottery also apply to the Navy and the Air Force. Face it, when there's a war, or the threat of war, nobody rushes to join the Navy or Air Force because he is overwhelmed by patriotism. He joins to avoid winding up in the same foxhole as a hostile named Boris or Ching Wang.

So let the luck of the draw decide who goes into the Army or the Navy or the Air Force. And maybe the Coast Guard, too.

An exception would be the Marine Corps, which probably should go on using only volunteers. Somebody who isn't wacky enough to actually *want* to be a marine won't get past his first day of masochism anyway.

Now for my most important recommendation.

President Carter said he would call for the registration of men between age eighteen and twenty-six.

Why stop at age twenty-six?

Why not make the maximum, say, age fifty, and let it apply to any able-bodied male who hasn't already been in the service.

I'm not saying we should draft the men of fifty, or those in their forties. They could be the bottom of the barrel.

But, having them register and making them subject to the draft would serve two good purposes: First, when a young guy moans to a middle-aged guy about the draft, the older guy could say: "Look, kid, we're all in this together." Second, the population of graying, balding hawks might be reduced if they thought they might have to suit up themselves.

Besides, what really makes a man of thirty or thirty-five or even forty any less eligible than someone of eighteen or twenty-six?

They definitely aren't less physically able. Go in any of the bars and discos along Michigan, Rush, or Mannheim. Have a pretty young thing ask the nearest thirty-eight-year-old High-rise Jogger: "Do you stay in shape, handsome?" And he will answer: "Listen, doll, there's nothing a twenty-two-year-old punk can do that I can't. Just try me."

So try them, Mr. President. Set up a draft board at the end of the Lincoln Park jogging path.

Oh, I know what the older men will say: "You can't take me now. I have a career, a business, big responsibilities."

Good. Then you have more to fight for. All some eighteen-year-old has to protect is his record collection.

Finally, the question of women. Yes, they, too, should be drafted. But not the more mature ones. I define mature women as those of the pre-*Ms.* magazine generations.

They shouldn't be drafted because they were not reared to think of military service as being part of their life's experience.

Younger women should be called, especially those who like to swear and swagger and beat men at racquetball and jogging and karate.

I will stay here and bake cakes to send to them.

Before anyone writes me any outraged letters, let me say that I'd rather not see the draft restored. I have two sons who will have to register.

I just want it run fairly.

If it is done my way, we might some day see Hamilton Jordan, John Travolta, Bob Dylan, and almost the entire Cub team in military uniforms.

That sight would be almost enough to make an international crisis seem nice.

Hopes Fade for the Green Bras

February 19, 1980

In recent days, three draft-age, unmarried women have told me that if called to the Army, they will become pregnant.

"And I'll stay pregnant," one of them said, "every year until I'm too old to go."

Frankly, this attitude disappoints me. Despite what some shrill female fanatics may believe, I have long admired the new, modern, liberated women, and have supported their goals. Although they rejected my suggestion, I once outlined how ERA could be passed in Illinois: by bribing the state legislature like everyone else does.

And I had assumed that as female-persons sought and won equality, they would also be willing to accept the same responsibilities as men.

So I'm surprised to hear liberated women now saying that if the need ever occurs, they don't believe women should be drafted. Or, if drafted, they should not be required to do anything but the safe jobs.

I just can't believe that able-bodied female-persons are now saying they don't want to serve as GIs, that they will have babies to avoid going.

Especially those women who so splendidly swear and drink and talk mean and jog and slam the racquetball around and learn karate. These, as I used to say before I became enlightened, seem to be very tough broads.

I had imagined an entire special forces army unit made up of the toughest of women. Something like the

Green Berets. It could be called the Green Bras.

And I saw myself baking cookies and fruitcakes and sending them off to Private Pam and Sergeant Jan and Lieutenant Tammy. Or standing at the dock, waving goodbye to their troopship, while singing "Over There, Over There," and "I Won't Sit Under the Apple Tree with Anyone Else but You," and shouting: "Give 'em hell, female-persons!"

I was even planning to volunteer to work at a local USO, serving coffee and cookies and little nips of bourbon to the female GI-persons.

Instead, I now have a frightening vision of millions and millions of young women, ages eighteen to twenty-six, tummies protruding with draft-dodging pregnancies. An entire new baby boom, brought on by the fear of being classified 1-A. Total collapse of pharmaceutical companies that make the Pill.

Oh, I'm disappointed. I hadn't imagined that the same female-persons who lope so aggressively down the street, jaws jutting, boot-heels thumping, and voice snarling, could now be saying: "I'm going to stay pregnant."

John Wayne never said that.

But more than being disappointed, I'm now worried. Although I don't expect this country to get into a shooting war, you never know. And I had counted on today's modern young female-persons to pull us through to victory, or at least a draw.

The reason I was counting on the female-persons is that I don't have much confidence in the young male-persons.

My final, flickering hope that America's young males could defend this country against an invasion by, say, the Cuban army, faded a few days ago.

That was when I picked up a newspaper and saw a picture of a group of students at Yale who were holding an anti-registration rally.

And in the front rank of the demonstrators was a young man holding a sign that said:

"Nothing Is Worth Dying For."

During the anti-war days of the 1960s and '70s, I saw a lot of placards bearing slogans like: "Don't Napalm Babies," "Make Love Not War," "Hell No, I Won't Go," and hundreds of others.

But I never saw one that put it as bluntly as: "Nothing Is Worth Dying For."

In a way, I respect that young man. He's not trying to kid anyone about moral issues, idealism, a love of peace, a hatred for aggression.

He just doesn't want anybody shooting at him, and that's that.

Had this kid lived 205 years ago, he might have stood up at the Virginia Provincial Convention, as Patrick Henry did, and shouted:

"Is life so dear or peace so sweet as to be purchased at the price of chains and slavery? Forbid it, Almighty God! I know not what course others may take, but as for me, give me liberty, or . . . uh . . . or if you can't give me liberty, OK, then I'll take chains and slavery, you know?"

Or in 1776 he might have stood on the British gallows, as Nathan Hale did, and said, as the rope was placed around his neck:

"I only regret that I have but one life to, uh, to uh—actually, what I regret is that I'm here. How about probation?"

And in 1961, he might have stood through a chilly inaugural address, as John Fitzgerald Kennedy did, and said:

"And so, my fellow Americans, ask not what your country can do for you: and ask not what you can do for your country. What I wanna ask is, will somebody please go do it instead of me, huh?"

I thought that maybe the liberated female-persons would do it instead of him.

But now I'm convinced otherwise.

So, with the new threat of mass-pregnancy, I hope this country doesn't have to start up the draft again. It was bad enough last time, with thousands of young men saying: "I'm going to Canada."

Now we'll have thousands of young women saying: "I'm going to bed."

Sexism and the Strike

February 24, 1980

An angry fireman was talking about "our LADY mayor." Not "our mayor." Not "Mayor Byrne." But "our LADY mayor."

During the past week, I've probably heard that a hundred times.

I've also heard her angrily referred to as "that WOMAN" and "that BITCH" and that . . . well, from here on, they are words I can't repeat—crude, sexual words often used to describe women.

Almost every reference to her that I've heard from firemen, or other males who sided with the striking firemen, contained some reference to her sex.

I'm not a shrink, but I cannot help wondering if their dealing with a woman didn't have something to do with the rage that seemed to grip so many of the striking firemen.

Firemen are, as a group, pretty macho guys. It's a physically demanding job. They play handball, a punishing sport, on their own courts.

I've heard them described as "urban cowboys," riding to someone's rescue, roaring through town on their fire engines like a posse, crashing through doors and walls.

Macho guys don't like having women defy them. Even more than being defied by a woman, they dislike having a woman tell them what to do.

And what man, especially a macho man, can stand having a woman double-cross them.

So there they are, being defied by Jane Byrne, a woman, when she wouldn't give them the kind of contract they demanded, and being told what to do by Jane Byrne, that woman, when she said they had to go back to work . . . or else.

Oh, what painful things for a macho man, for thousands of macho men, to suffer at the hands of one, short, grim woman.

If you want to play amateur shrink a little more, you can wonder how some of them, especially those who are divorced, might have felt when "that woman" had their supermacho leader, Frank Muscare, thrown in jail. Jail is where women have ex-husbands sent if they don't come up with the child support payments. (Muscare, incidentally, constantly referred to her as "that broad.")

So the questions I'm raising are these:

- Would the same wild events have occurred if the mayor had been a man and had treated the firemen exactly the same way?
- Was the mayor's sex a factor in the strike and the way tempers flared and events went out of control?
- Did firemen let the fact that they were dealing with a woman, or more correctly, that a woman was dealing with them, influence their thinking?

The answer is: I don't know. But my guess is, yes.

One reporter, who spent the entire week talking to striking firemen and their union officials, said: "They talk as if she had castrated them. In fact, I heard one of them say that she was trying to chop their . . . I think that every problem every one of them ever had with a mother or a wife or a girl friend was psychologically mixed up in the way they felt about her."

I don't know if that's true, but I do know that they never used parallel terms in talking about Mayor Byrne's predecessors.

For example, Mayor Bilandic refused to give them a contract. And when Muscare took a strike vote, Bilandic used vicious intimidation tactics to persuade many firemen to vote against striking.

Yet, I never heard angry firemen refer to Bilandic as "our JOCK mayor" or "that MAN" or "that STUD."

When they did call him a nasty name, it was usually something nonsexual.

Mayor Daley used to kick the firemen around regularly through Commissioner Quinn. When firemen talked about a contract, Daley would reach out and catch a few of them living in the suburbs to teach them a lesson. Or threaten bad assignments or no promotions.

But as bad as things were under Daley and Quinn, the firemen never called Daley *anything* but "the mayor," much less than something like "our FAT MAN mayor."

And speaking of Daley, the firemen and others seem to have forgotten some of his personality traits. Especially when they talk about Byrne.

I've heard them complain about how emotional, shrill, sharp-tongued, and blabby Byrne can be; how she loses her temper and flies off the handle; how spiteful and vindictive she can be, and how she can't stand personal criticism or people disagreeing with her. And they usually conclude their criticism by saying that Daley wasn't that way.

Well, I don't know where they were between 1955 and 1976, but during most of those years, I was watching Daley.

And I saw him become emotional and lose his temper and fly off the handle and make speeches and statements that were shrill and blabby enough to blow out windows. When criticized, he would fly into purple-faced, ranting rages. Remember how he shouted obscenities at Senator Ribicoff while the world watched on TV?

When has Byrne shouted obscenities for an audience of millions? Or when some lonely independent alderman would disagree with Daley during a city council meeting, remember how he would respond by shouting and becoming almost incoherent? Then he would have the dissenter's microphone turned off.

But when he did these things, was he called shrill and vindictive and capable of tolerating criticism?

Of course not. Being a man, he was described as tough and forceful and a strong leader.

Gents, I hate to say this, but I think your sexism may have been showing.

And in future dealings with groups of men, maybe Mayor Byrne ought to wear a false beard and a fedora.

Watch Out, Rollers!

May 11, 1980

I was driving through the Near North Side, not far from Lincoln Park. In the distance, I could see the usual parade of joggers panting and wheezing their way toward the perfect pulse rate or trimmer behinds. Nearby were some Frisbee tossers, jumping around like idiots and dreaming of being stars on Wide World of Sports.

As I rounded a corner, I had to hit my brakes. There were two young men roller skating in the street, which is the latest Lake-front fad.

They appeared to be wearing designer jeans. One wore a puffy-sleeved silk shirt open to his navel. The other had on a T-shirt bearing the name of a popular Division Street singles joint.

The tall, skinny one was spinning on one skate, like a mad stork. The other was doing what appeared to be a disco dance on wheels, undulating in a way that would have caused his immediate arrest in my old neighborhood.

I crept along behind them for about half a block while the Stork Man twirled on one foot, then twirled on the other foot, and the aspiring gigolo spun his hips faster than his wheels.

Because they had the street blocked, I had no choice but to poke along and watch them. They grinned at me as they twirled and pranced. I guess they thought that the reason I got in my car and drove on that street was just to see how nicely they could roller skate.

Then something came over me. I didn't even stop to think about what I was doing. You might call it an uncontrollable urge.

I came to a full stop and let them get about 200 feet ahead. I flicked a switch on my steering column. It's called a panic switch, and it came with my four-wheel-Bronco. You're only supposed to use it in an emergency, such as when you see a stranger crouching in your back seat. When you turn it on, the switch activates a piercingly loud siren.

With siren screaming, I stomped the gas pedal and roared straight at them.

When they heard the siren, they froze. When they saw my Bronco bearing down on them, with my face leering from behind the windshield, their eyes bulged and jaws dropped.

The Stork man dived off the street into a tall hedge. His disco friend tripped over the curb and banged into the trunk of a tree.

I slowed down, and in my rear view mirror I could see them scramble to their feet and shake their fists at me.

It really made me feel good.

So I'm serving notice on roller skaters. Get out of my way or I will hurl my two-ton Bronco at you.

I've put up with joggers running past my house, frustrating the natural instinct of my dogs to bite things that move. I've put up with female bicyclists who wear tight pants, which cause middle-aged motorists to suffer from heavy breathing and have dirty thoughts, thereby creating dangerous distractions in traffic. I've put up with the teen-age mutants who have grown loud portable FM radios where their right ears should be.

Now, joining the other urban nuisances, we have the mod roller skaters all over the place, and I'm not going to let them take over the streets.

I pay for a city sticker. I pay for state license plates. I pay taxes on my gasoline. I pay for a dozen parking tickets a year.

The roller skaters don't pay for anything except their Brut after-shave lotion.

They don't belong in the streets. It's against nature for them to be there. If God wanted them out in the middle of the streets, he would have equipped their bodies with piston engines and a gas cap.

I don't mind roller skaters when they are little children, who have been taught to move politely out of the way when an adult yells: "Look out, you little rat."

But I'm not going to tolerate supposedly grown men with wheels on their feet, especially when they are gyrating in a lewd manner on a public thoroughfare.

The place to gyrate lewdly, if that is what you must do for recreation, is in a disco, a high-rise apartment, a singles bar, or in the bleachers at Wrigley Field—but not in the middle of a Chicago street.

If they must do it outdoors, then they should stay on the sidewalks where they can't do any harm, other than knocking down a few old ladies. I'm not in favor of roller skaters knocking down little old ladies, but I'm not a little old lady, so that's their problem, not mine. If they don't like being knocked down, let them trip the skaters with their canes.

So from now on, roller skaters, it is war. Just keep this in mind—wearing your shirt open to the belly button won't look nearly as fashionable with radial tire tracks across your chest.

A Poll Cut on the Bias

June 3, 1980

The national polls show that an overwhelming majority of Americans oppose admitting any Cuban refugees into this country.

I've conducted my own poll, and it has the same results.

My poll was limited to only one person—my friend, Phil T. Slobb. I didn't have to poll anyone else because he has always been an accurate barometer of public opinion.

The poll consisted of the following questions and his answers:

Should this country have let in the Cubans?

"Hell no. We should never let in any kinds of foreigners."

None?

"That's what I said."

What are your feelings about Poles?

"We shouldn't have ever let them in. The big dummies can't even speak English. I got on the Milwaukee Avenue bus a few nights ago, and it was loaded with a lot of scrub ladies going home and they were all jabbering in Polish. Why do we let them come here and scrub the floors of our office buildings when we could hire good Americans to scrub floors. Did you hear about the two Polacks who hijacked a submarine? They asked for a million dollars and two parachutes. Hah!"

What about Italians?

"If we had kept them out we would have never been

wound up with Al Capone and Paul Ricca and other bums like that. We should never let in another Italian. Hell, what do we need them for? We can cook our own spaghetti. You know why Polish jokes are so short? So Italians can understand them.''

And the Irish?

''Are you kidding? The Micks are nothing but a bunch of political crooks. What have they ever done except run for office so they can steal my tax money. And the ones who didn't run for office became cops so they could shake me down. All the Irish ever contributed to this country was municipal corruption. By the way, do you know why Irish wakes last three days?''

Why?

''So they can make sure the guy is dead, and not just drunk.''

Do you have any feelings about Lithuanians?

''Yeah. They're almost as dumb as the Polacks, and they're twice as mean. The day we let the first Loogin in this country, the average IQ in America dropped by ten points. Do you know how a Lithuanian pilot navigates an airplane?''

How?

''By reading street signs.''

How about Bohemians?

''Look, those people are all the same—Bohemians, Serbians, Yugoslavians, Latvians, Hungarians, Slovaks. They're cheapskates, and all they want to do is stick a lamb on a stick and roast it, drink beer, and play loud music on their mandolins. You can't even pronounce their names. They're as bad as the Polacks and Loogins. You know how you can tell the mother-in-law at a Bohunk wedding? She's the one on her knees, picking up the rice.''

I don't suppose you care much for the Greeks?

''What do I need a Greek for? I know how to make a hamburger. I went in a Greek restaurant once and they were all jumping around to that Zorba music and snapping their fingers, and when I ordered some cheese they set it on fire. You know how many Greeks it takes to screw in a lightbulb? One to put in the bulb and the other one to burn the place down for insurance."

And the Chinese?

"No gooks of any kind. Chinks, Japs, Koreans, Vietnamese, none of them. We're always having a war with one kind of gook or another, so why do we let them in. And the rats have screwed up our economy with their little cars and TV sets. I say, no more gooks. You know what sound a Japanese camera makes? Crick."

What are your feelings about Jews?

"What do you think my feelings are. Every used car I ever had, I bought from a Jew and they were all clunkers."

What about the French?

"Those people eat snails, and anybody who eats a snail is a creep."

I won't even bother to ask you about blacks.

"Don't bother. You couldn't print it."

But they didn't ask to come here.

"Then they should leave."

I don't suppose you care for other Hispanics, besides the Cubans. Mexicans? Puerto Ricans?

"That's right, I don't care for them. You know why a Puerto Rican can't use a checkbook? Because it's too small for him to spray his name on. Hah! Pretty good, huh?"

Hilarious. I gather, then, that you think this country should not have let anyone in except the early English settlers.

"I wouldn't have let them in either. What do you think the hillbillies are? If the English hadn't come here, we wouldn't have had nearly as many hillbillies as we have now. We've had hillbillies in this country for 200 years, and what have they contributed? They invented stock car racing and the demolition derby, that's all. If we hadn't let the English in, we wouldn't have that peanut picker in the White House."

Then there's nobody you like.
"I like Americans."
What kind?
"The kind that are already here. Like me."

A Grand Old Hiccup

July 14, 1980

Detroit—These four Reagan people were having brunch
at the next table in the hotel coffee shop. They were
duded up in their best conservative finery. The two men
wore cowboy hats and white shirts with red and blue
trim. Their ladies were wearing red, white, and blue
scarves and sensible shoes.

One of the women began hiccuping during her
grapefruit. She tried a long swallow of water while
holding a spoon handle between her teeth. That didn't
help.

So she held her breath for more than a minute. That
didn't help, either.

Her plight led to a group discussion of hiccups. The
other woman said:

"My auntie had the hiccups once and they lasted for a
whole day. She felt just terrible."

The hiccuping woman asked: "How did she get rid of
them?"

The other woman said: "She drank a whole glass of
bourbon whiskey."

The hiccuping woman grimaced and said: "You
know I hate whiskey. It would make me just sick to my
stomach."

Her husband growled: "Yeah, but if it cured your hiccups, it'd be worth it."

"No it wouldn't," she said. "I'd rather have the hiccups than be nauseated."

The husband shrugged and said: "Then suffer." And after a moment's thought, he added:

"Besides, it's your own fault."

The others nodded in agreement. Even the woman with the hiccups.

And there it was, the spirit of the Reagan convention. They are so conservative that even a case of hiccups is "your own fault."

And if you don't have the guts, the strength of character, the macho boldness to cure yourself with a belt of bourbon, then you deserve to suffer.

The woman let out a loud hic as the waitress was serving the scrambled eggs.

"You have the hiccups, honey?" asked the waitress, who was black.

The hiccuping woman nodded.

"You know what you ought to do?" the waitress said. "Hold your breath. What causes hiccups is too much carbon monoxide. Or maybe not enough—I'm not sure. But it's carbon monoxide. I read that somewhere. So holding your breath will get rid of them."

"She already tried that," the husband grunted.

"Well, try again," the waitress said. "It'll work. You'll see."

The husband scowled and said: "Get me some more coffee."

When the waitress walked away, he said: "What does she know about carbon monoxide?"

"But she might be right," his wife said. "I'm going to try it again."

"Well, go ahead, hold your breath all you want. You'll probably bust a lung. I don't give a damn. Crazy women'll believe anything."

(And people are actually surprised that the ERA has been bounced out of the Reaganites' platform?)

The wife took a deep breath and held it. Her face was

getting red when the waitress returned with the coffee pot.

"That's the way, honey, it'll work, you'll see."

"Tell me," the husband said, "where'd you read about carbon monoxide, huh?"

"In a newspaper, I think," the waitress cheerfully said.

"Hah! A newspaper. You believe what you read in a newspaper? All you get in a newspaper is bull. Just plain bull."

"You watch," the waitress said, "it'll work."

When she left, the man said: "Jesus. Damned woman reads a newspaper story and she thinks she's some kind of chemical engineer."

Meanwhile, the wife's face was nearly purple from holding her breath. Her husband looked at her with disgust and said:

"Cut it out. People are going to notice."

She shook her head.

"Damn it, I said quit! You look crazy."

The woman's eyes were bulging, but she wouldn't exhale.

"I can't believe this," her husband said. "I just can't believe it. You must be goin' nuts."

Finally, with a loud "poof," the woman released her breath.

They all stared at her for several seconds. Then she beamed and said: "It worked. It really worked. They're gone."

The husband threw down his napkin, picked up the check, and said: "C'mon, let's get goin'."

As they stood up to leave, the wife said: "Well, she was right."

"Yeah?" said the husband. "Then tell me this: if she's so damned smart, what's she doin' waiting' on tables, huh?"

And he dropped one thin dollar as a tip.

Boy, there are no bleeding hearts at this convention.

Pilgrims' Progress

November 27, 1980

A woman strolling through Grant Park on a recent Sunday was horrified to see two men stalking pigeons.

One man would throw some breadcrumbs on the ground to lure the pigeons to him.

When the pigeons gathered, the other man would sneak up on them and slam a long-handled fishing net over one or two of them. Then he would stuff them into a canvas sack.

"They caught more than a dozen pigeons just while I was watching," the woman said.

She asked the men what they were doing. Neither man spoke much English, and they had difficulty understanding her. But finally one of them smiled happily, pointed at the sack, and said: "Eat, eat!"

"Can you imagine?" the woman said. "They were catching the pigeons to eat them. It's unbelievable."

Not really. People have been snatching pigeons out of the parks and eating them ever since there were pigeons in the parks.

The police say the practice has always been most popular among more recent European-born immigrants and some Asians who eat pigeons in their homeland.

When I told the woman that, she said: "Then it must be illegal. And isn't it unhealthy? I mean, they're such filthy little things."

No, it is not illegal to catch and eat a city pigeon unless it happens to be someone's trained homing pigeon. And in that case, it's doubtful that the owner would know you had eaten his trained homing pigeon.

Besides, if the little bugger doesn't have enough sense to go home, then he has to face the consequences.

I asked the Park District's main office if there is any law against catching pigeons, and spokesman Ben Bentley said: "The pigeons go in the park, but we're not responsible for them. We have enough to worry about with muggers without trying to keep an eye on the pigeons."

As for their being unhealthy, that is not true. The city's health office says that there is nothing harmful about eating a city pigeon, so long as you remember to remove its feathers first. And don't swallow the bones. Or the beak.

"Oh, my God, that's terrible," said the squeamish woman who brought this matter to my attention. "They're like pets—little tame things. How can anyone eat something that's almost like a pet?"

I'm sure many people share her feelings. And I feel their attitude ridiculous. What's wrong with eating something that's like a pet? People do it all the time.

After all, many people keep tropical fish or goldfish in their homes. They feed them, make sure they have enough air bubbles in the tank, and change the water. These fish are treated like pets.

But they will go to a restaurant and eat fried smelts, although these little creatures are just as cute and wiggly as their tropical fish.

People eat ducks all the time, although the duck is, in my opinion, a far more likable bird than the city pigeon. All a duck wants to do is paddle happily around a lake, sticking its rear end up every so often, just like a tourist.

Yet, people who might cringe at the idea of eating a Grant Park pigeon will eagerly plunge their teeth into the dead body of a poor little ducky-wuck.

Or consider the lamb. You won't ever run into a more pleasant, even-tempered, friendly, pet-like beastie than a lamb. There is no record in all of history of a lamb ever attacking a human being. All they do is go baa. Lambs are quite decent.

Compare the temperament of the lamb to that of the

cat. Cats are really vicious. They kill little birds, squirrels, tiny mice, and anything else that is defenseless. If a cat doesn't like your looks, he'll sink his claws into your arm. My elderly aunts all swore that if you dared sleep with a cat in the house, he would surely pluck out your jugular vein some dark night. Cats give people the evil eye.

Lambs never do any of those terrible things. But people are always eating lambs. They eat their ribs and shanks and all different parts of the little dears.

Yet, these same lamb-devouring people would turn green if you suggested that they eat a cat.

I don't see why. I've never eaten a cat. At least, not yet. But there are some parts of the world in which cats are eaten when they are available.

They're supposed to taste pretty good, if prepared properly, although I still haven't found a cookbook with a recipe for cats.

Don't misunderstand me. I'm not recommending that anybody go to Grant Park and catch themselves a Thanksgiving dinner, although there are many excellent recipes for pigeon—and I assume that you would cook up a city pigeon the same way as a commercial bird.

Nor do I recommend that anyone eat a cat—theirs or anyone else's. Whether one eats a cat or not is a personal choice, and I don't want to sway anyone one way or another.

But if you do, there is one obvious cooking tip: Always remember to remove the bell from the cat's collar before cooking. You don't want to make a tinkling noise every time you burp.

Deep-sea Dopers

January 7, 1981

Key West, Fla.—This is where the serious fishermen have always come. From one end of the fabled Keys to the other, they chase the great tarpon, the bonefish, the sailfish, the marlin. Other more glittery parts of Florida are for the beach worshipers, the swimming pool lizards, and the disco dandies. Here, you fish.

And as every fisherman would agree, an essential part of a day's fishing is when you come in out of the sun, grab a hamburger and a beer, and lean back and talk about it.

So at dusk, on my first trip here, I found myself in this bar, about half way between Key Largo and Key West. It's near a marina, and through the barroom window you can see the pelicans scrounging a handout from the people cleaning their day's catch.

The bar stools were filled with fishermen. The leather-skinned captains from the big deep-sea boats, the wiry professional guides from the smaller craft that prowl the back waters, as well as the serious amateurs.

It was in a place like this that Ernest Hemingway surely stopped before going home, to talk about the mystical meanings of a life and death struggle with a madly leaping sailfish.

I bellied up to the bar and waited to listen to the wisdom of the men to whom fishing is their life's work. I wanted to hear about the elusiveness of the bullet-fast bonefish, the great courage of the marlin, the slashing jaws of the barracuda, the arm-wrenching lunges of a giant jack.

"Where ya' from?" asked the man to my right. I told him. We talked about Chicago for a while. Then he said he was a native of the Keys.

"Do you fish?" I asked.

He shrugged. "That, and some other things."

"Tell me, when you go after sailfish, do you rig the bait so that the . . ."

He interrupted. "You're from Chicago, huh?"

"Right."

"How'd you get down here? Plane?"

"I drove."

"Ah, good. Lemme ask you something. How'd you like to make enough money to pay for your whole vacation, and then some?"

"Huh?"

"Money. A few thousand dollars, easy. And you really don't have to do hardly anything. Just deliver something in Chicago when you get back there."

"Deliver what?"

He smiled. "Just some merchandise. It'll fit in the trunk of your car. You just take it to point X and give it to somebody. That's all. No risk."

"Merchandise? What kind of merchandise."

"You know. Some, uh, merchandise."

"Hey," I said, "you mean you want me to run some dope back to Chicago? Marijuana or some other kind of dope?"

He winced, closed his eyes, sighed, and said: "Please, keep your voice down. Now, are you interested?"

"In transporting dope? Of course not. A guy could go to jail for something like that."

He looked at me in a puzzled way, shook his head, and said: "Oh, man, are you really from Chicago?" He picked up his beer and drifted down the bar.

The bartender was standing nearby and heard me muttering: "Dope. Imagine that? Dope."

The bartender eagerly said: "Yes, sir, what is it you want?"

A little later I was talking to a former Chicagoan who

now lives in the Keys. He moved there because of his love for fishing.

"What's the best day you every had?" I asked him.

He thought for a moment, and said: "Last year. I was out with my brother-in-law. All of a sudden, I dropped my rod, grabbed the gaff, and leaned over the side. My brother-in-law said: 'What in the heck are you doing?' It was a bale. A whole bale, wrapped in burlap."

"A bale?"

"Yeah, a whole bale of marijuana. A smuggler must have thrown it overboard when the Coast Guard closed in. It happens around here all the time. People have bales wash right up on their property. So I sunk the gaff into it and hauled it aboard, but when I did that I punctured the plastic inner-wrapping and water got in and got part of it wet.

"So I raced back to shore and rushed home and borrowed two microwave ovens from my neighbors and me and my brother-in-law were up half the night drying that stuff out. I took it to a guy in Miami and made myself a fast $3,000. Yeah, that was the best day I ever had fishing.

"You want to know the worst day? It was when I saw a boat way out, and nobody was on it. I ran my boat over and it was abandoned all right. They must have jumped into another boat and took off when they thought the Coast Guard was going to grab them.

"Well, when a boat's abandoned, you have salvage rights. That's the law of the sea. So there I was with this abandoned boat that must have been worth at least $50,000. And I don't know how much marijuana there was on it.

"So I tied a line on and started to tow it in. I was gonna be rich. Rich! I'm heading for shore and counting all the money I'm gonna make. I was gonna be set for life. I was gonna trade in my little twenty-two-footer for a yacht.

"All of a sudden, a Coast Guard boat comes roaring up, and they tell me to cut it loose. I said it was abandoned and I had salvage rights.

"They must have been staked out at a distance, watching it to see if the smugglers would come back for it, and I came along and goofed things up for them.

"They kept telling me to cut it loose, and I kept telling them that it was mine, by my right of salvage.

"Finally the captain said that if I didn't cut it loose, they were going to just steer their boat right at the line and cut it. So I cut it loose. It still breaks my heart to lose something like that."

I asked: "Is everybody down here involved in dope?"

He motioned to the bar. "See those guys? What do you think they're talking about."

"Fishing, of course."

"Are you kidding? Don't you know the biggest industry down here? The biggest industry in the state of Florida?"

"Tourists."

"Not any more. It's dope. Right at this moment, there are big ships coming in from Colombia, loaded with grass. Millions of dollars worth. When they get near here, they transfer it to smaller boats. And they bring it in. Who do you think has all the small boats and the know-how to do that?"

I motioned toward all the fishermen. "You mean they . . . ?"

"Every one of those guys can get you anything you want. By the time this joint closes, you can get high just sitting here."

"Aren't they ever caught?"

"One out of a hundred. But so what if you're caught? Everybody here is involved in it. The politicians and the cops and the prosecutors. You know what happened to the state's attorney in this county? The governor suspended him from his job. The FBI said the guy smoked grass and popped Quaaludes in the presence of their agents. And he was supposed to prosecute the dope smugglers!

"So the worst that'll probably happen to you if

you're caught is that you'll lose your boat. They con-
fiscate it. But chances are you'll get off, and you'll have
made so much money from the times you didn't get
caught that you can buy another boat with your pocket
money.''

I looked at all the sea-weathered fishermen at the bar.
They weren't talking about marlin and sailfish after all.
What would Ernest Hemingway have thought?

I put one final question to the former Chicagoan.
''I'm going out fishing in the morning. Any suggestions?''

''Yeah. Keep your eyes open for any floating bales.
And if you get one, give me a call. I can get those micro-
wave ovens again.''

Fun in Blahsville:
Spring Along 'til April

January 11, 1981

We've entered the dullest, most depressing time of the
year in Chicago. People suffer from the post-holiday
blahs. The miserable weather keeps us indoors. Election
excitement is over. Football is winding down and baseball hasn't started. Wallets have been tapped out by
Christmas spending and the social security bite.

So the question we face is how to glide through
January, February, and March as painlessly as possible;
how to find a way to brighten our spirits and keep busy
and make the time fly by until spring arrives.

I've talked to several experts in the fields of psychology, social work, and recreational therapy, and
they've helped me put together a list of things to do that

will help you through these long, gray months until the sun and the muggers come out again.

Here are some of their ideas:

DRINKING: Getting roaring drunk has always been a remedy for the doldrums, especially in parts of the world that have long, cold winters. In Finland, for example, so many people use this means of fighting off the blahs that the government provides free hangover stations to administer oxygen and massive vitamin doses. So you might consider throwing a log on the fire and becoming absolutely stinko. Every so often, throw on another log, bite the top off another jug and before you know it, April will be here, all the loudmouthed birds will be chirping and you can take a bath, shave off your three-month growth of beard, throw all the empties out in the alley, stagger outside for a breath of fresh air, and walk down to the neighborhood saloon for a drink.

BROODING: Brooding is so often overlooked as an absolutely great way to pass dull time. And it's something you can do any time by yourself. Just pick out all the things that you hate about yourself; or think back to all the terrible mistakes you've made with your life, things that make you feel guilt and shame. Or think about all the cruel and thoughtless ways your friends, relatives, co-workers, and neighbors have ever hurt your feelings. Then sit in front of the fire or in a dimly lit room and dwell on them at length. Go over them time after time, reliving each awful and shameful detail. The hours will just fly by. (You can combine your brooding with drinking and have one heck of a time.)

CHANGE LIFESTYLES: By that I mean, you say to your wife or husband and kids: "I have cabin fever— I've got to get out of the house for a while." Then clean out your bank accounts, move into a high-rise apartment, join a racquetball club, hang out in urban cowboy bars, take a loveboat cruise, run amok with your credit cards, and carry on with some attractive but shallow and empty-headed young thing. And in the spring, return home looking dazed and tell your loved ones, "Quick, give me Volume A of the encyclopedia. I've got to look up amnesia!"

WINTER SPORTS: Cross-country skiing has become very popular and downhill skiing is still growing. There are also winter camping clubs, and ice fishing. But I don't recommend any of these. They can give you a heart attack, frostbite, or broken legs. The best winter sport is shooting pool. You meet really fascinating people in pool halls or bars that have pool tables. You can gamble and swear and get in fights and buy and sell stolen merchandise. And even if you're not a good pool player, don't worry. You can play the pinball machines or just hang around. Something is bound to happen.

CORRESPONDENCE: People don't write letters any more, and they should. It's a wonderful form of human contact. And it's an inexpensive but constructive way to fill empty time—especially by writing hate letters. So make a list of the ten or twenty people you hate most and write them long, totally honest letters telling them why you hate them in vivid detail. They don't have to be famous people, although that's always fun. Friends, relatives, neighbors, co-workers, and old flames will do. If you have illegible handwriting and don't type, then consider cassettes. With a cassette, you can growl, snarl, hiss, shriek, weep, and say any obscene old thing that pops into your head.

NOVELS: You might consider writing an obscene novel. Make yourself the hero or heroine. You might be surprised at how well you write, and the colorful ideas you can come up with. Your book could even be published. And even if it isn't, later in the year you can give it to someone—a friend, loved one, or a stranger to whom you are attracted—as a birthday or Christmas gift.

BINOCULARS: Powerful binoculars are great fun for high-rise dwellers whose windows look out at other high-rise dwellers. If they are strong enough, you're bound to find someone whose drapes are open. You can watch other people eating, sleeping, talking to each other, having sex, exercising, murdering each other, and all kinds of things. Or you and a friend can open your drapes and pretend to murder each other, and if the police show up, you'll know that somebody was watching.

HOLDING SOMEONE HOSTAGE: Usually, husbands take their wives and kids hostage, although boyfriends occasionally seize their girl friends. Whatever the case, it's a lively winter time activity. Just fling a chair or lamp through the front window, scream some crazy threats and in no time the police will have your place surrounded and will be talking to you through bullhorns. The TV cameras will show up, so after an hour or two, or even longer, you can surrender to a TV reporter. You might wind up spending a couple of weeks in a nuthouse, which could be a surprisingly interesting way to get through the winter doldrums. And when it's over, you'll have your very own videotape of the police dragging a hysterical *you* to the paddy car.

Those are just a few of the things the experts recommend. And if you have any pet ways of fighting off the winter blahs, just send them in and I'll be glad to share them with the other readers.

But, please, don't suggest the old reliable "send out for a cheese and sausage pizza." It's loaded with cholesterol and I don't like to recommend anything dangerous.

Pity Poor Jenrette

January 15, 1981

If you just look at the bare facts, it's not easy to feel sorry for someone like John Jenrette, Jr., the disgraced former congressman from South Carolina.

He has been convicted in the Abscam bribe case. He was a lush, a skirt-chaser, and an all-around sleazy guy.

And he's being punished, as he should be. And he could go to prison. He had to slink out of Congress before being thrown out. He could lose his license to practice law. His name and reputation are dripping mud.

But, holy cow, should even a crooked politician— even a dog—have to endure what Jenrette is being subjected to?

I am talking about his wife, Rita, the new star of the press, TV, talk shows and *People* magazine—and one of the most terrifying women I've ever seen.

By now most people know their story. Jenrette had been convicted and was washed up in Congress. But he wasn't well known. He was just one of several congressmen involved in Abscam.

Then the beautiful Rita decided that her husband hadn't been punished enough. So she went into action. She told the *Washington Post* what it was like to be young, beautiful, and married to a middle-aged lecher like Jenrette.

Suddenly, it was all over the front page of the *Post* and hundreds of other newspapers, on TV, and in the magazines.

Rita telling how she awoke one morning and went

downstairs to find her husband drunk, naked, and on the floor in the arms of a woman "old enough to be his mother."

Rita talking about the first time they met and how in an instant he said: "How would you like to go to the Virgin Islands with me? We'll lie in the sand nude all day long and make love all night?"

Rita telling how Jenrette's cronies took loose ladies to the beach "to shack up . . . in one of the dirty cabins."

Rita telling how she picked up phone extensions only to overhear her husband talking dirty to a female acquaintance.

And Rita saying what kind of bumpkins her husband's constituents were.

This is the kind of stuff that sometimes oozes out of divorce hearings. But amazingly, Rita did her blabbing while she and Jenrette were still together and said they planned to remain together. Rita said it was just something she had to get off her chest.

And Jenrette, poor wimp that he has become, just walked around looking dazed and saying something like: "Gosh, it could have been worse."

They went on TV talk shows, gave interviews, and almost overnight Jenrette had easily become the biggest jerk in America. While beautiful Rita sat there coolly revealing what a creep he was, he blinked his puffy eyes and mumbled things like: "Ah have now reformed. Ah sure do love her."

Then when the Jenrettes seemed to be mercifully fading from our consciousness, the beautiful Rita did it again.

It seems that Jenrette recently went to Florida, supposedly to do some fishing. But when Rita tried to call him, the phone number turned out to be a phony.

That got Rita mad all over again. But I can't blame Jenrette. Any man who was married to someone like Rita would probably want to sneak off and hide from her. And if you gave her your real phone number, she would probably just phone and say:

"Hi! I just gave an interview to the 'Today' show. I

told them that you are impotent and are afraid to sleep without a night light, and that you have a bed-wetting problem and are probably gay. How's the fishing?''

But Rita was so angry that she said she was now going to go ahead and get a divorce. Realizing that Jenrette might consider that good news, she also gave him some bad news.

She revealed to the world that Jenrette had a shoe, containing $25,000, hidden in their home.

In leaped the FBI to see if the hidden money was something more with which they could whack Jenrette.

And Jenrette, now looking like a punchy fighter, went on network TV to try to explain the beautiful Rita's newest disclosure.

Some of the money in the shoe, he said, came from friends for his legal defense. Some of it was money he had saved. And some of it, he said, with his voice cracking, was left to him by his old mom to spend any way he wanted.

He was asked about another of Rita's disclosures—that she had seen him taking some of the money out of the shoe only a few weeks ago.

And that is when Jenrette became Super-Wimp.

Looking like he was about to blubber on camera, he said, yes, he had taken money out of the shoe. But he used it to buy a Christmas gift for his Rita—a diamond ring with emeralds.

Then he shuffled away, probably wondering what Rita would do next—sell the diamond ring and use the proceeds to put out a contract on him?

Under our system of law, we forbid cruel and unusual punishments. No floggings, tearing out fingernails, walking on hot coals, or other tortures.

There are even agencies, public and private, to protect animals from mistreatment.

But there is nothing to protect someone like Jenrette from the terrors of Rita. There is no Anti-Cruelty Society for wimps.

I suppose you could say he brought it on himself. When he decided to marry, he didn't have to be dazzled by a young blond who aspires to a career in show biz. He could have done the prudent thing and gone to an undeveloped nation, found an illiterate native woman, brought her back here, and never taught her English or how to turn on the TV. A wife like that would have been true-blue and Jenrette would be a happier man today.

Jenrette is just the latest male victim of the alarming tendency among many modern women to tell all.

When Elizabeth Ray and Fanne Foxe blabbed, Congressmen Wayne Hays and Wilbur Mills were on their way to fast retirement.

Actresses now give interviews and write books about all the famous men they have slept with. Gloria Swanson has written of her ancient affair with the late Joe Kennedy. Big Shelley Winters even threw a party and invited the many Hollywood stars she named as bedpartners in her book. And Peter Sellers' life may have been shortened by embarrassment when one of his ex-flames decided to reveal shortcomings in his amorous techniques.

Men don't do such unchivalrous things. You don't see men writing books about the women they've slept with. Men don't give interviews ridiculing their former girlfriends. Men don't tell their wives' secrets to the *Washington Post*.

I don't know why women are acting this way, but I have some advice for them. Ladies, please try to act like gentlemen.

In the immortal words of Professor Henry Higgins: "Why can't a broad be more like a man?"

Hostage to Hoopla

January 23, 1981

Patriotism is breaking out in so many places that it is hard to keep up.

The National Football League has grandly invited all of the hostages to attend the Super Bowl in New Orleans this Sunday on their way home from Iran.

The hostages haven't even seen their families yet, and they are going through a period of trying to become normal again. But apparently Pete Rozelle, the football peddler, figures that if they are normal Americans, watching large thugs pound on each other comes first.

The hostages won't be at the game, of course, but you can count on some kind of special tribute. Maybe the players will all wear yellow ribbons.

And baseball has grandly announced that all fifty-two hostages will be given lifetime passes to all major league baseball games. (The story did not make clear whether this includes playoffs and World Series games.)

In Chicago, a yellow ribbon was wrapped around Arnie's, a slick restaurant-bar on Rush Street, popular with the fast-buck, fast-broad set, and this patriotic gesture was reported in a newspaper-items column.

This touched off a wave of phone calls from other restaurant owners and barkeeps to their press agents, demanding to know if they, too, could get public attention by wrapping yellow ribbons around their businesses. I'm sure we will soon be seeing the hostage cocktail.

New York is going to have a huge ticker-tape parade, and other cities want to do the same. It's a chance for mayors to show voters how patriotic they are, and for patriotic downtown businesses to sell some yellow ribbons and other baubles to parade goers.

TV is planning countless specials and dramas. Hollywood producers are already in a race to see who can make the first hit movie. Publishers are getting their money ready for a bidding war on the hostages' stories.

What will be next? A lifetime coupon for all at McDonald's? A lifetime pass for Disney World?

Or appearances on Johnny Carson's show? Or the "Hollywood Squares"?

Mayor Jane Byrne moved quickly and has already had her hostage ceremony at the Daley Center, with hundreds of yellow balloons being released, and the mayor making a solemn speech about the hostages' "sacrifice," and the crowd displaying their yellow ribbons, singing patriotic songs, and waving at the TV cameras.

I'm not sure what the mayor meant by "sacrifice," since it wasn't the hostages' idea to be locked up for fourteen months. Essentially, they were victims of a crime, as any kidnapping victim would be, and normally one doesn't talk about a crime victim's making a heroic sacrifice. Rather than make a heroic sacrifice, most crime victims would just as soon run like hell, as the hostages would have preferred to if they had the chance.

But I have to admit that holding emotional rallies for crime victims is an interesting idea, and the mayor might consider doing this regularly.

She could hold another rally and bring in some old guy with his head wrapped in bandages and make a speech about the "sacrifice" he made when he was whacked on the skull with a brick and his pay envelope was stolen.

Then the crowd could sing: "Tie a yellow bandage 'round the old guy's head, the old guy's head, the old guy's head. . . ."

We could have the victim of the week. And at the end of the year Super-Victim—somebody who was robbed, kidnapped, tortured, raped, and ticketed for overtime parking, all in the same day.

All of this makes me a little sad at how much earlier Americans missed.

For example, what about the Revolutionary War troops who spent that long, cold winter at Valley Forge. They didn't do any fighting. They just sat there starving, freezing, and wondering when they could go home.

How nice it would have been for them if, when spring came, someone had said to them:

"Hi, I'm Peter Rozelle, commissioner of the Colonial Turkey-Shoot League and I am inviting everyone who was at Valley Forge to attend the annual Super-Turkey Shoot. As my guest, free!"

"I just want to go home and take a bath and see my wife."

"Well, here's a couple of tickets anyway. Give 'em to a pal."

Or they might have been greeted in the spring by someone who said:

"Hi, I'm Arnie, and I own Arnie's Ye Olde Inn—best mutton, ale, and dry martinie in the colonies. And I want you to know that I have tied a tattered stocking to my inn's door in your honor."

"Gee, that's great. You're a terrific patriot."

"Think nothing of it. By the way, if you'll autograph this picture, I'll put it on the wall of the inn. Just say: 'To my old pal, Arnie, from the guys at Valley Forge.'"

Some people are also talking about having an annual holiday—Hostage Day.

A great idea. I can just see the ads and the signs in the window:

"Hostage Day Sale. Fifty Percent Off on Everything. Seventy-five Percent Off on Yellow Ribbon."

Killer Gets Two-timed

March 6, 1981

It was obvious all along that Jean Harris did it. When you put two bullets into somebody and don't even nick yourself, attempted suicide makes a weak excuse.

Right up to the verdict, most people I talked to didn't buy her story, that she was aiming at herself when she shot Dr. Herman Tarnower, the Scarsdale diet author. But they still wanted her to be let off. And they were disappointed when the jury found her guilty.

I'm not talking about women. They might be expected to sympathize with a fifty-seven-year-old woman who was cast aside by her longtime lover for a younger doll.

But what surprised me was the number of men who told me they wished Harris had been acquitted, even though she was guilty.

One of them is a conservative, law-and-order type— forty years old, a combat veteran of Vietnam, divorced once. He said:

"Sure she did it. But he deserved it. If this was France, it would be an open-and-shut case. They'd let her go. A crime of passion. They understand these things. When a guy breaks a woman's heart and she does him in, the French are sympathetic. This country has no romance in its soul."

Then there is my friend who has been divorced, pays heavy support money, and isn't getting along too well with his second wife. You wouldn't think he would be the kind who would sympathize with any woman.

"To tell the truth," he said, "if my first wife shot me, I wouldn't have blamed her. She caught me cheating on her with the woman who became my second wife. That Tarnower treated [Ms. Harris] rotten, so he got what he deserved."

And I heard that kind of comment from several other men.

I'm not sure what it means. Maybe men really do have romantic souls. Or guilty consciences.

I sort of agree with them. After reading about the many years Dr. Tarnower strung along Ms. Harris, I wouldn't have felt bad if the jury came in and said:

"Look, we don't buy that story about a suicide attempt, but he was a louse and he did you wrong, so you can go now. But watch your temper in the future."

One has to feel some sympathy for Ms. Harris. She is a victim of a double standard that still exists.

The fact is, a man who gets up in years has a better deal than a woman. I mean in terms of chasing each other for reasons of romance, lust, and whatever else they have in mind.

Men in their forties and beyond are still considered desirable creatures, although you wouldn't think so if you saw us coming out of the health club shower.

But they are. Men in their forties and fifties and sixties frequently dump wives near their age. Unless they are exceptionally worn out or financially flattened, the men can not only find youthful companionship, but sometimes they are in great demand.

In many bars across the North Side, you will see older men—hairpieces firmly glued on, waistlines sucked in, baggy eyes concealed behind tinted aviator glasses—wheezing sweet nothings into the cars of the lithe young ninnies.

And where are the women these rogues shed? You have to look hard to find a bar where women in their forties or fifties are being looked at adoringly by a lot of John Travoltas.

When a mature woman is dumped, she usually gets the kids. She might have to go to work for the first time in years, or ever. That makes playing the wild singles game difficult. "Hi, my name's Midge. This is my teenage son, Rudy. And I have to be up for work at 7 A.M. Your place or mine?"

When a mature man develops wrinkles in his face, they are marks of "character." That's why we have male movie stars old enough for social security still doing torrid smooch scenes.

But when a woman picks up the same wrinkles, the reaction is: "I'll bet she was a doll—once."

Do you remember when paunchy Henry Kissinger became a sex symbol and was always being seen with gorgeous younger women? The explanation was that he was powerful, and power is sexy.

Oh yeah? Then how come nobody was trying to pinch old Golda Meir's bottom?

So it's not fair. And Dr. Tarnower was a cad for stringing along Ms. Harris for all those years, then giving her the brush and taking up with a younger sex object.

On the other hand, shooting someone is a pretty extreme way to say, "You have hurt my feelings."

If we say that what Ms. Harris did was all right, that might touch off a wave of spurned women plugging selfish men. And as someone who believes in gun controls, I have to oppose that.

As it is, women are getting more violent in their dealings with men, and judges and juries tend to be sympathetic.

I'm not talking about those cold-hearted women who decide that they don't want the bother of a divorce, and instead try to hire a hit man to make them single. While that is one way to avoid bruising the unwanted husband's ego, murder isn't the best way to say, "The magic is gone."

But more and more women, who are brutalized by wife-beaters, are striking back and getting away with it. As they should. I have no sympathy for a guy who punches his wife around, then doesn't have the sense not to turn his back on her while she has a hot clothing iron in her hand. That's his headache.

That's not new, though. Even before the attempted efforts at liberating women, society has been tolerant of women who tire of being punching bags.

Years ago, there was a murder case involving an immigrant woman who took about ten whacks a day from her hulking husband.

After a couple of decades of this, she got fed up, picked up an ax, and let him have it.

Then she had a problem. She wanted to hide the body, because she figured the law wouldn't understand what she had been through. But her husband was too big for her to budge.

So she reduced her husband to several manageable parts. And by making several trips with her shopping bag, she was able to dispose of him in various parts of the Northwest Side.

When the husband began turning up here and there, the police were baffled. Then they found a part that provided fingerprints, which led them to the man's house.

And the wife shrugged and confessed everything.

But as I recall, she either got off completely or served a very short term.

And I'm sure the leniency was due to what she said when an incredulous prosecutor asked:

"Madam, are you sure you didn't have any help in what you did?"

She looked at him in a puzzled way and said:

"But where does someone find *that* kind of help?"

Toeing the Line

March 17, 1981

With some people, the problem is always the back. With me, it's feet.

So I wasn't really surprised during the past weekend when I suddenly found myself howling and hopping on one foot around my kitchen. The thought went through my mind: "It figures, it figures."

The reason I was hopping on one foot was that I had been cooking some spaghetti. But instead of pouring the boiling water into the sink, I aimed badly and poured it off on my bare foot.

On the way to the hospital, I watched without sympathy as my foot changed colors.

If it hadn't been for the pain, I might have pointed a finger at it and said: "Foot, you got exactly what you deserve."

The fact is, I dislike my feet. At times the feelings border on hatred. As far back as I can remember, they've been nothing but trouble.

You might wonder how a person can hate his own feet. I don't think that's unusual. Some people hate their own noses. Or their teeth.

At least they can go to a plastic surgeon and get a nose job, or have their teeth capped.

But when you hate your own feet, there's not much you can do about it except try to ignore them or swear when you happen to see them.

And that's one of the problems with feet. They're

hard to ignore. The first things I see every morning are my feet, stcking up at the other end of the bed.

So I start each morning by saying: "Hello, you lousy, ugly, gnarled, painful b——s. I hate both of you!"

That's not the best way to begin the day, I suppose, but it does get me into the proper frame of mind for my job.

As I lie there looking at my feet, I'm always struck by how ugly they are.

Most feet aren't very good looking. I can't remember anybody being renowned for his or her stunningly attractive feet, although there are strange people whose pulses race at the sight of a toe. Or so they say, when they write about their fantasies to *Penthouse Forum*.

But for ugliness, mine have always been in a class by themselves.

When I was born, the first thing my mother said to the nurse was: "He takes after his father. Look at those feet."

She was right. My father had size twelve feet. And so did I—on the day I was born.

And the doctor later said that I was the only infant he had ever seen come into the world with calluses and corns and cracked toenails.

My toes are longer than most people's fingers. If the toes were extended, I'd probably wear a size twenty shoe. But they curl under about three times so they look more like large, clenched fists than feet.

They're also very wide. They might be as wide as they are long, which has always made it difficult for me to find shoes that fit properly.

When I was a kid, we'd spend hours at the shoe stores looking for shoes that were wide enough. One salesman finally gave up and said:

"Lady, the only place you'll find a shoe that fits this kid is at a blacksmith's shop."

We finally found something that fit perfectly. They were comfortable, but a lot of people looked twice when they saw somebody walking around with two baseball gloves on his feet.

Then there's the arch. Basically, there are two kinds of arches.

The normal arch curves upward, providing the foot with flexibility and acting as a shock absorber for the spine.

The flat foot has little or no curve.

Mine is in a class by itself. The arch curves downward, sort of like the bottom of a rocking chair.

This makes it difficult for me to stand up without swaying back and forth, which has led to considerable misunderstanding, especially in bars.

When I was in the service, we'd all be standing at attention. Then the wind would blow. With my arms stiff at my side, I'd sway forward, then backward. Pretty soon, I'd be going back and forth like a rocker, first my nose, then the back of my head, grazing the ground.

The commanding officer didn't know what to do with someone like that, so he finally assigned me to the base orchestra, where I was used as a human metronome.

You can learn to live with feet like mine, but you have to take certain precautions.

For example, I took a vacation along the seashore once. In the evening, I'd take long, barefoot walks along the beach.

One morning, I noticed a crowd of men studying my footprints in the sand. They were from the police, the Conservation Department, and the local zoo.

One of them shook his head and said: "I don't know what kind of creature it is, but we'd better post some armed men here at night."

My feet have probably sensed how I've felt about them, and they've retaliated by getting themselves stubbed and stepped on every chance they get. I don't even take it personally when someone steps on my foot any more. I just say: "Don't apologize, he had it coming. Step on the other one, too, he's just as bad."

And I wouldn't have even gone to the hospital when I burned my foot, except that I have to live with it.

When the doctor came into the emergency room, he asked me what happened.

"I poured a pot of boiling water on it."

He shook his head and said: "Yeah. Boy, it really does look awful."

"Doc," I said, "it's the other one."

Killers as Guinea Pigs

March 18, 1981

The lady was upset. She is one of those kind-hearted people who was appalled by the recent execution of rapist-killer Steven Judy.

"Now that he is dead," she said, "what has society accomplished, other than to demonstrate that it is just as capable of murder as he was?

"Would it not have been far more intelligent to keep him alive and in prison so that he could be studied by psychiatrists?

"If we are ever to eliminate violence in our society, it will be done through knowledge. Steve Judy would have provided a wonderful opportunity for psychiatrists to expand that valuable knowledge."

That, of course, is one of the most popular arguments against capital punishment—that killers should be kept alive so that they can be studied by the shrinks.

And one day, the argument goes, the shrinks will tell us why some people commit murder. Then society will be able to take precautions to prevent the murders.

But there are several flaws in this argument.

For one thing, the psychiatrists really didn't need Judy to do research. There are already more than enough murderers behind bars to keep the nation's psychiatrists busy for the next fifty years.

There is not only a huge surplus of killers, but the

selection is without bounds. There are stickup-killers, wife-killers, husband-killers, gang-member killers, gay killers, killers of gays, straight killers, children killers, old people killers, cop killers, random sniper killers, and even a couple of crime syndicate hit men.

People such as that unhappy woman should remember that very few killers are executed. The odds against it are almost as long as winning the state lottery. There would be even fewer executions of people like Steve Judy if they didn't decide that they'd rather go to the chair than hang around a prison.

And at the rate people are killing each other today, there won't be a shortage of imprisoned killers during our lifetime. If anything, the surplus is going to keep growing.

Besides, what makes anyone think that psychiatrists are all that eager to look into the frightening brain of somebody like Steve Judy?

For one thing, most convicted killers can't afford to pay a shrink fifty dollars or seventy-five dollars for a short hour of couch time.

And any self-respecting shrink would much prefer to be in his quiet Michigan Avenue office, making seventy-five dollars an hour for listening to a well-heeled business executive complain that he is unable to make love except on days when he has successfully cheated a business associate.

Then there is the time factor. Even if you appear to be perfectly normal and have never killed anything beyond a fly or a drink, it might take a shrink ten years at three visits a week to figure out whether you like your father or hate him. And regardless of how it turns out, he's going to wind up telling you that you're right to feel that way about the old man.

Most important, it should be remembered that shrinks *have* been studying killers for years. There are probably several tons of research material available on the homicidal mind.

All this information hasn't done anything to reduce the murder rate. And if you ask a psychiatrist what to

do if somebody shows up with a wild look in his eye and
an ax in his hand, his best professional advice will probably be:

"Run like hell—he's probably nuts."

So for the time being—which means as long as people
like Judy are committing atrocious crimes—I'm really
not that interested in whether Judy liked or disliked his
ma and pa. It's enough for me to know that he disliked
women and children enough to murder them.

And before I listen to a shrink explain that Judy was a
victim of an unhappy childhood (who ever had a really
happy childhood?), I'd prefer to hear a return to the
good old days of meaningful sentencing speeches by
judges.

The following sentence was handed down in about
1881, somewhere in the Old West. It's been credited to
several hanging judges, such as Roy Bean and Judge
Parker. Nobody is really sure who made it, and it might
have even come out of the imagination of some folklor-
ist.

In any case, the Old West judge supposedly said:

*Jose Manuel Miguel Xavier Gonzalez, in a few short
weeks it will be spring. The snows of winter will flow
away, the ice will vanish and the air will become soft
and balmy.*

*In short, Jose Manuel Miguel Xavier Gonzalez, the
annual miracle of the years will awaken and come to
pass.*

But you won't be there.

*The rivers will run their soaring course to the sea, the
timid desert flowers will put forth their tender shoots,
the glorious valleys of this imperial domain will blossom
as the rose.*

Still, you won't be here to see.

*From every treetop, some wild woods songster will
carol his mating song, butterflies will sport in the sun-
shine, the busy bee will hum happy as it pursues its accustomed vocation, the gentle breeze will tease the
tassels of the wild grasses and all nature, Jose Manuel
Miguel Xavier Gonzalez, will be glad but you.*

You won't be there to enjoy it because I command the sheriff of the county to lead you away to some remote spot, swing you by the neck from a knotting bough of some sturdy oak and let you hang until you are dead.

And then, Jose Manuel Miguel Xavier Gonzalez, I further command that such officer retire quickly from your dangling corpse, that vultures may descend from the heavens upon your filthy body until nothing shall remain but bare, bleached bones of a cold-blooded, blood-thirsty, throat-cutting, chili-eating, sheep-herding, murdering son of a bitch.

And we never did find out if Jose liked his father.

N.Y. Bowled Over

April 30, 1981

Every so often something comes along that reminds me again of how provincial New York City is. I mean, they have people in that town who are real rubes.

Not all New Yorkers. In Queens and Brooklyn they have some genuinely sophisticated belly-scratchers who could easily be Chicagoans.

I'm thinking more of Manhattan. And especially those residents of Manhattan whose lifestyle seems to reflect the glossy pages of *New York* magazine.

This is the magazine many New Yorkers depend on to discover who is in or out, where to live, eat, drink, be entertained, and what is chic and what ain't.

It also contains such examples of inspirational reading as the story of how Diane von Furstenberg, who peddles high-priced dresses, found her new truelove, a bronzed young guy named Paolo, while strolling on the beach at Bali. (She says Paolo isn't very ambitious, which gives him time to iron her skirts.)

But the most important function of *New York* magazine is to ferret out new trends so that its trend-hungry readers don't miss a chance to be trendy.

And in a recent issue of *New York,* the writer of the Nightlife column excitedly told how he had discovered a new trend.

He said that a new activity had been found "to fill the notoriously empty evening hours of 11 P.M. to 1 A.M.— *after* chic little dinner parties, *after* the theater lets out, and *before* the rock clubs and discos are at full power. Where is the crowd to go then? Elaine's or Odeon or Mickey's? No, not again!"

So where do bored in-people now go after the chic parties and theater, and before the discos are in full power?

Bowling.

That's right, gushes *New York* magazine—actors such as Christopher ("Superman") Reeve, models, fashion photographers, artists, and other members of the so-called "fashion pack" have discovered the existence of bowling alleys—and it is simply blowing their minds.

For one thing, they were deliciously stunned to find that they could not walk in any time and get an alley, regardless of how fashionable and beautiful and chic they might be.

"The first time I went," says a fashion photographer named Jen, "it was right in the middle of league play.

"Well, there was no way they were going to let us play. This isn't '21' or 'Studio 54.' They don't care about who you are or what you look like. It's a different world!"

The magazine has also determined that bowling has what it calls "reverse-chic appeal: Prices are low."

I don't understand why low prices would be "reverse-chic." I always figured that the cheaper something is, the more chic it is. But, then, I prefer a twelve-dollar pair of jeans from Sears to a pair of sixty-dollar jeans with some gigolo's name on the rear end.

Some of the chic New York bowlers put as much thought into finding just the right ambience in their bowling alleys as they do in seeking out a chic little restaurant. "I really scouted out a few lanes," said an art critic who was planning a "bowling party." "I wanted something kind of small. So I went with Beacon Lanes. . . . It was very small, just ten lanes."

But, the magazine says, most of the Manhattan bowlers want bowling alleys that are the *real thing. The real atmosphere.*

As a *New York* writer described his search for atmosphere: "When I went bowling, I wasn't going to do anything in Manhattan. I wanted the real thing. You know—*Jersey.* Of course, if I'd had the money I'd have flown everyone to Detroit."

Too bad he couldn't afford it. If a horde of chic New Yorkers showed up at some Detroit bowling alleys, they'd be given enough atmosphere to last them until the doctors said they were well enough to go home.

The magazine went on:

"Most non-bowlers are surprised by the bowling culture. 'My God, they have everything here,' says Edie Vonnegut, the artist and daughter of novelist Kurt, as she glances at the Bowlmor bar, the pinball machines and the twenty-five-cent ballpoint pen dispenser for those who forget to bring along a pencil for their score-cards."

(They aren't called scorecards, dummy, they are scoresheets. And bowling alleys provide pencils.)

Edie Vonnegut, the artist, goes on to say: "Is this really going to be the next thing?" Then she sees a "fashionable group" and points out a man who has a "familiar face . . . one of *those* faces we see around town."

Ms. Vonnegut whispers to the *New York* magazine writer: "He's very fashion-conscious. He was one of the first to be into complex roller-disco dance steps."

"Bowling," says Ms. Vonnegut, "can't be far behind."

Ah, Manhattan. What a wonderful collection of hicks.

I hate to be the one to bring this to the attention of *New York* magazine, but out here in the rest of the country, bowling is not "far behind." It's probably the most popular participation sport in America.

A few statistics:

In one month, more people go bowling than attend all the pro football games during an entire season. There are about 10 million regular league bowlers. But in a year's time, with families, kids, couples on dates and others, about 70 million people will go bowling at 8,700 bowling centers. There are 165,000 bowling lanes, and each year about 2 million balls are sold.

New York magazine, which prides itself on its critical eye, did not hesitate to warn its readers about something it considers distasteful in bowling. The magazine said:

"Bowling is a sport, and as such it takes its toll. The balls, used constantly, tend to acquire a layer of grit and human grime that then transfers to one's fingers.

"And there's something rather unappealing about putting on and taking off shoes that others have rented before."

We can only hope that *New York* magazine never discovers golf. On a dewy morning, you can find *worms* crawling on the greens.

Eeek!

The Great Shootout
of Cullerton Street

May 18, 1981

He was soft-spoken and courteous, a pleasant change
from most of the handgun lovers I hear from.

He said he just wanted to ask a few questions, and
since he was polite about it, we talked.

"Have you ever used guns?" he asked.

Sure. I've fired pistols, shotguns, and rifles. I was a
good rifle shot in the service, even outscoring a lot of
country boys who said they grew up shooting.

"But did you have guns at home when you were a
child?" he asked. "The reason I ask that is people who
didn't grow up around guns are often those who are the
most opposed to them. But those of us who grew up
with guns in our homes are less frightened by them."

I could tell that he thought he had me. But I crossed
him up.

Yes, we had guns at home when I was a kid. My
father was in the tavern business, which meant he kept a
pistol behind the bar. He also had a pump-action shotgun in our flat behind the tavern.

"Ah," the gun advocate said, beginning to sound excited. "Then your father had the guns to protect himself
and his business. Did he ever actually use them for that
reason?"

Sure, I said. He used a gun once.

He pounced: "Then you have to *admit* that people
do use guns to protect themselves. So how can you
want to deny others the right to do so, when your own
father . . ."

He really thought he had me. So when he finished his lecture, I told him about the Great Shootout of Cullerton Street.

That's where the tavern was. A neighborhood saloon on a side street of wooden two-flats and cottages. A sweat-stained, blue-collar street.

It was Saturday afternoon, and the poker game was going at the end of the bar. Before TV flooded the weekends with professional sports, the local gentlemen spent their leisure time trying to fill a flush.

Among the players was Gorilla Joe, a barrel-shaped man with the hairiest arms this side of the Lincoln Park Zoo.

Gorilla Joe had one very bad habit: He couldn't resist trying to fill inside straights. So he usually lost. And when he lost, his temper, which was foul when things were going well, got even worse.

That day, he must have set a record for failing to fill inside straights.

Finally, when he was betting the mortgage money, he filled one. And he raised and raised, then slammed down his cards in triumph.

The trouble was my father had a higher straight.

My father had many bad habits, one of which was laughing sadistically when he won a pot—especially when he won a pot from Gorilla Joe.

Gorilla Joe's temper snapped. First he threw his cards into my father's face and said: "You no-good Polack."

Naturally, my father responded by throwing his cards in Gorilla Joe's face and saying: "You goddamn Bohunk."

So Gorilla Joe threw his shot glass, which bounded off my father's brow.

Well, a certain amount of levity was permitted in the tavern, but not bouncing shot glasses off the owner's forehead.

My father came around the bar and hit Joe three times. Each time, Joe reeled backwards about ten feet. After the third punch, he was out the door, down the steps and sitting on the sidewalk.

Gorilla Joe got up, shook his fist and said: "Awright, I'm going to get my shotgun."

My father responded: "And I'll get mine."

Joe lived only two doors away, and he headed for home. My father went for the door to our flat, with the rest of us following and trying to persuade him not to get his shotgun.

We were standing in the kitchen arguing with him when we heard the roar of a shotgun outside the tavern. And we heard a howl of pain.

My father, shotgun ready, rushed to the street. We got there just in time to see Gorilla Joe sprint into his house. And in time to see our dog disappear around the corner at the end of the block.

It seemed that Gorilla Joe had arrived with his gun just as our dog, a Doberman named Duke, had been taking a stroll. So he let go with a blast at Duke.

A few drops of blood on the sidewalk let us know that he hadn't missed.

Dog lovers shouldn't weep. We quickly caught up with Duke. He had only one superficial pellet wound in his thigh and was more frightened than hurt.

Meanwhile, my father went to the front of Gorilla Joe's house and shot out both front windows and put a hole in the door.

Gorilla Joe did not reappear. Maybe he was afraid. Or maybe, being a Bohemian, he was too thrifty to use up any more ammunition.

Somebody called the police, and when they arrived, they hit Gorilla Joe on the head and charged him with a variety of crimes. They also congratulated my father for his coolness under fire. The police were always understanding with tavern keepers who made monthly payments to the captain's bagman.

The police court judge didn't send Gorilla Joe to jail, but he ordered him never to set foot in the tavern. A form of exile.

So Joe never came in again, and peace returned to the neighborhood.

But a couple of months later he made the mistake of walking past the tavern just as Duke the Doberman was taking in some sun.

Duke chewed his leg like somebody gnawing an ear of corn. It was the only dog-bite case I can remember in which people came out on their porches and cheered for the dog.

So my answer to the handgun advocate was: Based on my boyhood observations on the use of guns for self-defense, I'm still for strict control of handguns.

But I did learn certain rules of safety from the Shoot-out on Cullerton Street, and most people would be wise to follow them:

Never try to fill an inside straight; never hit a Pole in the head with a shot glass; and don't ever get a Doberman mad at you.

Shish-ka-bow-wow

June 5, 1981

Animal lovers will be disheartened by this story, especially those who are opposed to people eating dogs and cats.

It was discovered recently that immigrants from Southeast Asia had been catching stray dogs in San Francisco and having them for dinner.

Naturally, this horrified native Americans, most of whom don't believe in the eating of dogs and cats, even though they have more nutrition than your average TV dinner.

California animal lovers were distraught, even after it was explained to them that dogs and cats are considered fine table fare in many parts of Asia, as well as dozens of other places in the world.

There are all kinds of fancy dog recipes in those countries: Roast puppy and sweet potatoes; stir-fried dog; rice-stuffed dog; smoked dog; and Coconut-Cream-Marinated Dog on Skewers.

While this probably disgusts you, you can imagine how these Asian immigrants reacted when they came to this country and saw vast numbers of dogs and cats wandering around loose.

It would be something like an American going to some other part of the world and seeing hundreds of stray filet mignons and Big Macs and pizzas hopping down the street.

But the animal-lovers protested, and a state legislator from Menlo Park, where wealthy Californians own all kinds of fancy dogs they don't want eaten, submitted a bill to make dog- and cat-eating illegal.

The bill provided a punishment of six months in jail and a $500 fine for anyone who killed a dog or a cat with the intent of eating it.

The bill was sent to a committee and witnesses rushed to testify. Many of them wept, as Californians are inclined to do, as they pleaded with the committee to protect Fido and Fifi from voracious Asians.

Somebody brought in a spaniel that had a sign hanging from his neck that said: "I am for loving, not eating."

It was assumed that the bill would quickly be passed into law, since the vast majority of Americans oppose the eating of dogs and cats.

But to everyone's amazement, the dog-cat bill didn't pass. It didn't even make it out of the committee, where it fell one vote short.

It failed because some people apparently thought the law showed a lack of sensitivity to the sensibilities of Asian-Americans, since the bill was inspired by their dining habits.

One legistator, whose district has a large Asian population, decribed the bill as being "racially and culturally insensitive."

A Japanese-American psychologist, who works with refugees from Southeast Asia, didn't like the idea of people going to jail for eating a dog. He said:

"Being incarcerated and taken into the legal process could be very traumatic."

Another Oriental witness said the proposed law discriminated against him. "The assumption," he said, "is that because of the way I look, I eat dogs."

Well, I'm as sensitive to the feelings of immigrants as the next bigot.

But there have to be some limits to how liberal we are about permitting newcomers to practice their native customs.

That psychologist is right when he says that "being incarcerated and taken into the legal process could be very traumatic" for a recent immigrant who did nothing more than innocently whip up a pot of pooch stew.

But consider the trauma of someone who takes a dog to the park for a romp. He throws a stick for his dog to retrieve. The dog happily chases the stick. Suddenly some hungry Asian jumps out of a bush, snatches Spot and rushes off to turn him into shish-ka-bow-bow.

How does a guy explain that to his wife and kid when he gets home?

"Where's Spot, Daddy?"

"Spot isn't coming home any more."

"Why not?"

"Somebody ate him."

That's real trauma.

I'm surprised that this dog-eating law would fail in California, of all places.

California leads the nation in vegetarian population. If you bite into a steak out there, you run the risk that someone at the table will shriek: "Monster! Cannibal! Unclean, unclean! You dig?" And it might be the waiter.

Everyone in that state is on some kind of strange diet.

Some won't eat red meat. Some won't eat any kind of meat. Some cringe when they see a child put its thumb in its mouth.

Even the vegetarians have pangs of conscience. They think they hear faint cries of pain when they bite into a carrot or avocado.

The Californian ought to reconsider this dangerous precedent. Remember, this country is always letting in new people, unfamiliar with our ways.

And the next time, the new immigrant group might come from a culture in which it is normal to eat crazy people.

If that ever happens, Rhode Island would wind up with a bigger population than California's.

It's All in the Wristwatch

July 5, 1981

When digital wristwatches came on the market several years ago, I wrote that people who wore them were some of the worst bores I had ever met.

They were always showing them off, poking buttons that made the time, day, and year appear on the tiny screen.

As new models with more advanced features came out, they became even worse bores—constantly jabbing at the buttons and saying: "Look, it's also a stop-watch," or "Look, it shows Paris time," or "Look, it beeps every hour on the hour."

However, I recently received a digital watch as a gift. And now that I have one on my wrist, with buttons of my own to push, I realized I was wrong: People who wear digital watches are not bores. We simply want to let others know what wonderful devices they are.

And now I'm amazed at the way some people react when I begin showing them what my digital watch can do. They actually act bored.

For example, I was in a bar the other day and somebody said: "The price of beer in this joint must have gone up twenty percent in the last year."

I quickly punched a button on my watch, which activated the calculator mode, and said: "Let's check out that figure."

Then I hit a few buttons, triumphantly displayed the numbers on the tiny screen, and said: "No! Beer hasn't gone up 20 percent. It is 21.89 percent higher."

There was sullen silence until someone said: "Big deal. What's the difference."

I pointed out that there was a difference of 1.89 percent—so why be inaccurate when a digital watch/calculator can provide precise data.

Someone else sneered at my watch and said: "I could have figured that out with a pencil and paper."

I couldn't let that challenge go unanswered. So I poked a button that shifted the watch from the calculator mode to the stopwatch mode and said:

"Paper and pencil, eh? Can you use a paper and pencil to determine exactly how long it takes the bartender to draw that stein of beer from the tap? Of course you can't. But I can. It just took him 7.38 seconds to fill that stein."

And I held the watch aloft for all to see.

There was a snicker and someone asked, "Who cares how long it takes to draw a beer?"

"Time is money," I quickly responded, while punching more buttons on the watch. And in a few moments it began making a beeping sound.

"It sounds like you got a sick mouse in your pocket," one of them said. "Why is it making that noise?"

I triumphantly explained that I had shifted to the alarm-clock mode and the watch was emitting a thirty-second signal.

More sneers, and someone asked, "What do you need

an alarm clock on your wrist for? You figure on falling asleep on the stool?''

I patiently explained that some people have important appointments. Let's say that I was supposed to meet with the president. The alarm would let me know when it was time to leave the bar.

And as I poked more buttons, I told them that if our appointment was in a different time zone, that would be no problem because the watch had a special mode for other time zones. I knew exactly what time it was in Washington.

Jabbing another button, I explained that I was also ready if I had to deal with military types who prefer to say twenty-hundred hours instead of 8 P.M. The watch had a military-time mode.

There was no stopping me then. I showed them how it could be put in a mode to measure laps as well as hundredths of seconds.

And how it could add, multiply, divide, and provide decimals into the ten-thousandths.

Also, the button to push to make it light up at night.

Then one of them peered at it and asked, "What's that? Why are all of those numbers appearing on the screen?"

"Oh, that's nothing," I said, trying to shove my arm in my pocket.

"What do you mean, nothing? Look at all those numbers, and it's making a beeping sound. What's it doing?"

I was forced to explain. The watch also has a game mode. And it was playing a game.

"A game?"

"Right."

"How do you play it?" someone asked.

"I don't know."

"You don't know?"

"I don't know how to play it."

"You have a watch that plays a game, and you don't know how to play it."

"Right."

"That's the dumbest thing I ever heard."

He was probably right. When I received the digital watch, I was able to figure out how to make it calculate, emit an alarm, act as a stopwatch, and most of the other marvels.

But the directions that came with it were in Japanese. And it is not easy to understand the rules to a mathematical game you play with a wristwatch if the directions are in Japanese.

The hoots and jeers were still ringing in my ears an hour after I left the bar.

So if anyone out there has the English directions for playing a game with a Casio CA-80, I'd appreciate seeing them. By now, I've probably lost a thousand games to my wristwatch without even knowing it.

Maybe more than a thousand. And I could come up with a precise figure in just a few seconds if you're interested.

I'll just shift to the calculator mode. . . .

Stress and Drain

July 24, 1981

Diet books have become about the hottest products in publishing. There are curently three diet books on the *New York Times* best-seller list.

And soon there might be a fourth.

I recently interviewed Ralph Peptic, author of the soon-to-be published book: "The Stress and Misery Diet Book."

Peptic, formerly an accountant, used to be a typically overweight American male: 5 feet 11 inches tall, 225 pounds.

Now he's still 5 feet 11 inches. But he weighs 125 pounds.

I asked him how he did it.

"To begin with," he said, "I had tried all the diets. Carbohydrate diets. Protein diets. Weight Watchers. Pritikin. You name it, and I tried it. But none of them worked for me.

"Then I discovered my own plan, which I call the Stress and Misery Diet. In my diet, you don't count calories. You don't omit this food or that food. You don't worry about eating three small but well-balanced meals a day. You don't even think about what you eat or when you eat it."

That's incredible. How does it work?

"The way it worked with me was this. One day I came home and found a note on the table. It was from my wife. It said:

" 'Dear Ralph: You remember that piano-bar player we both liked so much when we went out to celebrate our last anniversary—the one who played "our song" and you tipped him five dollars? Well, I liked him even more than you did. In fact, I liked him so much that I have moved out and I am now living with him. Best of luck, Norrine.' "

That's awful.

"Yes, it was. But it led me to my diet. I went into total shock. I was in a deep depression for weeks.

"Then one day I ran into an old friend, and he said: 'Ralph, you really look good.' I said: 'I do? But I really feel bad.' And he said: 'I don't care how you feel, I haven't seen you look this trim in years.'

"So I got on the scale and weighed myself. I had dropped about thirty-five pounds."

How?

"After my wife left me, I was filled with such stress that I couldn't eat. My stomach was knotted up."

But you've since lost a lot more weight than that.

"Right. You see, just about the time I was getting over my wife leaving me, and my appetite was starting to come back, my wife returned. She said she had realized that she had made a terrible mistake.

"I was so happy I started eating again, and in one month I gained about ten pounds."

"Then she left me again."

That's terrible.

"No, I didn't feel as bad the second time around, but what really clobbered me were the bills she left behind. She had bought a whole new wardrobe, jewelry, she took off for the Bahamas and put everything on my credit card and cleaned out the bank accounts. I was hopelessly in debt. I had bill collectors coming at me from every direction.

"I was a total, psychological wreck. The stress was incredible. In two months I had dropped another thirty or forty pounds. And everyone I met told me how great I looked, except for the haunted look in my eyes. So I wore sunglasses.

"About that time, my boss told me that my work had fallen off. Of course it had. The stress and misery from my personal problems were driving me crazy.

"But he told me that if I didn't shape up in one month, he was going to fire me.

"So for a month, I worked night and day. I was like a man possessed. I was taking a Maalox pill every hour. I had stomach cramps, anxiety attacks, I hyperventilated, and I couldn't eat a bite.

"At the end of that month, I looked like a marathon runner. But my boss didn't fire me. He said I did fine. Except the company went bankrupt, and I was out of a job anyway.

"About that time, the divorce papers came through, and my wife got the house, the furniture, the car, the camper, the kids, and I got the debts and the child-support payments.

"By the time that was over I was down to my present weight of 125 pounds."

How have you kept it there?

"By trying to pay off the debts, trying to find a job, trying to stay out of jail for failure to pay the child support, and brooding about being rejected by my wife. The stress is terrific. Look, here's an experiment. Here's a paper bag. Reach in the bag and take out the contents."

I reached in the bag and took out a piece of plain bread.

Peptic began retching. He bent over and moaned in pain. Then he gasped and said:

"See? I'm so filled with stress and misery that even the sight of a plain piece of bread revolts me."

That's amazing. But shouldn't a diet be combined with exercise? That's what all the experts say.

"Right. And mine gives a lot of exercise. My legs are in terrific shape from nervously pacing the floor for hours. Look at the muscles in my forearms. I've developed them from constantly wringing my hands. And my shoulder muscles have become much more powerful from slamming my fists into walls as I cry out in frustration and agony at the wretchedness of my life. My stomach muscles are hard as boards from the constant stress spasms. And there's the constant trembling of my hands. Look at the way they shake."

Is that much exercise?

"It is when your hands shake even while you're asleep."

But if this book is a success, you're going to make a lot of money, and you'll be able to eat again. You'll be able to clear up your debts, pay off your wife and you won't have anything to be stress-filled and miserable about. You could gain weight again.

"I know. And I'm terribly worried about that, too. The thought of all that success is causing me terrible stress. But I think I have the answer to all that money."

What is it?

"I'll worry about my taxes. That'll get me down to one hundred pounds."

Good luck.

"Don't say that—it would ruin my life."

Belushi's OK, But . . .

September 27, 1981

At least a hundred people have asked me for my reaction to the movie *Continental Divide,* which recently opened.

Even radio and TV stations want to interview me on the subject.

It isn't that I'm a movie expert, because I'm not. I just like to look at them, especially ones with Bo Derek.

But the male star of *Continental Divide* plays a chain-smoking newspaper columnist who regularly appears on page two of the *Chicago Sun-Times.* And the movie's publicists have said that he is supposed to be a "Royko-like" character.

So, obviously, part of my reaction is that I feel flattered.

Of course, I'm not the first newspaperman to be portrayed in a movie.

In *All the President's Men,* Bob Woodward was played by Robert Redford, whom many women consider to be the world's handsomest man.

In the same movie, Carl Bernstein was played by Dustin Hoffman, who many women say has an intense, electric sexuality about him.

And in that same movie, editor Ben Bradlee was played by Jason Robards, who many women say has a craggy-faced, tough, worldly, mature sex appeal.

But me? My character was played by a pudgy John Belushi, who became famous as Bluto, the gluttonous, disgusting fraternity slob in the movie *Animal House.*

Many women say that he makes them want to throw up and dial 911.

So as much as I like Belushi personally, I think the producers might have made a mistake in casting my part.

I think Paul Newman would have been a better choice, although he's older than I am. And in appearance we're different because he has blue eyes and mine are brownish-green.

And I would have been satisfied with Clint Eastwood, although he's taller than I am. Or even Burt Reynolds or Alan Alda.

Some of my friends have said John Travolta would have been the perfect choice to play me. He's probably too young, but I suppose if they touched his sideburns with a bit of gray, he would have been believable in the part.

As to the plot of the movie itself, I had mixed reactions. Some of it was realistic, and some of it was ridiculous.

Some examples:

The movie began with the columnist picking on a dishonest Chicago alderman. That's realistic. I can no more ignore a Chicago alderman than a dog can ignore a fireplug.

However, the alderman soon has the columnist beaten to a pulp by two Chicago cops. That's unrealistic. Chicago cops haven't beaten up a newsman since the 1968 Democratic convention, and most of those newsmen were from New York and Washington, so they had it coming.

After the columnist is hospitalized by the beating, his editor is so concerned for his safety that he gets him out of town, sending him into a remote mountain wilderness to try to interview a female, hermit-like bird-expert who lives in the mountains and studies eagles.

That's unrealistic. For one thing, I'm afraid of heights. And I'd never climb a mountain to interview a bird-watcher. I'd ask her to come down the mountain for dinner so we could study such birds as coq au vin, or rock cornish hen and wild rice.

On the way up the mountain, the columnist loses his supply of liquor and cigarettes and is heartbroken. That's stunningly realistic. In fact, I wept during that part of the film.

But he goes on without them. That's unrealistic. I would have immediately gone back down the mountain to the nearest bar to get new supplies. Then I would have grabbed the next train back to Chicago.

When he finally finds the female bird-watcher, she turns out to be beautiful, self-reliant and brilliant, and she thinks the columnist is a jerk. That is so grimly realistic that I almost left the theater.

But later, she becomes fond of him, and they ended up more or less sharing the same sleeping bag, which wasn't very realistic, since a bird-watcher's vision couldn't be *that* bad.

Then he leaves her in the mountains and comes back to Chicago, where he just mopes around feeling miserable, low, blue, and filled with self-pity. That's realistic because I feel that way when things are going good.

But soon he pulls himself out of the dumps by chasing the crooked alderman again, and that's realistic. There's nothing like good, clean sport to make a person feel better.

Then the beautiful bird-watcher turns up in Chicago and they resume their romance, and he takes her to eat in the restaurant on the ninety-fifth floor of the John Hancock. That's unrealistic. At that joint's prices, she'd have to eat cheeseburgers in Billy Goat's.

I won't describe the finish of the movie, although it has a happy ending. And that's unrealistic, especially considering that once he got back from the mountain he had a chance to replenish his liquor supply, and when she came to Chicago, she had a chance to meet lean young men who wear gold chains and Gucci shoes.

There was one other thing that bothered me (and made my friends hoot and jeer and snicker at me): the sex scene, which wasn't at all explicit, except that the columnist didn't have any clothes on from the waist up.

As I bluntly told Belushi when he asked me about that scene: "John, I didn't like it because I don't have a hairy back."

And he answered: "Yeah? And you don't have a hairy head, either."

See? They should have cast Yul Brynner in my part.

Algren Paved the Way

October 2, 1981

I'm not sure what the late Nelson Algren's reaction would have been to Mayor Jane Byrne proclaiming a citywide Nelson Algren Day and arranging to have a street named for him.

Even in his writing prime, had Algren shown up near any previous mayors, he would have been pinched for vagrancy.

But, then, Nelson always did have a way with the ladies.

So city officials, cultural bigwigs, business mucky-mucks, and even a few people who actually appreciated Algren's back-alley literary genius did what should have been done long ago.

They got together Thursday at a luncheon to finally express Chicago's appreciation for Algren's work.

Mayor Byrne declared the day Algren Day in Chicago.

Chicago magazine established a yearly cash award in Algren's name for the author of the nation's best new short story.

And Byrne will rename a four-block stretch of

Evergreen Street, along Wicker Park, as Algren Street.

(I have to admit being especially pleased about the street name, since it was my idea. That makes it the first time a Chicago mayor has ever accepted any idea of mine.)

Evergreen Street was chosen because it's where Algren lived all the years he wrote books like *The Man With the Golden Arm, The Neon Wilderness,* and *Chicago: City on the Make.*

These were the books that made Algren a major literary figure—in cities like Paris, France.

But they didn't do much for him here. Algren's vision of Chicago wasn't quite the same as those of politicians, chamber of commerce types, and bankers with constipated literary views.

They surely didn't care for Algren's wonderful 1951 description of Chicago, in *City on the Make:*

For it isn't so much a city as it is a vast way station where three and a half million bipeds swarm with a single cry, "One side or a leg off, I'm gettin' mine!" It's every man for himself in this hired air.

But even they would have to see the beauty in the paragraph that followed:

Yet once you've come to be part of this particular patch, you'll never love another. Like loving a woman with a broken nose, you may find lovelier lovelies. But never a lovely so real.

Unfortunately, Nelson couldn't be there to enjoy a free meal, which he usually needed, or to cheer for himself, which he wasn't above doing—because he died five months ago.

But we, his friends and admirers, are enjoying it for him.

The Algren Day proclamation, for example. Nelson might have let out a few giggles. It begins:

"Whereas Chicago has in its brief history produced people who have won the respect, honor and admiration of the world, as well as of other Chicagoans, and . . ."

History? Algren's version of Chicago history isn't found in textbooks. A sample, about early settlers:

Yankee and voyageur, the Irish and the Dutch, Indian traders and Indian agents, halfbreed and quarterbreed and no breed at all. In the final counting they were all of a single breed. They all had hustler's blood. . . .

They hustled the land and hustled the Indian, they hustled by night and they hustled by day. They hustled guns and furs and peltries, grog and the blood-red whisky-dye; they hustled with dice or a deck or a derringer. And decided the Indians were wasting every good hustler's time.

Slept till noon and scolded the Indians for being lazy.

Paid the Pottawottomies off in cash in the cool of the Indian evening; and had the cash back to the dime by the break of the Indian dawn.

They'd do anything under the sun except work for a living, and we remember them reverently . . . under such subtitles as "Founding Fathers," "Dauntless Pioneers" or "Far-Visioned Conquerers."

Meaning merely they were out to make a fast buck off whoever was standing nearest.

The resolution also says:

"Whereas the late Nelson Algren has earned a special place in this group of famous Chicagoans, and whereas the City of Chicago belatedly wants to join . . . in honoring him for his love and understanding of people and his singular talent in showing it and . . .

"Whereas Nelson Algren didn't much care for establishment recognition in his life, it is time to give him his due."

Yes, I guess it could be said that Algren didn't care for "establishment recognition." He wrote:

Make the Tribune *bestseller list and the Friends of American Writers, the Friends of Literature, the Friends of Shakespeare . . . will be tugging at your elbow, tittering down your collar, coyly sneaking an extra olive into your martini or drooling flatly right into your beer with the dullest sort of flattery and the cheapest grade of praise: the grade reserved strictly for proven winners. But God help you if you're a loser. . . .*

Algren was a knocker in a time of boosters. But he

claimed that right because, as he put it:

Before you earn the right to rap any sort of joint, you have to love it a little while. You have to belong to Chicago like a crosstown transfer out of the Armitage Avenue barns first; and you can't rap it then just because you've been crosstown.

And I'll close this modest tribute to Algren with some of his advice that's still worth following:

It isn't hard to love a town for its greater and its lesser towers, its pleasant parks or its flashing ballet. Or its broad and bending boulevards, where the continuous headlights follow, one dark driver after the next, one swift car after another, all night, all night and all night. But you never truly love it till you can love its alleys too. Where the bright and morning faces of old familiar friends now were the anxious midnight eyes of strangers a long way from home.

Happy Algren Day.

The No-fat Polka

October 18, 1981

Hardly a day passes without a new book being published on exercise and physical fitness. Authors of these books, male and female and debatable, turn up on the TV shows to flex themselves and demonstrate methods for staying young, fit and boring.

But despite the national craze for daily strenuous exercise, many people still refuse to take part.

You mention jogging, the most popular form of exercise, and they say: "I hate running." Or: "It hurts my knees." Or: "I'm too old and I don't want to die of a heart attack alone and unloved on a jogging path."

If you suggest one of the court games, such as tennis, racquetball, or handball, they say: "It costs too much"; or "I don't have time"; or "I don't want to die of a heart attack alone and unloved in a strange shower."

You can propose one of the clubs that has all those muscle-building machines and they'll respond: "I don't want to get a hernia"; or "It's boring"; or "I don't want to die of a heart attack alone and unloved and with 200 pounds of iron on my chest."

They even reject brisk walking, which many fitness experts now say is just as good as jogging. "It takes too long." "It's dull." "I don't want to die alone and unloved after some mugger hits me with a brick."

But now these many shirkers will no longer have any excuses, because a new fitness book is coming out that will surely become a best seller and turn hundreds of thousands of lazy people into converts.

Although it hasn't been written yet, the planned title is: *The Fitness Book for People Who Hate Running, Walking, Cycling, and Hitting Balls, But Have Got Good Rhythm*.

I will be the co-author of this book, with Fats Grobnik, who is my friend Slats Grobnik's lesser-known brother.

The idea for the book was conceived this way:

While out strolling on Milwaukee Avenue the other day, I saw in the distance a man who appeared to be dancing a polka as he moved along the sidewalk.

As I drew nearer, I could see that he had his arms extended as if he was dancing with a very fat lady, except that he was dancing alone.

He was doing the traditional brisk polka steps, frequently stomping his feet, bouncing, whirling in circles, but all the time moving steadily along the sidewalk.

As I passed him, he called my name and said hello.

"Do we know each other?" I asked.

"Don't you recognize me?" he said. "I am Fats Grobnik, your friend Slats Grobnik's lesser-known brother."

"No!" I said. "But you are so lean and catlike. You look no more than twenty-two, and I know you must be at least forty-five."

He flashed a Robert Redford grin and said: "I'm forty-seven, actually."

"And you used to weigh 300 and became exhausted just from riding an escalator."

"Actually, I weighed 330 and became winded just from the exertion of snoring. But that was the old me. Before I found my secret fitness plan."

"Running? Nautilus machines? Bike riding? What is it?"

He shook his head. "None of them. It's the polka."

"I can't believe it."

"It's true. I discovered it this way. As you know, I am the leader and accordionist in the Fats Grobnik Whoopee Polka Band, and for years I've been playing hundreds of Polish weddings and other society events."

"Yes, you're my favorite recording star."

"Thank you. Anyway, I noticed something. Over the years, I kept seeing the same people, decade after decade, doing the polka at these weddings. And as they got older, they got spryer and healthier and lived to incredible ages. Meanwhile, those who didn't polka, but instead drank shots and beers and danced an occasional tango, were dropping like flies.

"So I began doing scientific research, wiring the old polka dancers to record their pulse, respiration, and things like that. I discovered that dancing every polka at a wedding provided as much exercise and burned up as many calories as running in the Chicago Marathon or singlehandedly moving all the furniture in a two-flat."

"Amazing."

"And if you danced with a large enough woman, it would increase your biceps by two inches, your shoulder width by ten percent, your neck size by three inches, assuming you tried to dance cheek to cheek."

"I can't believe it."

"It's true. So I decided to try it myself. Every day I

danced. First for two minutes, then five, then ten, steadily increasing my stamina and strength.''

"What happened?"

"I was evicted by my landlord downstairs. And that's when I started traveling this way."

"What way?"

"By doing the polka. I no longer walk anywhere. I polka where I'm going. Instead of walking to the corner bar, I polka there. When I go shopping, I polka to the store. When I go to the bus stop, I polka there while I'm waiting. And if the bus isn't crowded, I polka in the aisle. I never just walk anywhere. I polka there. Even when I go to the bathroom. And when I add it up, I'm polkaing about five to ten miles a day."

"Incredible. You look like a new man."

"Ah, but there are other benefits. When you're walking or even jogging, a criminal can sneak up behind you, right? But not me. Because I'm constantly whirling as I polka along, so I see everything around me."

"So you lower the crime rate as well as stay fit?"

"Right. If everybody did this, we would have a much safer, happier and healthier city."

"Yes, I can see it—millions of Chicagoans doing the polka everywhere they go. This city would be unique. Why, we should write a book about it."

"I'm all for it," Fats said as he whirled off down the street.

So those of you who want to get in shape in a new way, just watch for the book and for Fats flashing across your TV screen on all the talk shows.

I'll begin writing it just as soon as I can stop whirling.

Kerosene for Christmas

October 28, 1981

We're in an era of hard eyes, cold smiles and: "Sorry, I gave at the office. Actually, I didn't give at the office, either. I'm not giving anywhere."

Maybe the David Stockman spirit is spreading. When Stockman watches Dickens' *A Christmas Carol,* he probably applauds Scrooge for firing Bob Cratchit. And does Tiny Tim *really* need that operation or is he on the mooch, too?

Whatever the reason, anybody who dares put his hand out with the palm up in these times runs the risk of his fingers being broken.

The other day I watched a seedy old panhandler approaching people on Michigan Avenue, where most pedestrians figure to have a few spare coins jingling in their pockets.

He was working a stretch of street that has stores that sell blue jeans for $100, Italian shoes with paper-thin soles for $150, coffee tables for $1,500 and necklaces for what a bungalow used to cost.

He was walking slowly because he didn't look strong enough to walk any faster.

Of the fifteen people I watched him ask for a quarter, eight ignored him completely. Six shook their heads without breaking stride. And one hesitated and then scrunched up his lip and nose as if he smelled something bad, which couldn't have been the case because the bum was downwind.

The panhandler finally gave up and shuffled off Michigan toward the West. He was probably heading toward Clark Street's Skid Row, where he might at least get a toothless but friendly smile.

It wasn't a scientific survey, but zero for fifteen for a panhandler on a rich street should give us some idea what the national mood is. And he didn't even look like a wino. He looked more like somebody's old grandpa. Who knows, maybe he is somebody's old grandpa, and the kids threw him out.

If so, it will be a long winter for him. I've talked to a few people in the charity fund-raising field, and they're expecting a lean Christmas.

One of them said: "From what I hear, everybody thinks this will be a tougher year than last year, and last year wasn't good. The only ones who are doing well are the fundamentalist preachers. But there's no way I can promise a donor that I can destroy a liberal or bomb a Russian or stop a teenager from groping in exchange for a donation."

Maybe the spirit of these times was expressed best by a city commissioner in Fort Lauderdale, Florida.

During a recent meeting of the city commission, the owner of a beachfront restaurant showed up to complain about bums.

He was upset because the bums were making a habit of looking through his garbage bins for something to eat. He wanted the city commissioners to do something about it, since the sight of a bum plucking a discarded fried shrimp out of a garbage bin was not the kind of ambience he wished to provide his regular customers.

Up spoke Commissioner Robert O. Cox, who said: "We should get rid of them the same as we get rid of the cockroaches."

Before anyone could get the idea that Cox wanted the Orkin Man called in to exterminate the bums, he added:

"You cut off the food supply."

He went on to explain his plan: The city should spray the garbage cans of all beachfront restaurants with kerosene. "They won't eat the stuff if it smells bad," he said.

Which is probably true. Even the most desperately hungry bum would turn up his nose at a leftover caesar salad if the dressing was kerosene.

After hearing about Cox's starve-the-bum plan, we called him to see if he was really serious about using kerosene to deprive them of their ration of garbage.

"I just tossed out the idea of kerosene off the top of my head," he said. "But there are hundreds of other ways you can spray the cans. You can use insecticides or vinegar or ammonia. There's a lot of stuff you can use. Just look under your sink.

"This isn't India or Bangladesh, you know. People here eating out of garbage cans can pose a problem."

(Actually, people eating out of garbage cans in India and Bangladesh pose a health problem, too. If they don't eat, they starve to death.)

Cox said he is not without sympathy for the truly needy, such as "little old bag ladies" and the truly poor.

But he said most of the people who forage in restaurant garbage cans are capable of honest work and are nothing more than "real scum" or "dirt bags."

Unfortunately, Cox said, his idea and a promise by the mayor's office to look into the feasibility of garbage-spraying touched off a hostile reaction.

He said the city has heard from "little old ladies" who think he wants to poison people and from civil libertarians who say garbage might be considered "abandoned property," which can be eaten by any garbage fanciers.

Despite the protests, Cox said he would vote for the garbage spraying if he gets a chance.

And it will work, he said, because he's already tested it. Sort of.

"I used to have raccoons that came around my garbage cans. They'd get the lids off and get into the cans.

"Then I sprayed insect repellent inside the cans and put the lids back on, and they poked their noses around once and never came back.

"There's no real difference between a real animal rummaging through garbage cans and a human doing the same thing."

Right. And they shoot raccoons, don't they?

Has anyone ever tried wearing a human-skin hat?

Back from the Dead

October 29, 1981

I received some startling information today. It happened while I was reading the cover story in the latest *Time* magazine.

The story itself wasn't depressing. It was about the obsession for physical fitness that has become a part of American life.

I don't mind reading about how millions of people jog, whack balls, wrestle with exercise machines, ride twelve-speed bikes, and otherwise punish themselves to squeeze into a pair of designer jeans. Just as long as I don't have to take part.

But at the end of the story there was one of those self-testing quizzes that magazines and newspapers like to print.

You've seen them. They're usually labeled something like: "Do You Drink Too Much?" or "How Happy Are You?" or "Are You Under Stress?" or "Are You Courting a Heart Attack?" or "What's Your Rating as a Lover?"

You answer the questions, then add up the points, then look at the bottom to find out what kind of shape you're in. And depending on the kind of quiz it is, it says something like:

"Ten to twenty points—You are a deeply unhappy person and will probably jump off a bridge soon."

Or: "Ten to twenty points—Your heart probably sounds like a slush maker."

Or: Ten to twenty points—You are a terribly inadequate lover and your mate is surely carrying on with somebody else."

I usually skip these quizzes because I know the results in advance. If you don't know if you drink too much by the red of your eyes, then you're probably too shaky to take the quiz in the first place.

But the headline on the quiz in *Time* had a title that made it impossible to ignore. It said:

"How Long Will You Live?"

That is an intriguing question. If you know the answer to it, then you have time to make plans for your future. For example, you might buy a new Mercedes-Benz, knowing your children would be stuck with paying it off. Or you could stop slobbering on your boss's shoes and tell him what you really think of him and his wife.

So I took the quiz, which consisted of about thirty questions in two categories: personal facts and lifestyle status.

The personal facts included whether I lived in a city or small town; the longevity of my grandparents; health of my parents' marital status; and earnings. The lifestyle questions had to do with how much I smoked, drank, exercised, slept, weighed, and whether I was easygoing or an aggressive, angry person.

It was a simple test. I started with seventy-two points, each of which represented a year. Then each question was worth plus or minus points or years. I just added or subtracted as I went along.

When I finished I looked at the final number. Then I looked for further instructions. Most quizzes tell you to multiply by two or something like that.

But there were no further instructions. The final number was it.

"That can't be right," I told myself. And I took the

quiz again. But the results were the same.

According to that test, I died seven years ago.

I couldn't believe it. I went to a co-worker and said: "I just took this test in *Time* magazine. It says that I died seven years ago."

He nodded and said: "I'm not surprised. You haven't looked well lately."

Hoping to show that the test gave inaccurate results, I asked a friend who doesn't drink, smoke, swear, get mad, and stays in perfect physical shape, to answer the questions. The final figure was eighty-two years.

"How did you do?" my vice-free friend asked.

"I died seven years ago."

"Nonsense. Only the good die young."

At first I was depressed. I've always known that my life style isn't recommended by most phys-ed instructors, but I didn't think the situation was that serious. After all, I take vitamin pills and get regular exercise by walking down escalators.

And I know others who have the same habits and have made it to ripe, old ages. After I took the test, I sought one of the oldsters out in the nearby bar and asked him: "Oldtimer, how long have you been living this way?"

"As far back as I can remember," he cackled.

I looked at his wrinkled, withered face, his frail, stooped shoulders, the liver spots on his hands, and said: "To what do you attribute your remarkable old age?"

He said: "What the hell are you talking about? I'm only thirty-eight."

The joint does have poor lighting.

Now that the initial shock has worn off, I don't feel as bad about the test results. In a way, I find them complimentary.

For one thing, I took the test again, basing the answers on the condition I was in seven years ago.

Those results showed that I wouldn't have died until last year. So that tells me *something*, although I'm not sure what.

You can look at it this way: I must be a truly amazing physical specimen if I'm in such awful shape that I should have died seven years ago, but I'm still walking around today.

Nevertheless, there's a warning in the test results, I guess. So I'm going to immediately change some of my bad habits.

By doing so, I can make a dramatic shift in the results and add about ten years.

For one thing, I lost three points (or years) by answering "yes" to the question: "Do you work behind a desk?"

I'm going to add those three years by moving out from behind my desk and sitting on my sofa when I write.

Also, I failed to pick up two years by answering "no" to the question: "Did any of your grandparents live to be eighty-five?"

Actually, one grandfather would have surely made it, but he died at eighty-two in a barroom brawl with a sneaky young Greek who had a knife hidden in his sleeve.

Finally, instead of losing three points by being "intense, aggressive and easily angered," I'll gain three by becoming "easygoing and happy."

And I'll drink to that.

Why I Moved to the Lakefront

November 22, 1981

Because it's already been the subject of an exposé by Walter Babytalk, the TV commentator, I might as well make a full confession.

Yes, I have moved into a condominium along the city's lakefront. As Walter indignantly raved, I am no longer a resident of one of the city's inland neighborhoods.

However, Walter, despite all his angry bouncing, failed to explain why I have moved to the lakefront. So I'll explain:

In anthropological terms, I was born Bungalow Man. Or, Bungalow Baby, to be more precise.

Later, during a period of family hard times, I became Basement Flat Child.

Still later, I became Flat Above a Tavern Youth.

For a while, I was Barracks Man.

Then, in early manhood, I was Attic Flat Man. Then Two-flat Man.

Most recently I was Bungalow Man again.

From childhood on, I never lived more than staggering distance from Milwaukee Avenue, and thought I never would.

But in recent decades, a new kind of creature has evolved in Chicago. I was the first to name him Highrise Man.

As an amateur anthropologist, I was familiar with the ways of Two-flat Man, Bungalow Man, Tavern Man, and all the other species that form the general classification of Neighborhood Man. That's because I was one, from my shot glass to my long underwear from Sears to my new linoleum.

And I had an extensive understanding of such mutants as Suburb Man and such lesser creatures as Downstate Man.

High-rise Man was a different matter. I could study him only from afar, getting a fleeting glimpse as he jogged past or whizzed by on his ten-speed bike. Or try to gain insights by eavesdropping as he ordered a Perrier and lime, or spoke his quaint pidgin French to a waiter.

But it was difficult to gain a solid understanding of High-rise Man's culture because he is such an elusive creature, flitting from trend to trend, dashing from disco to country bar, from Baltic ethnic restaurants to

French restaurants to Sichuan restaurants to pasta parlor.

I decided to follow the example of Margaret Mead, the late, great social anthropologist, whose method was to become part of the tribal culture she studied.

So to study High-rise Man, I set out to join the Lake-front Tribe and become High-rise Man.

Like Margaret Mead and other anthropologists and explorers, I couldn't embark on my expedition without proper equipment. The outfitters for this expedition included Gucci on Michigan Avenue, The Season's Best on Michigan Avenue, Robert's on Walton, Morrie Mages, and Shutter Bug.

The result can be seen in the picture that accompanies this column, which shows me in my new High-rise lifestyle, with many of the trappings of High-rise Man.

They are numbered for identification purposes.

1. The magazines include *People,* the Gucci

catalog and, of course, *Chicago* magazine, the
bible of those who seek new experiences and
the perfect pesto sauce for their pasta.

2. High-rise Dolly. (Also known to some anthro-
    pologists as Disco Dolly.)
3. Vidal Sassoon blow drier.
4. Pasta-making machine.
5. Mega-Vitamins. High-rise Man needs strength.
6. Video recorder.
7. Gold Rolex watch.
8. Peugeot ten-speed bike, for those mad dashes
    through Lincoln Park.
9. Irish walking hat, for those melancholy strolls
    through Lincoln Park.
10. Trak Nowax cross-country skis, for those in-
    vigorating treks through Lincoln Park.
11. Perrier water.
12. Soft contact lenses. The better to see you with,
    High-rise Dolly.
13. Funny little cigarettes.
14. Vegetable steamer. High-rise man must be
    lean.
15. Racquetball racquet. High-rise Man must be
    fit.
16. Harvey's Bristol Cream. (Or Amaretto on the
    rocks, if you prefer.)
17. Another High-rise Dolly. High-rise Man al-
    ways carries a spare.
18. HIS AND HERS roller skates. High-rise Man
    swoops and spins.
19. Useless little dog. They're very good, inciden-
    tally, on a Ritz cracker.
20. Cognac-colored, reverse-leather Gucci loafers,
    at $185 a pair. High-rise Man loafs in style.
21. Nike jogging shoes. For running off the calo-
    ries of the perfect pesto pasta.
22. Head jogging suit. For looking suave while
    running off the perfect pesto pasta sauce cal-
    ories.

23. Funny white powder for High-rise Dolly's nose. Inside of nose, not out.
24. High-rise Man's credit cards and membership card for East Bank Club, in greedy clutches of High-rise Dolly.
25. Gold chain and medallion, to accent High-rise Man's manly chest.
26. Sony Walkman portable stereo. High-rise Man must hear beauty wherever he jogs, bikes, glides, or strolls.

There is much more, of course, such as the Tony Lama boots, Calvin Klein jeans, bomber jacket, goose down vest, keys to BMW car, coffee bean grinder, Cuisinart, microwave oven, futon mattress, Eames chair, George Kovacs lamp, L. L. Bean catalog, and glassware and other doodads from Crate and Barrel. I didn't show them all because High-rise Man doesn't want to appear ostentatious.

So that's the story of my evolution from Bungalow Man to High-rise Man. Or my decline, if you prefer.

I will have regular scientific reports on my findings of various aspects of this culture. Is there a perfect pesto sauce? Does walking a useless little dog help High-rise Man meet High-rise Dollies who are also walking useless little dogs? Can a French ten-speed bike outdistance a Chicago high-speed mugger? Does potential class war exist between Coho snaggers and High-rise joggers?

Meanwhile, I must go. My capuccino machine is hissing at me.

Save the Office Party: Bah on the Bluenoses!

December 6, 1981

It's about time someone spoke up in defense of the office Christmas party.

Every year at this time, the tradition of holding office Christmas parties is condemned by clergyman, journalists, housewives, the police department, teetotalers, and other meddlers.

A few days ago, Ann Landers' column contained a lengthy letter from a lady who called for the abolition of Christmas parties, and Ann agreed, which probably makes her the only newspaper person on this continent who is against any kind of raucous parties.

The result of all this goodness-mongering has been that the office Christmas party has just about faded away. Personnel directors, who have the thinnest lips and quiveriest nostrils of all corporate executives, except possibly the controllers, have declared office parties to be counterproductive.

In fairness, I will concede that most of the critics of office Christmas parties make some valid points.

For example, it is true that a few employees do become so carried away with enthusiasm for their office Christmas parties that they arrive home a little late for their own family celebrations.

That happened to a friend of mine, whose company used to have a party that began at about midafternoon every Christmas Eve.

When my friend arrived home after one such party, his loving wife met him at the door and began alternately shrieking and weeping. His children sat at the top of the stairs in their pajamas and just stared sullenly at him. Even his faithful old dog growled.

My friend, pained by the surprising coldness of their greeting, finally focused his borscht-colored eyes on his watch and said:

"But it's only 8:15 P.M."

And his wife wailed: "Yes—on December 26th."

It's also true, as some wives have complained, that after a Christmas party their husbands aren't as clear-headed as they'd like them to be.

Mr. Grobnik, who was my friend Slats Grobnik's father, once had a few eggnogs too many at the annual party held at the toilet seat factory where he was chief quality control inspector. He should have known better, since too much egg with his liquor always did addle his brain.

But he was in high holiday spirits when he came bursting through the front door that evening, dancing about, waving his arms and joyously shouting: "Ho, ho, ho—how's 'bout big kiss for the old man, honey."

Unfortunately, Mr. Grobnik had gone in the front door of the wrong house, and the resident old man broke a chair over his head.

And it's probably true that during an afternoon of holiday high jinks, as the fast set calls it, some things are said and done that can cause strained relationships in an office. They can result in post-holiday conversations that sound something like this:

"Uh, sorry about your office rug, chief. I hope there's no hard feelings."

"Not at all, Wilkins. Those vomit stains give it character."

"Miss Smith, I hope that nothing I've said or done has offended you. You're the best secretary I've ever had and I wouldn't want a few casual remarks to be misinterpreted and affect our working relationship."

*"Not at all, Mr. Collins. Shall I order us something
from room service?"*

"Say, thanks for getting me home after the office
party, Bill. I was in no shape to drive. By the way, where
did you leave my car?"

"What? I was going to thank you for getting me
home, and ask where you left *my* car."

*"What do you mean lipstick on my collar? That's not
lipstick. I cut myself shaving."*

"You shave the back of your neck?"

Yes, Christmas parties have their flaws, and maybe
they are unnecessary. After all, with thousands of good
bars in the Chicago area, what's the sense of leaning on
a filing cabinet while having a drink?

But they serve one valuable and humane service: They
are the stockboys' biggest day.

In every company there are stockboys. They might
have other titles and duties, but it amounts to the same
thing: They have the lowest pay and the least respect.
They have to call everyone mister or miss or mizz or sir
or ma'am. And nobody calls them anything but hey
you.

For them, the office Christmas party was always the
social highlight of the year—the safety valve when, after
sufficient lubrication, they could air their grievances
and express their opinions in an informal atmosphere.

Those were the best parts of any Christmas party—
when a stockboy could be heard saying:

"Mr. Brown, you're not a bad guy, you know that—
for a fat, creepy old lech."

*"Say, Mr. Sims, can I tell you a secret? You know
how one of us has to go down to the cafeteria to get you
coffee every morning and every afternoon, and you
scream if we forget the cream or the sugar and you never
buy us a cup? Well, the secret is, we spit in your
coffee."*

"We've never talked before, Mr. Reeves. I work in
the shipping room. But I'd like to say how much I ad-
mire you for the way you've really moved up in this

company. I mean, you're not much older than I am and you're already a vice president. Do you think that the fact that your father owns this outfit had anything to do with it, you arrogant son of a. . . ."

"You can't fire me—I quit."

III.

1981–1983, THE SUN-TIMES

Hats Off to the Cold

January 12, 1982

John Ruane, who observes the passing scene, wonders why some men don't wear hats even in the coldest weather.

"I really can't understand it," he says. "I wonder if they walk around without hats because they're over-concerned about their looks. Do they believe it's not chic or cool to wear a hat?

"Since you have moved into a swinging apartment, and are now considered chic and cool, you might be the person to explain this."

Yes, in matters that involve being cool and chic, it's widely known that I'm the person to consult. So I'll explain about hats.

It's true that a hat is essential for warmth, since much body heat escapes from the top of the head.

But basically there are two kinds of men: Those who wear hats and those who don't.

Men who don't wear hats are generally youthful, vigorous, impetuous, and have a devil-may-care glint in their eyes. They're inclined to be dashing, adventurous risk-takers.

On the other hand, men who made a habit of wearing hats are, I'm sorry to say, fuddy-duddies.

As you may recall, President John F. Kennedy seldom, if ever, was seen wearing a hat. In contrast, Herbert Hoover always wore one, even to bed.

Because of their attitudes toward hats, Kennedy is remembered as being youthful and dashing, while Hoover is dismissed by many historians as a dusty old coot.

Naturally, I don't wear a hat, since I've always had a youthful, devil-may-care nature. I'd rather have a numb head, which I often do, than identify with Herbert Hoover.

But hatmakers themselves must share the blame. The fact is, most men's hats look funny, and some of us would rather not put objects that look funny on our heads, especially those of us whose heads look funny enough already.

Let's consider the most popular hats.

First, there is the standard man's hat, which has a brim and comes in a variety of shapes and styles.

They range from the narrow-brimmed porkpie to the wide-brimmed cowboy hat. In between are the standard fedoras, which often come with some poor bird's feather sticking out of the band.

The main trouble with the brimmed hats, besides their appearance, is that in a city as windy as Chicago, they are always blowing off.

To avoid the indignity of chasing your hat down the street, which isn't very dapper, you have to walk with one hand holding your hat on your head.

This causes you to raise your arm high, thus exposing your armpit area to the icy winds. I see no point in keeping the top of my head warm if the price is a chilled armpit. To compare the discomfort of the two options, make this experiment: Press an ice cube to the top of your head; then press an ice cube to your armpit. See? It's far worse.

Some men get around the wind problem by jamming their fedoras down on their heads as far as they can.

But when they arrive at their indoor destination and remove their hat, they have a deep indentation around their head, as if someone had been squeezing it with a vise.

After years of jamming their hats down on their heads, the indentations become deeper and deeper. Eventually, the upper part of a head seems to bulge until a person looks like a science-fiction creature. Having a two-piece head is a pretty steep price to pay just to retain a little body heat.

That's why many men choose hats other than the standard fedora.

Among the most popular is the Irish walking hat, which is rumpled and tweedy, or the cheaper American version, which looks like it is punched out on a machine in Taiwan. In either case, the Irish walking hat makes you look like you have your head stuck in a funnel, which isn't very suave.

Then there is the Irish cap. It's a sturdy, simple cap, and just the thing to wear if you want to look like a 1930s cab-driver.

The Russian hat, in wool or fur, is very popular, especially among commuters. As they swarm out of Union Station in the morning, they look like thousands of suburban Leonid Brezhnevs.

When the weather turns bitterly cold, the most popular hat is the plain, wool stocking cap, often pulled down over the ears. It gives you the sophisticated look of a rural mail carrier.

Some men wear black berets, because they think they look dapper. And they are, if being dapper means looking like a French pimp.

So my answer to John Ruane is, yes, those of us who refuse to wear hats in cold weather do so out of vanity.

We like to give the appearance of being undaunted by the cold, jauntily strolling with bare heads held high into the teeth of a forty-below wind-chill factor. Oh, sometimes you have to have a blackened earlobe removed by a doc, but that's the price of looking jaunty.

Being cool and youthfully dashing, the only concession I make to extreme cold is to put on a pair of quilted long underwear from Sears, wool stockings, heavy, insulated boots, a thick scarf, earmuffs, a ski mask, and mittens pinned to my sleeves so I don't lose them.

Of course, if I'm getting out of bed I'll wear even more.

A Lost Job Isn't the End

January 19, 1982

He didn't waste any time getting to the point. His letter began:

"Please excuse me for infringing on your privacy, but I just had to tell someone before I take my life."

It was written on lined notebook paper and the handwriting was erratic.

He went on: "I am a thirty-year-old male, married with a family of three, living on the Southwest Side. I am a religious person and never been in trouble with the law.

"For the last five months, I have been frantically searching for some kind of employment but with no success. I am at the point now of no return.

"My family and I are about to be evicted because I can't pay the rent. I wouldn't feel so desperate if it wasn't for the debts and bills piling up.

"I really would like to live longer and enjoy my family, but I can't support them because of no job.

"I have tried seeking employment. No matter what it may be, factory, gas attendant, office work, or retail clerk, but it seemed that no one has a job opening.

"I'm not asking for charity or a handout. All I'm asking for is a chance to work and support my family.

"I'm a human being with pride and integrity, but you understand that integrity can't pay the rent, gas, and food bills. If a person can see light at the end of a tunnel, he can have hope. But when you can't see any light, there is nothing.

"When you have a job it makes you feel like a man to accept responsibility. When you don't, you feel lower than dirt itself.

"How do you explain it to school-age children when they say 'daddy, why can't I have boots for the snow?' When you don't have a job, you have to cut back on everything just to survive. But small children don't understand.

"I never thought that anything could cause me to break down to this point of suicidal tendencies. I'm at the brink of taking myself from this society. Maybe it is a better life hereafter.

"I always believed that one must help himself before he can get help from someone else. I tried everything outside of robbery and stealing just to survive. I'm desperate, totally desperate. But I can't find it in my heart to rob and steal from someone who is more fortunate.

"When you run out of hope there is a deep mental strain that causes you not to function properly.

"Please tell anyone who has a job that they are the luckiest people in the world, no matter what the pay or conditions. At least they can tell their family when payday comes that they can buy food, clothes and pay the rent."

And he signed his letter: "No Hope—Please help."

Well, Mr. No Hope Please Help, I'm sorry, but there isn't much I can do to be of help.

For one thing, when you write a suicide threat and ask

for help, you really should sign your name. An address and phone number would help, too.

You are one of almost 9.5 million Americans who are out of work, so it wouldn't be easy to track you down to offer help.

But I can offer some advice.

To start, I'm not going to plead with you not to kill yourself.

You know better than I whether you, at the age of thirty, presumably in good health since you didn't mention illness, with a wife and kids you obviously care about, are ready to end it all because you have been out of work for a few months.

I'm sure you've had it rough. But I have to be honest: Thirty is still pretty young, so many more difficult events await you. There are rougher things in life than being unemployed.

As you get older, you could experience a long, lingering, painful illness. Every day, people go to hospitals for chemotherapy treatment or repeated surgery. It can be terrible. But they hang on.

Even worse, it could happen to someone close to you. Someone you love might die. That's part of life, and it's more painful than being without a job. And it happens to people every day. Just read the death notices. But most of the survivors endure the pain and hang on.

So if your present problems are enough to drive you to suicide, it might be that you just aren't strong enough to handle the more severe jolts that will inevitably come your way if you decide to stick around.

But before you take shelter in the great beyond, you might give some thought to what you will be accomplishing.

You'll probably be the object of sympathy—especially if you leave a farewell note saying that being without a job drove you to the grave. It's a natural news story, and some of your friends will say: "Poor Joe, life just wore him down."

On the other hand, some of your friends might decide that you were more coward than victim. After all, 9.5

million Americans have the same problem and few of them jump from bridges or swallow everything in the medicine cabinet.

I don't think your wife and kids would be impressed by your decision. Most kids prefer the presence of a living, though unemployed, father to the memory of a dead one. If your kids don't have winter boots while you are alive, how is your being dead going to make their feet warmer?

And considering all the other unpaid bills you have now, it's really inconsiderate to stick your wife with the additional burden of paying for your funeral. Undertakers aren't any more understanding than Commonwealth Edison or a landlord.

Look, you married her, took various oaths, and brought the children into the world. They have a vested interest in your existence. So it would be only fair for you to sit down with your family and tell them that you are going to kill yourself, and get their opinions. Simple courtesy, really.

You might also consider that as painful as it is to be unemployed, you aren't alone, and it's not something to be ashamed of. Most jobless people have no control over the national and international trends that cost them their jobs.

You might also consider that no matter what happens, you and your family aren't going to starve, you aren't going to be out in the cold freezing to death, and you will have medical care if you need it. As chaotic as our welfare system is, it does provide the bare basics. People have survived on less.

So give it a little more time. And drop me another note with your name and address on it. Who knows, some employer out there might read this and have an opening.

But if you must do it, go somewhere isolated and do it quietly. Your wife will have enough problems without cleaning up after you one last time.

Algren Street Farewell

February 14, 1982

One of the marks of a good Nelson Algren story was the wry, sometimes bizarre, ending.

So Algren, who wrote so many wonderful stories set in Chicago, would have been delighted with the way this story ends.

But first, the beginning of the story.

Algren, who was a friend of mine, died last year. I wrote one of the many eulogies about him.

In it, I noted that despite his international literary reputation, he had never been given much recognition in this city, where he had lived most of his life and where he had done almost all of his writing.

It wasn't just indifference, although there was a lot of that. In most civilized countries, someone with Algren's literary credentials would have been given a professorship at a university, so he would be assured of a roof over his head and eating money while he wrote.

Oh, we even do that in this country. But most such professorships are given to pretentious bores who write novels about literary professors and the agony they go through in writing novels.

None of the Chicago-area universities wanted someone like Algren on their faculty. They considered his manners too crude. He wouldn't have blended well at the dean's dinners.

Beyond the indifference, there was outright hostility. Algren's big best seller, the book that established his reputation, was *The Man With the Golden Arm*. It was set in the Humboldt Park area, where Algren lived, and most of the main characters were Polish-Americans.

The book was good enough to win the first National Book Award, which is something like a literary Oscar.

But all it received in Chicago were jeers. Alleged leaders of the Polish community felt that it was an insult to Poles because the characters were something less than high society. Using their logic, Danes should have a grievance against Shakespeare because Hamlet was kind of a weird guy.

So with the connivance of City Hall, Algren's book was virtually banned from the libraries.

Also, the politicians didn't like another brilliant Algren book—*Chicago: City on the Make*—because it portrayed Chicago's crooked, money-grubbing, thickheaded, bigoted politicians as crooked, money-grubbing, thickheaded, bigoted politicians.

Anyway, when Algren died I wrote a column about these and other high points and low points in his career.

And I suggested that it might be nice if City Hall named a street for Algren. Specifically, Evergreen Street, where he lived in an old third-floor walk-up for so many years.

Much to my surprise, Mayor Byrne liked the idea and told an aide to draft an ordinance changing the name of the street. Not the entire length of Evergreen, of course, but only a four-block segment between Damen and Milwaukee avenues.

The ordinance was submitted to the City Council. Naturally, I was delighted, especially when the mayor's office gave me one of the "Algren St." signs.

And a few weeks ago, a city crew went to the neighborhood and took down the signs that said "Evergreen" and put up signs that said "Algren."

How did the neighborhood react? Were they pleased that someone who had lived there was being honored? Did they welcome the opportunity to tell their children: "See? A man who used to live right down the street here was a very famous writer."

Not quite.

My phone immediately began ringing. The callers said things like: "Hey, are you the jerk that messed up our street signs?"

Some people in the community, it seems, were not pleased that their street had been renamed. They moaned that they were being inconvenienced. Their relatives couldn't find their homes any more. Their mail would not be delivered. They would have to change their driver's licenses.

A handbill, printed in English and Spanish, began circulating in the neighborhood. It was signed by a person or group that called itself "The Concerned Residents of Evergreen Avenue" and it said:

"Do you know that the street on which you live, Evergreen Avenue, is in the process of being renamed to Algren Street??? Do you know why it's being changed to Algren Street??? Robert Algren was a poet who died recently. Sun-Times Columnist Mike Royko thought it would be nice to name the street after him.

"Why is our alderman, Michael Nardulli, supporting this street name change without inquiring of its residents????"

The handbill went on to claim that it would cost every resident a small fortune in postage stamps to change the address on various documents.

And it urged the residents: "It's up to us to try to stop this proposal. So place a call to Alderman Nardulli at his city office to voice your objection. We must act NOW before it is too late!!! Just think of how much you will save. For example, to change the address on your driver's license alone amounts to $5, not to mention the 20 cents postage for each family and friend you have to notify. SO CALL NOW."

By the tone of the handbill, you'd think they were being threatened with bubonic plague. And the fact is, the secretary of state's office doesn't charge anything to change the address on a driver's license when a street has been renamed.

But enough people were horrified at the thought of the name change to call Alderman Nardulli. Some said that if they had to spend twenty cents or more in postage because of the change, they would never again vote for him.

Nardulli, fearing that he would be tossed out of office and forced to find honest work, scampered down to City Hall to see what he could do about the street signs.

And, it turned out, there was something he could do.

It seems that the city signs department simply assumed that because the mayor wanted the street name changed, the City Council would automatically approve it. So it put the new signs up before the Council made it official.

But when Nardulli wailed that he might lose a few dozen votes, his colleagues took pity on him. And they voted against the street name change.

So Evergreen Street never officially became Algren Street.

And a few days ago, a city crew went to the neighborhood and took down the "Algren Street" signs and put the "Evergreen Street" signs back up. So much for literary glory.

It was a typical Nelson Algren ending. And he would have liked the touch of calling him "Robert Algren" in the handbill.

And he'd even have liked Alderman Nardulli's comment:

"I didn't even know duh guy."

That's all right, alderman. He didn't know you either. And I don't think he felt a sense of loss.

My Belushi Pals

March 7, 1982

Like so many Chicagoans, last Thursday night I was watching a rerun of the original "Saturday Night Live" show.

I was rewarded when John Belushi came on to do one of his outrageous skits.

As happened whenever I saw John perform, I felt a mix of emotions.

Amusement, of course. All he had to do was lift a brow and curl his lip and he could make me laugh.

But I also felt pride. As I wrote here once before, I go back a long way with the Belushi family. John's late Uncle Pete was one of my closest friends and was godfather to my first child. John's father and I were also friends. I first set eyes on John when he was about five years old, running around his uncle's back yard while I devoured his Aunt Marion's wonderful Greek cooking. I don't remember that he was very funny then. But he and the other Belushi kids were sure noisy.

So when John became successful, I suppose I felt something like a distant uncle and was proud of him.

But, as I watched him on my TV or in a movie theater, I always felt puzzled. Where had this incredible comic instinct come from? His parents were good people, but not visibly humorous. Yet they produced two sons, John and Jim, who have the rare gift of being able to make strangers laugh.

I remember when I first learned that John had become an entertainer. It had to be, oh, a dozen years ago and I was at an independent political rally at a big restaurant on the South Side. A young man came up to me and, in a shy way, said: "Uncle Mike?"

I guess I blinked for a moment because he said: "You don't remember me?"

I said: "I know you're one of the Belushi kids by your goofy face, but I'm not sure which one."

He laughed. "I'm John. Adam's son."

I asked him if he was there because he was interested in politics.

"I just joined Second City. We're going to be doing a few skits here tonight."

I was impressed. Second City was already a nationally known improvisational theater group. I wish I could say that after I saw him perform, I knew he would one day be a big star. But I didn't. I could see he had a flair, but I wouldn't have bet you money that by the time he was thirty, he'd have one of the most familiar faces in America. A lot of people are funny, but very few have a talent that might be called genius.

As I said, I always had a mix of feelings when I watched John. And last Thursday night, I also felt a twinge of sad nostalgia.

That's because he was playing Pete the Greek, the owner of the short-order diner. You know the one: "Chizbooga, chizbooga, cheeps, cheeps, cheeps."

Whenever I watched him do that character, it was like flipping back in time almost thirty years.

I'd be sitting in a short-order diner in Logan Square, waiting for my wife to finish work upstairs in a doctor's office. The diner was where Eddie's Barbeque now stands, just across the side street from where the old "L" terminal used to be.

John's Uncle Pete would be at the grill, slapping cheeseburgers on the grill, jiggling the fries. Marion would be serving the food and coffee and handling the cash register.

I don't remember if Pete said "chizbooga" and "cheeps" exactly the way John later did. His thick accent was Albanian, not Greek. But it was close.

And somewhere in another neighborhood, in another short-order joint, Adam Belushi was slapping cheeseburgers on another grill. Everybody in the family was chasing the American dream. And they were doing it the way immigrants have always done it. Whatever works—and never mind how many grease burns you get on your arms.

If it was a Friday, we'd probably wind up in Peter's third-floor flat or my attic flat, drinking Metaxa and talking about the things we might do some day. If I ever got off that weekly neighborhood newspaper and he and Adam could pyramid those short-order grills into the restaurant of his dreams.

We were all together the night a few years later that the dream restaurant opened. Adam, Pete, and me and our wives. The place had thick carpets and cloth wallpaper, oil paintings, a piano player in the bar and the best prime rib I've ever had. Maybe you remember it—Fair Oaks, on Dempster, in Morton Grove. It's now a big Mexican restaurant.

We toasted their success. It was a long way from tending sheep in Albania, and they had earned it. It didn't stop there, either. Before long there were other businesses. Pete figured he might as well go on and become an American tycoon.

But life has a way of giving you the gladhand. Then slamming you with a fist.

A few years ago, Pete, still in his forties, died. At the funeral, we talked about John and how he had gone to New York and was starting to make a name, and how proud everybody was.

And the last time I saw John, we talked about those times and my friend Pete. It might surprise those who saw him only on the TV or in movies, but he was still shy and often quiet. And he had not let his success and wealth turn him into a jerk. He was still a genuinely nice kid.

That was the night his movie *Continental Divide* opened in Chicago and there was a party after the show.

A reporter for *Rolling Stone,* who covered the evening, later wrote that as the evening ended, John and I were hugging.

I guess we were. When you feel like a proud uncle, and see the kid up there on a movie screen, you ought to give him a hug.

This column seems to have rambled. I'm sorry, but I just heard about John a few hours ago, and I have difficulty writing when I feel the way I do right now.

He was only thirty-three. I learned a long time ago that life isn't always fair. But it shouldn't cheat that much.

Don't Write Off Belushi

March 16, 1982

The moment it was determined that drugs caused John Belushi's death, they snatched up their pens and paper to express their self-righteousness.

"You have been caught with your pants down!" was the triumphant message from Mrs. Martha McMinn, of Portland, Oregon.

I assume Mrs. McMinn means that because I wrote a column expressing sadness at the sudden death of a friend, I should now be embarrassed because of the circumstances surrounding his death.

She went on to say: "Life was certainly not unfair to Belushi. He had fame, money, adulation and he blew it on dope and a broad who was not his wife.

"He got what he deserved!

"Sincerely. . . ."

And I'm sure Mrs. McMinn is sincere. At least I

would sincerely hope that people would not be *insincere* when expressing what almost amounts to glee at some-one else's death.

Mrs. Pauline Olson was not exactly bubbling with compassion, either. She said:

"Boy, I'll bet your face is red! You give us a song-and-dance about what an All-American kid your friend Belushi was. But now it turns out that he was just another show business dope user.

"Frankly, I never liked him much on TV. He was fat and crude, so I'm not surprised that he came to such a bad end.

"He was not deserving of our sympathy, and I think you owe your readers an apology for portraying him as a decent person when he was no such thing."

There were many others, and their letters are still coming in, but you get the idea.

Well, I hate to disappoint Mrs. Olson and Mrs. McMinn and all the others, but no, I'm not embarrassed and, no, I'm not going to apologize.

When I wrote about Belushi, he had been dead only a few hours and nobody knew what had caused his death. Later, I was surprised to learn that he had been using drugs. When I had seen him in Chicago last fall, he appeared to be leading a clean life. Soft drinks, a sensible diet, regular exercise, no outward evidence of drug use.

Had I known about his drug use, I wouldn't have been any less sad. If anything, I would have felt worse because of the wastefulness of his death.

Nor does the way he died mean that he was, as Mrs. Olson so harshly contends, not "a decent person."

The fact that he stuck needles in his arms could mean that he was capable of stupidity; that he might have been weak, self-indulgent, or guilty of whatever character flaws make otherwise intelligent people perform self-destructive acts. But that didn't make him a monster.

Belushi hurt no one but himself, and his family. But until his family condemns him for their pain, I think outsiders like Mrs. McMinn ought to reserve their condemnation.

Actually, I have more difficulty understanding the workings of the minds of people who are so quick to dance on somebody's grave. Obviously, no sensible person approves of drug use. But Belushi wasn't exactly selling the stuff to kids in schoolyards.

I wonder if they fire off notes like that whenever somebody they know dies.

If you think about it, the opportunities are always there. Drugs aren't the only form of self-indulgence that can lead to death.

For example, one could write a note like this:

"Dear Lucille:

"I was saddened to hear of the untimely death of your dear beloved husband, Rudy. Because I was out of town at the time, I could not attend the funeral.

"However, I must say that Rudy brought it on himself! And you didn't help, either.

"As your friend for many years, I could not help but notice that Rudy was always thirty or forty pounds overweight. Lugging around all that fat couldn't have done his heart any good. And you must share the blame for cooking him all those high-calorie meals.

"Dietitians keep warning that being overweight can shorten a person's life. But did Rudy stop shoving food in his mouth? Noooooo!

"So as much as I can sympathize with you in your time of sadness, you and Rudy got exactly what you deserved!

"Sincerely, your friend. . . ."

Or one could always write a note like this:

"Dear Mary:

"I didn't want to bring this up at John's funeral because you were busy greeting mourners.

"But I have to say that I can't understand why you and everyone else was so surprised that John dropped dead so suddenly.

"After all, he did smoke two packs a day, and any

idiot knows that the U.S. Surgeon General has warned that smoking is dangerous.

"If he had the will power that my William has, and had quit the filthy habit, he'd probably be alive today. And his teeth would have been much whiter. But, nooooo, he just kept on puffing away.

"So in your time of sorrow, I just want you to know that John got what he deserved!

"Sincerely, your friend. . . ."

Or this one:

"Dear Lucille:

"Just a note to let you know we are thinking about you in your time of sorrow.

"But as I was telling my dear Ed the other day, it was just a matter of time.

"Your George just wouldn't slow down, would he? Sure, all that drive and aggressiveness got you a big house, and two cars, and those fancy clothes and expensive vacations. But it also got George hypertension, anxiety, and high blood pressure.

"So you and George got exactly what you deserved!

"Sincerely, your neighbor . . . (We're the ones in the much *smaller* house, with the *older* car, and the *cheaper* vacations. But at least my husband is still around!)"

So Mrs. McMinn and Mrs. Olson and all you other grave-dancers, feel free to use any of the above letters when the occasions arise.

Or have you already been doing it?

Home on the Scalp

March 21, 1982

I was pleased to read that Chicago is having its worst outbreak of cooties in forty years.

For those who are not familiar with the word "cooties," it is a polite, refined way of describing head lice.

Public health officials say that there are more cooties strutting around more young heads today than at any time since the 1940s.

Cooties, being democratic little creatures, recognize no economic or social barriers. To them, a head is a home, so they are being found on the scalps of youths in the city and suburbs, among the poor, the middle class, and the rich.

This cootie epidemic probably seems like a strange thing for somebody to find pleasing, so I should explain.

There are those who say that today's technology-oriented youths have little in common with past young generations. With their Walkman headsets and their Pac-Man games, their electric musical instruments and the various herbs and spices they sniff or smoke, they have less contact with reality than past generations did.

I don't know if that is true. But there is no greater sense of reality than discovering that tiny creatures have decided to live on your scalp.

And this gives today's young people and older people a common ground. I find it heartwarming that some cootie-infested teen on the North Shore and his old gramps have an experience they can share.

"I have cooties, grandpa."

"Yep, I noticed that, sonny. You're scratching with both hands. That's the most physical activity I've ever seen from you."

"Did you ever have them, gramps?"

"Sure did. But they don't make cooties like they did in my days. They were big, mean buggers back then. Chomp your head right off."

One thing that has changed are the remedies. There are a wide variety of cootie-killing shampoos, hair sprays, and various lotions sold in drugstores.

When I was a youth, there were only three standard cures.

One was something called Larkspur Lotion. Not only was it an effective cootie-killer, but it had such a powerful odor that everybody within fifty yards knew immediately what your problem was. You could always be sure of getting a seat on a streetcar.

The other, for economy-minded families, was nickel-a-quart kerosene, sold in the gas station or at the hardware store.

You could immediately tell when there was an outbreak in our neighborhood. Half the kids would be standing in line at Moore's gas station, holding an empty milk bottle with one hand and scratching with the other.

Mrs. Ruby Peak had the largest brood. She had between twelve and fifteen kids, but nobody was sure exactly how many because they all looked alike—flat heads and eyes that touched. They weren't very bright.

When the cooties invaded, Mrs. Peak's kids were always the first to have them. The gas station owner once said: "I sell enough kerosene to that family to have lit the lamps of all the early settlers in Fort Dearborn."

Then there was the cure favored by Slats Grobnik's father, Mr. Grobnik.

Being a fiscally prudent man, he didn't believe in spending money for Larkspur Lotion, saying, "First you buy the Larkspur Lotion. Then you have to buy a fine-tooth comb to comb out the cooties' dead bodies. Then a month later, he's scratching again and I have to buy some more lotion and another comb. In my old age I could wind up broke just because Slats ain't got enough sense not to sit next to Ruby Peak's lousy kids at school.''

And he didn't believe in the less-expensive kerosene treatment, explaining, ''It's too dangerous. I put that stuff on Slats' head and somebody lights a cigarette. Poof, his hair is on fire. That would be a tragedy because if Slats panicked and ran around, he could set the curtains on fire and my whole house would burn down, and I don't think my insurance would cover it.''

So Mr. Grobnik's remedy was simple. As soon as he saw Slats start scratching, he would reach for the scissors and razor and shave Slats' head.

Slats would loudly protest, saying, ''Why am I always the only bald kid in my class. I'm fourteen years old and there are girls who have never seen me with hair.''

But Mr. Grobnik would say, ''This is the best way. Without your hair, they have no place to hide. Then I've got 'em.''

As soon as Slats' head was bare, Mr. Grobnik would start smacking away with a rolled up newspaper. In later years Slats said, ''It was lucky for me that the only newspaper my old man ever read was the *Racing News.* If we had subscribed to the Sunday *New York Times,* I would have died of concussions before I was twelve.''

I can recall only one other remedy, and that was used only by Crazy Archie's father. I don't remember his full name. He was known only as Crazy Archie's father. It was better than having no sense of identity, I guess.

What he would do was shave a bare spot, about three or four inches across, on top of Crazy Archie's head. Then he would sit there waiting and watching the bare spot, with a heavy soup spoon poised. When one of the little creatures would try to scamper across the open space, Crazy Archie's father would smack it with the spoon.

We lived next door to Crazy Archie, and during a cootie outbreak, all evening we would hear: "Boing! Oww! Boing! Oww."

Crazy Archie's father once explained why he did it that way: "Sure, it's slower, but there's a lot more sport involved. I can't afford to go on hunting trips, you know."

Crazy Archie put up with that until he was about sixteen. Then one day, during dinner, he suddenly snatched up a ball peen hammer and hit his father on the head with it.

When the old man regained consciousness in a hospital three days later, he said, "Archie, why did you do that to me?"

Archie smiled and said, "Biggest bug I ever saw, Pa, but don't worry—I got 'im."

After that, Crazy Archie's father used Larkspur Lotion and a comb. And everybody agreed that Crazy Archie wasn't so crazy after all.

Put a Lid on That Crock Plot

April 11, 1982

Suddenly there's all this serious talk about civil defense planning and how many people could survive a nuclear war.

Whenever that subject comes up, I recall a conversation I once had with Carl Sandburg, the great poet, when I was a young reporter.

It was about twenty-two years ago, when the Cold War was really frigid and digging fallout shelters was one of this country's most popular pastimes.

Sandburg was visiting Chicago and I was assigned to interview him.

Before I left the office, I was called aside by an editor who was building his own home fallout shelter.

He said, "I want you to ask Sandburg what he would stock a fallout shelter with."

"Why should I ask him that?" I asked that editor.

"Well, he's a brilliant, world-famous man, and I think a lot of people would be interested in knowing what somebody like him would think was important to have."

When I put the question to Sandburg, we were in a dining room with some of Chicago's wealthiest, most socially prominent citizens, who were honoring him.

He pondered the question for about twenty or thirty seconds, pursing his lips and looking toward the sky, while everyone sat silently awaiting his profound thoughts.

Then, in that dramatic, rumbling voice, he said very, very slowly and deliberately:

"I would be sure [pause] to take with me [pause] a sufficient number of receptacles [pause] to hold that [pause] which Norman Mailer [pause] calls shit."

At the sound of that word, all the fine ladies in gowns and fine gentlemen in dinner jackets gasped. Sandburg stifled a grin.

"Is there anything else?" I asked.

"No," he said, "that is what comes to mind when someone talks about survival after nuclear war."

I returned to the office, wrote the story and turned it in. The editor yelped, "We can't print this!"

"Why not? He said it."

"Because it's crude."

"But I think Sandburg was trying to make a point."

"Well, I don't understand his point and it's not going into this newspaper."

And it didn't.

But I've always remembered it because Sandburg pretty well summed up in that one blunt word what all of these serious discussions about crawling into holes or evacuating the cities really amount to: It is just a crock.

It was a crock back then, when millions of frightened Americans stocked their basements with bottled water, canned foods and first-aid kits, and politicians donned civil defense uniforms and blew off sirens to show that they were ready for anything.

And it's a crock now, as the Reagan administration unleashes a double-barreled propaganda barrage.

Propaganda Barrel one: We are woefully behind the Russians in nuclear strength, so we have to have a huge military buildup costing billions of dollars.

This buildup, of course, terrifies many people. We build more bombs and the Russians build more bombs. So we build more and they build more. And along the way, a lot of other, smaller countries build their bombs. And one of these days, poof!

So that's where Propaganda Barrel two comes in. It goes something like this:

Don't worry about the nuclear buildup. The more bombs everybody builds, the safer we'll all be. Besides, we *can* survive nuclear war. Not nearly as many people would die as we might think. Sure, millions would not make it—but many, many more millions would survive.

All we have to do is be prepared with plans to evacuate the cities. Then when we see the Russians evacuating their cities, we will know they are going to attack us, and we can evacuate our cities.

Or something like that.

This kind of talk is almost funny when it comes from those eccentric people who call themselves survivalists and plan for the day when they will barricade themselves in their vacation homes and wait with shotgun cocked to blast the looters who want their homes.

But the talk isn't funny when it comes from officials in the present White House administration.

They talk about evacuating the cities. Every day at about 4 P.M., people get in their cars to go home from work. Every day there is a huge traffic jam.

And that's with only a fraction of the population being on the move.

What would happen if *everybody* tried to get away at the same time?

Nothing would move. It would be chaos.

Ah, but Washington tells us that wouldn't happen because we would have about four days in which to evacuate the cities.

I don't understand why they think there would be a four-day grace period before we and the Russians began bombing each other. Maybe they have an optimistic computer.

But even though it's ridiculous to think there would be time to evacuate the urban areas, let's go along with this crazy thinking and assume there would be time.

We would have 200 million people wandering around the countryside with no food, no shelter, no medical care, no organized society.

Then when the bombs went off and the radiation and fallout got to them, they could die slowly instead of quickly. And those who survived the blasts and radiation could die of the diseases that would quickly spread.

Since most experts on the subject agree that planning for survival is a waste of time, why is there so much official talk about it?

The answer is that if the government wants to engage in a nuclear buildup that we don't need, since we are already as powerful as the Russians, they have to soothe us into thinking that we can survive a nuclear war.

That is supposed to make the buildup, and the possibility of nuclear war, less frightening to us.

It's a sales job. Even worse, a con job.

All they're doing is talking a lot of that which Carl Sandburg said Norman Mailer described as. . . . Well, you know what they're talking.

Your Shelter or Mine?

April 21, 1982

The fact that young people engage in pre-marital sex more frequently than in the past is nothing new.

There have been all sorts of theories as to why.

The most obvious is that the Pill makes it less risky. But that seems to be contradicted by the soaring illegitimacy rate.

Some preachers contend that it's all the fault of rock music, which they say arouses animal, jungle instincts in the young people. But as far as I can tell, the only physical effect rock music has on the young is to make them prematurely hard of hearing.

Others blame drugs, such as marijuana. That might be true, but the youths I've seen using marijuana don't seem active enough to do more than stare at a light bulb and say: "Wow, dig that crazy color."

Because more and more youths are replacing drugs with liquor, some experts say booze is the cause of increased sexual activity. But I doubt that. Liquor doesn't make young people passionate. It makes them throw up.

Now, a sociologist from the University of Wisconsin has come up with an explanation that I hadn't heard before.

He was testifying before a congressional subcommittee that is sticking its nose into the sex habits of the young. (You would think that a congressional subcommittee could find far more titillating material if it looked into the kinky sex habits of congressmen.)

Anyway, Professor Ray Short testified that his research has shown that many young people are doing it (my generation referred to it as "it") because they fear the coming of nuclear war.

This, he says, makes them insecure about the future. And so they decide that they might as well engage in sex before a nuclear holocaust deprives them of the opportunity.

Ahah! It's just a variation on the old "Baby, my outfit is shipping out in the morning and I don't know what's going to happen to me" trick.

I'm sorry to deflate the professor's findings, but this routine isn't new. Young men have been using the old "Baby, this is our last chance" line since long before the atom was first split.

One of its most adept practitioners was my old pal Slats Grobnik.

The very day he registered for the draft, he began roaming the neighborhood, a grim set to his jaw, telling all the young ladies:

"Well, it looks like this is it. I don't know if I'll be coming back. But I love this country and if I get killed, well, it's the least I can do."

Then he'd pause for dramatic effect and say: "SO LET'S DO IT, HUH?"

After Slats was still around for a year, the girls started to wise up, even though he told them he was doing undercover Army intelligence work. As one of the girls said: "Who does intelligence work in a pool hall?"

But the pitch became effective again when Slats finally went into the service, enlisting in the Coast Guard.

Then his line became: "My ship is leaving in the morning. At dawn. It could be rough. Baby, this is our last chance. LET'S DO IT, HUH?"

Of course his ship was leaving in the morning. It left every morning to chug around looking for drunken pleasure boaters. And it came back every evening.

Until the professor testified, I had wondered if the old "Tomorrow I might be dead" line was outdated. Without the draft, its use would be limited only to those joining today's volunteer armed forces.

But I can see how easily it could be adapted to the nuclear threat.

And especially today, with the Reagan administration trying to scare everyone into thinking that the Russian finger is only an inch away from the doomsday button.

Why, every time a young man picks up a newspaper today, he can wave it at a nubile young thing and say:

"Look! The Russians have nuclear superiority. They have first-, second-, and third-strike capability! And we have left open the window of vulnerability!"

"Oh, my goodness, that's terrible."

"You're damned right it's terrible. So the question is: What are we going to do about it?"

"I don't know."

"Well, I know. YOUR PLACE OR MINE?"

If the professor is right, then it could explain something that has been puzzling me recently.

We had a big ban-the-bomb rally in Chicago a couple of weekends ago.

There was a huge turnout, but it appeared that the vast majority of the people at the march and rally were middle-aged or elderly.

I've been asking myself why there weren't more young people in the march. Aren't they concerned about nuclear war? Don't they care?

The answer, according to the professor, is yes, they do care, they are concerned, they are worried.

Maybe they didn't march.

But that doesn't mean they're not active.

View from the Hoosierdome

June 3, 1982

I hadn't realized that people in Indiana are so excitable. Every time I've been there, they've seemed tranquil. So tranquil that many appeared to be asleep on their feet.

So you can imagine my surprise at the wild-eyed way they reacted to a bit of mild criticism I directed at their state in a recent column.

All I said was that I thought the Indianapolis 500 race was America's most stupid major sporting event, that Indiana is probably the most miserable state in the nation, and that Indianapolis was the dullest of big cities.

I quite accurately said: "For most males in Indiana, a real good time consists of putting on bib overalls and a cap bearing the name of a farm equipment company and sauntering to a gas station to sit around and gossip about how Elmer couldn't get his pickup truck started that morning. . . ."

And I noted: "Its only large cities are Indianapolis and Gary, which give you the choice of dying of boredom or of multiple gunshot wounds."

Now, most mature people can accept constructive criticism, which is exactly what those comments were. What could be more constructive than telling the residents of Indiana how unfortunate they are to live in such an awful place?

But did they take it that way? Just the opposite. They got mad and started shrieking and hopping up and down.

After that column appeared in an Indianapolis paper,

Mayor William H. Hudnut III called a press conference to denounce me.

Mayor Hudnut said, "It's easy to write out of ignorance, but not very responsible." And he added that my mind was like concrete: "All mixed up but too set to change."

The state's lieutenant governor, John M. Mutz, fired off a statement saying: "You know those nasty things you said weren't true." And he challenged me to come to Indianapolis so he could show me the city's exciting sights.

Even worse, my phone has been clanging with calls from those people who are the worst threat to clear, logical thinking—hosts of radio call-in shows.

"Why did you say all those things?" demanded one talk show babbler.

"Because they were what I had in my heart," I honestly told him. "And somebody had to say them."

He became angrier. "You talked about Indiana men wearing bib overalls and farm caps hanging around gas stations and talking about whose pickup truck wouldn't start?"

"That's right, I did."

"But I've seen men do that in Ohio and Arkansas and even in downstate Illinois."

"That doesn't make it right," I said. "Just because they do it in other places is no excuse."

Another airwave defender of the faith snarled:

"You said Indianapolis is a big hick town. Are you aware that we have a new convention center? And that we are building a domed stadium—the Hoosierdome?"

I showed admirable restraint by not laughing aloud. Can you imagine—the Hoosierdome?

If there is anything that marks a town as being a genuine hicksville, it is the innocent belief that a new domed stadium is the height of progress.

The greatest cities in America do *not* put protective plastic bubbles over the heads of their dumb athletes. Yankee Stadium has none. There's none in San Francisco. And, of course, none in Chicago.

And they're going to call it the Hoosierdome. The Hoosierdome?

Of course they are, since they call themselves Hoosiers.

Do you know why they are called Hoosiers?

There are two explanations. One is the one they prefer, and it's not accurate. The other is accurate, but they don't like it.

The Hoosiers will tell you that the word hoosier came from the tendency of early Indiana settlers to say: "Who's here?" when somebody rapped upon their cabin door.

Over the years, their habit of saying "Who's here?" evolved into something that sounded like: "Hooshere?" and finally "Hoosier."

(That could explain why so many settlers kept going west when they got to Indiana. Who'd want to stay in a place where everybody was yowling: "Hooshere? Hooshere? Hooshere?"?)

But most reputable scholars, which are the only kind I deal with, say that the word "hoosier" came about this way:

The early settlers of southern Indiana were mainly unwashed, uncouth mountain folk from Kentucky.

They were usually referred to as "a hoojee" or a "hoojin." As in: "Quick, lock up the girls and the livestock—there's some of them hoojees and hoojins comin'."

And as years passed, the words "hoojee" and "hoojin," meaning "a dirty person," according to one reference book, evolved into "hoosier."

So maybe they should call their new stadium the "hoojee-dome," or the "hoojin-dome."

A lady who phoned one of the call-in shows said: "But what about all of the famous people who came from Indiana?"

I had to tell her that I wasn't aware of any famous people coming from Indiana, but later I realized I was wrong.

Indiana should receive credit: John Dillinger, America's most famous bank robber, was a Hoosier. But Chicago's Biograph Theater must be credited with being the place where he was finally shot down.

And further research has shown that George Ade, a wonderful writer at the turn of the century, came from Indiana. It was Ade who once said:

"Many smart young men have come out of Indiana. And the smarter they were, the faster they came out."

But I have an open mind. So I'll probably accept the invitation of the lieutenant governor to take a tour of Indianapolis and see all the great sights. It shouldn't take me more than an hour.

And when I get there, I'll take the advice of an airline stewardess who was on a plane that recently landed in Indianapolis. She cheerfully announced to the passengers:

"We have just arrived in Indianapolis. If you wish, you can turn your watches back twenty-five years."

Indiana's Not Alone

June 6, 1982

"What about Arkansas?" the man on the next barstool bellowed at me. "C'mon, what about Arkansas?"

He was a transplanted Hoosier, and he was objecting to my description of Indiana as the most miserable, least interesting state in the union.

"Have you ever been in Arkansas?" he shouted.

I told him I had been there several times.

"Then how can you say that Indiana is a more miserable place than Arkansas? Have you ever eaten in a restaurant in Arkansas, for God's sakes?"

He had a good point. And I had thought long and hard about Arkansas before I rated Indiana at the bottom.

There probably is no place in America where you can get a worse meal than Arkansas. They eat something there called "chicken-fried steak." I don't know what it is. I tried it once, swallowed one bite, and was in bed sick for two days.

The worst hamburger I've ever seen was in a town called Flippin, Arkansas. It dripped enough grease to lubricate a pickup truck.

So as not to offend the owner of the diner, who was 300 pounds of menacing redneck, I asked him to wrap the hamburger and I'd take it with me.

When I left, I tossed it into a lake. A carp surfaced, took a bite of the hamburger, and threw up.

There's no question that Arkansas has few redeeming qualities. It has more bumpkins than even southern Illinois and Indiana.

But it does have the Ozarks, which provide some of the best scenery in America. It has beautiful, unspoiled lakes like Bull Shoals. So I'd have to rate Arkansas ahead of Indiana, although not by much.

Somebody else at the bar said: "Yeah, well, what about Mississippi? Nobody can tell me that Indiana is a more miserable place than Mississippi. Have you been there?"

Many times, I told him.

"Then you know that there are more rubes and bigots per square foot in Mississippi than anywhere in this country, if not on the face of the Earth.

"You go into a bar in Mississippi and every guy in the place has a scar on his face from a bottle fight. If you don't say 'Howdy' just right, one of them is going to lay a bottle upside your head.

"They got a lot of those Cajuns, or whatever you call them. They live in the swamps and eat snakes and other rotten things, and they talk some kind of combination French and hillbilly language that nobody in the world can understand.

"You turn on your radio and every station is playing either hillbilly music, or there is some right-wing preacher, or it's Paul Harvey."

He's right. Mississippi is one of the most unpleasant

states. But most of his criticisms of Mississippi could apply to almost any state in the South.

But for one reason alone, I have to rate it ahead of Indiana.

Mississippi shares part of what is known as "The Redneck Riviera." This is the Gulf Coast that stretches from Louisiana to the Florida panhandle. It has excellent beaches, fine fishing, and beautiful old plantation-era homes. So if you can avoid getting into barroom brawls with grown men named Junior and Bubba, you can have an enjoyable time in Mississippi.

The discussion continued. Names of states were flying from all over the bar.

"New Jersey, what an armpit. . . . You ever been in Nebraska? A guy could go crazy in Nebraska. . . . Nothing's worse than Oklahoma. . . . Oh, yeah? Have you ever been in Nevada? . . . Hey, what's wrong with Nevada? At least hookers are legal in Nevada. . . . How can any decent American not hate New York?"

They all made valid points. There are some awful states in this country.

And maybe it is simply a matter of taste: I just happen to find Indiana more awful than the other awful ones. I've tried to think of even one thing I like about Indiana, but I can't.

"What about Notre Dame?" said the transplanted Hoosier. "You're going to tell me that you don't like the great football they play at Notre Dame?"

Of course, I like Notre Dame, but that has nothing to do with Indiana—it's my pride as a Chicagoan. The fact is, Notre Dame is a Chicago school. It gets most of its huge Polish, Italian, Black, and even a few Irish, players from Chicago. Without Chicagoans, Notre Dame could not beat St. Mary of the Woods.

The Hoosier brooded about that a while. Then he said:

"All right, but I'm going to tell you one more thing: You made a serious error. A factual error. And you ought to correct it."

What was the error?

"When you explained the origin of the word

'Hoosier.' You said it was from when the early settlers used to ask people who knocked at their door 'Who's here?' "

That is one theory, yes.

"Well, it's wrong. I'll tell where the word 'Hoosier' came from.

"It was back in the early days, and a lot of the early settlers were real tough guys. They used to have terrible brawls in the bars and gouge each other's eyes, and bite off ears.

"So when the fights would be over, the owners of the inns would be cleaning up the mess, and they'd be asking: 'Whose ear? Whose ear?'

"And that's where the word 'Hoosier' came from."

I finally found something about Indiana that I like—a great heritage.

Iowa's the Real Pits

June 27, 1982

All those unflattering comments I've made about Indiana in recent weeks—I take them all back.

It appears that I've made a terrible mistake and I owe the people of Indiana an apology.

I discovered my error this way:

A friend of mine, who is a Hoosier, had suggested that he take me on a tour of Indiana.

"Believe me," he said, "when I show you what a wonderful place it really is, you'll change your mind."

"Never," I said. "I've been to Indiana and nothing you show me can convince me that it is not the dullest, most miserable state in the union."

"That's what has me confused," he said. "I don't understand how you could say that about such a lovely state."

"Because it's true," I said.

"Why don't you take one more look," he said. "I appeal to your sense of fairness."

"All right," I said. "But I warn you that nothing you can show me will change my mind because I've already seen it."

So we set out for Indiana.

Within an hour, I knew something was wrong.

"Isn't that a pretty sight?" he said, pointing out a part of the countryside.

"You're right," I conceded. "I don't understand how I could have overlooked it."

A little later, he showed me something else.

"Isn't that beautiful?" he said.

Once again I had to agree.

Finally I blurted out, "Something's wrong. I'm thoroughly confused. I've never seen any of these things before."

He said, "I can't understand that. If you've been to Indiana, then you couldn't have overlooked these pleasant sights."

"Are you sure this is Indiana?" I said.

"Of course," he said. "I lived here most of my life."

"Then there's something I have to confess," I told him. "I don't think I've ever been in Indiana before. This is all new to me."

He said, "But you said you had been in Indiana. You wrote that in your column."

"I meant it. I thought I had been in Indiana. But none of this is familiar."

It was a baffling mystery. But we finally got to the bottom of it and discovered how I had made the mistake.

First, I have to explain that I'm not very good at reading road maps. They all look the same to me and I'm always turning onto the wrong highway.

Also, I have a poor sense of direction—especially when I go beyond the city limits, which is why I seldom travel outside the city. I was once lost in Schaumburg for two days. It was such a frightening experience that my hair turned white almost overnight.

So what apparently happened was this: When I went to Indiana, I must have turned onto the wrong road. And I ended up somewhere else.

But the question was, where?

My friend provided the solution. He got out a book that has pictures of towns, cities, and the countryside in every state. And we went through the book, page by page, hoping that I would see something that looked familiar.

"How about this?" he asked.

"No. There was no mountains where I was at."

"All right. What about this?"

"No. There was no seashore with a rolling surf. I'd remember something like that."

"And this?"

"No. Those are skyscrapers. I didn't see anything taller than a silo. Lots of silos."

We were about to give up, when he turned a page and I said: "That's it! I've seen that town before—that's Indianapolis."

My friend shook his head. "No, that's not Indianapolis."

"Then what is it?"

"That's Des Moines, Iowa."

"Iowa?"

"That's right. When you thought you were in Indiana, you were actually in Iowa. And when you were in Des Moines, you thought you were in Indianapolis."

"So all those things I said about Indiana. . . ."

"You were really talking about Iowa."

"Amazing."

"Well, mistakes will happen. But you really should apologize to the people of Indiana."

He was right.

So, in the immortal words of Emily Latella, the lady on the original Saturday Night Live shows:

Never mind.

Where There's a Will . . .

July 11, 1982

It's widely believed that news people and politicians don't get along too well.

What nonsense. Why, some politicians and news people are downright chummy.

For example, there is the warm relationship between President Reagan and George Will, one of the country's most influential and widely read syndicated columnists.

It's been well known, at least in Washington, that Reagan thinks so much of Will, who shares many of Reagan's conservative views, that Reagan has been a dinner guest in Will's home.

But only recently was it disclosed that Will, while writing a column that appears in many papers, has done some speech-writing for Reagan.

After Reagan prepared the speech that he intended to deliver to the English Parliament, he showed it to Will and asked him what he thought of it.

Will didn't like it. So he sat down and wrote a speech for Reagan.

Reagan then wrote another speech, using some of the material that Will had provided. And that was the speech he finally used.

I'm sure there are some people who question the propriety of a newspaper columnist, who writes about the Reagan administration, being sort of a part-time member of that administration.

I know that there are people who feel that way because they've said so.

For example, there is Fred Friendly, former president of CBS news and now a professor at the Columbia

School of Journalism, who said:

"The public has a right to know that what a columnist says is originally his—not a reflection of a cozy relationship that journalist has with some political figure. We owe our readers detachment.

"Journalists can't have it both ways. We're supposed to stand on the sidelines and call it as we see it. As soon as we get cozy, we lose our independence."

Then there is Ben Bagdikian, former ombudsman at the *Washington Post* and one of America's most respected press critics. He said:

"I think he [Will] stopped being a news columnist and became a presidential speech writer the instant he did that. You have to decide on doing one or the other. You can't do both.

"It's a problem with every political writer. You're either an independent observer as a journalist or you're a member of 'the team' that you're observing.

"Very early on, George became a semi-team member of Reagan's. He would consider any semi-conservative politician worthy of his time, so I'm not surprised to hear that about him.

"George is filled with wit and Presbyterian self-righteousness. He thinks he's smarter than anyone else and, therefore, purer than anyone else. But he's neither."

Will, of course, doesn't see it that way. When a reporter called him and asked about his speech-writing chore for Reagan, he said:

"I give him advice all the time in the press, whether he wants it or not. But it's a sign of the times that I can't do him a favor like this without people blubbering about it.

"I have not yet had anyone intelligently explain the ethics part of this. By asking me about ethics, YOU are moralizing. Who are you to moralize? Whoever said that journalism is value-neutral? I have a right to do what I want.

". . . If the president is going off to do something important for his country and the president calls, through someone else, and asks me to help him out, what am I to say? That I'm too goddamn grand as a journalist to help a president? Or that I'm too noble to perform a service for the president? That's silly."

I had never thought of a newspaper columnist's role that way, but now that Will—a former college professor —has explained it, I can see the logic of it all.

Let's say that Mayor Byrne has written a speech, but she's not sure about it.

Because I frequently write about Chicago government and politics, let's also say that she asks me to look at it.

Let's say I don't think it is a good speech. So I sit down and write one for her.

Then, let's say, she uses my speech, or parts of it.

What's wrong with that? Nothing, now that George Will has explained it.

After all, she is the leader of this city, and I am a resident of this city, and am I too grand as a journalist to help a mayor? Am I too noble to perform a service for a mayor?

As Will says, that's silly.

I suppose somebody might ask how I could be an objective observer of the Byrne administration if I was, in effect, part of her administration.

They might say: "Hey, how can I trust what this guy writes about her in his column, if he's writing speeches for her on the side?"

And my answer—now that Professor Will has shown us the way—would be: "That's silly."

But I'm not sure how that would go over in Chicago. The journalistic tradition in this town is that newspapermen try to act like watchdogs.

In Washington, it appears, some are more like lapdogs.

Make It King Ron

July 22, 1982

What this country needs is a king.

Not a genuine king, ruling and giving orders. We need a figurehead of a king—smiling, looking attractive and reassuring, making stirring speeches, but not having any genuine authority.

He could appear regularly on the ten o'clock news, telling us what a great country we have and what salt-of-the-earth folks we are, and send us to bed feeling good.

He could get on and off airplanes, wave at TV cameras, grin, chuckle, utter a few comfortable clichés, and make the nation's little old ladies feel that all is well in the land.

The kind of person I have in mind is someone like President Ronald Reagan. In fact, the person I have in mind is Ronald Reagan.

It's obvious that when we elected Ronald Reagan president, he was the right man for the right job at the right time.

The only problem is, the right job for Reagan is not a job that is allowed by the Constitution.

Reagan was elected because he looked good, sounded good, and said things that most people wanted to hear.

Now, there is a lot to be said for looking good, sounding good, and saying things that most people want to hear.

These qualities are useful to car salesmen, TV talk-show hosts, and beauty contest winners.

But Reagan was elected to the office of president, a position that requires qualities more substantial than looking good and sounding good—qualities such as knowledge and judgment.

He came in preaching an economic philosophy that has become known as "Reaganomics." It was the result of many years spent as a mediocre show-biz figure listening to rich, crotchety Republicans yearning for a return to the good old days.

And in only a year-and-a-half, Reaganomics has brought us closer to the good old days of Herbert Hoover than any sane person would want to be.

Census figures show that we now have more people below the poverty level—a family of four living on $178 or less a week—than at any time since 1967.

Entire industries, such as housing, automaking, and savings and loans, are on the brink of going under.

A few years ago, the only time the word "depression" was used was when referring to the past. Now you can't read the business pages without encountering an economist or businessman using the same word to refer to the present or the near future.

We see federal cheese giveaways to the poor. We see people standing in line for free bags of groceries. More and more people are out of work.

Even those who aren't unemployed or below the poverty level are feeling the crunch.

They're getting their local real estate tax bills now. And as jolting as the 50, 100, and 200 percent increases are, they're just a preview of coming attractions.

When Reaganomics achieves its goal of stripping cities and states of federal funds, local taxes will be staggering.

Meanwhile, Reaganomics rolls on. At the same time that Reagan is preaching to Congress about getting big government off the people's backs, he's talking about building more and more billion-dollar toys for the Pentagon.

In Washington, the pundits and other comic figures cry: "Do we have a foreign policy?"

In the rest of the country, the question is: "Is there a policy for us?"

So no matter how you look at it, Reagan has managed

to goof things up in record time.

The economy is crashing: the rest of the world is going crazy and we can't do anything about it, and it is going to get worse before (or if) it gets better.

But Reagan shouldn't be blamed for any of this. All he has done is what he said he would do.

It was all there in his campaign speeches and his confused, meandering question-and-answer sessions with reporters who covered his campaigns.

Most of the big brains agreed that running a country this big, in a world this small, was the most demanding job there is. And anybody who tried it had to be smart and filled with a clear vision of the future, not an obsession with the past.

But along came Reagan with a chuckle, a grin, a wealth of simple-minded stories about his boyhood, and his country-club-green economic philosophy.

The more he talked, the more obvious it became that here was a guy who didn't know what the hell was going on. Not in America's desperate cities, not in foreign policy, not in economics, not in anything but his memories of Life in Small Town U.S.A. Circa 1922.

But that was what people wanted to hear. It sounded good and he looked good. And that was what won their votes.

So it shows that there was a need in this country. We wanted that comforting figure, assuring us that everything would turn out all right because we, as Americans, are destiny's darlings.

And I suppose there's nothing wrong with that. With Cronkite retired, we probably did need a national Good Uncle Figure.

But we should also have a president who knows his ear from a hole in the ground. Maybe a dull-sounding and dull-looking fellow who couldn't inspire emotion in a coke-head. But somebody who knows that you can't spend billions on bombs, shove the middle-class and poor deeper and deeper into financial misery, and wind up with a prosperous society.

So the only answer is to have both.

We need a constitutional change that will permit us to

have Reagan, or somebody like Reagan, as king—an English-style figurehead to tuck us in every night with a few encouraging words.

We also need somebody in charge who can understand that poverty, unemployment, and interest rates that stun a loan shark are not what this country needs.

An American royal figure. Why not?

If anybody ever sneaked into his royal bedroom and sat on the edge of his bed, all he'd have to do is start talking economics, and the creep would panic and run.

Who's the Patriot?

September 3, 1982

Stanley was in a rage. He was glaring at the TV set at the end of the bar. It showed Polish cops smacking Polish citizens on the head, spraying them with water guns, and lobbing tear-gas bombs.

"Those lousy rats," Stanley finally shouted. "Those no-good bastards!"

"You mean the demonstrators?" I asked.

Stanley looked at me with amazement. "The demonstrators? No. Are you crazy? I meant those cops or soldiers or whatever they are."

"You mean you're on the side of the Solidarity demonstrators?" I asked.

"Of course I am," Stanley said. "I'm Polish, ain't I? And even if I wasn't Polish, I'd be on their side. Any decent, right-thinking person would be."

I shook my head and said: "You sure have changed, Stanley."

"What do you mean?"

"I mean that you used to be a real law-and-order guy. I remember when you would have been cheering those cops, when you would have been wondering why they weren't using live ammunition."

"What are you talking about?" Stanley said. "I'd never do anything like that."

"Stanley," I said, "think back to the 1960s. Think back to those days when people were demonstrating in the streets. When they were joining hands and singing 'We Shall Overcome.' When they were marching on the Selma bridge. When they were marching from Selma to Montgomery, and when children were demonstrating in the streets of Birmingham and other cities. Do you remember what you said then?"

"Uh, I'm not sure. It's a long time ago."

"I remember, Stanley. You said they were trouble-makers, and when the cops bashed them in the head and rode them down with horses, you said they were getting what they deserved."

"They were. I mean, that was different."

"Different in what way?"

"Well, the Poles want rights. They want to be able to have a say in what's going on in their own country. And they don't want their leaders thrown in jail just for speaking their minds."

"Stanley, the demonstrators in the South just wanted their rights. In many parts of the South, they weren't being allowed to vote. They were segregated in schools, discriminated against in jobs and housing. And their leaders were being thrown in jail just for speaking their minds. Don't you remember?"

"Uh, what did the Cubs do today?"

"Never mind the Cubs, Stanley. Do you remember how you felt when Martin Luther King came to Chicago?"

"That troublemaker. All he wanted to do was come here and stir things up and get everybody upset."

"Stanley, what was Lech Walesa doing?"

"Uh, how did the Sox do?"

"Never mind the Sox, Stanley. Do you remember what happened when Martin Luther King said he was going to march into your neighborhood?"

"I can't remember everything."

"You said you were going to throw a brick at him."

"Well, what did he want to come in my neighborhood for?"

"Poland for the Poles, right, Stanley?"

"Right."

"Well, King was an American. America for the Americans, right?"

"Yeah? What about the riots, huh? What about the way blacks threw rocks and Molotov cocktails? Is that peaceful demonstrating?"

"Stanley, some of the Poles are throwing firebombs and rocks, too."

"That's different."

"In what way?"

"I'm not sure, but it is."

At that point, I heard a cackle from down the bar. It was Patrick, and he was pointing at Stanley. He said:

"He really got you, Stanley."

"Oh yeah?" Stanley said. "Well, what about you, Patrick?"

"What about me?"

"You're always talking about how the Irish-Catholics are right, when they blow some Englishmen or Irish-Protestants up."

"And they are right," Patrick said, with a fine glower on his face. "They're patriots."

"Yeah, well I remember when you were cheering for the cops when they were cracking everybody's head at the Democratic convention in 1968."

"Of course I was. Those lousy bums were nothing but troublemakers."

"They were just against the Vietnam War, making free speech."

"Well, they should have made it quieter."

"And I remember how you felt about all the civil rights crowds, too. You felt just the way I did."

"So what? Listen, those people were just causing trouble. And they caused their own problems. You know what their trouble is? They have too many babies and they drink too much, that's their problem."

"Who are you talking about, Patrick?"

"The blacks, of course."

"Oh, I didn't think you'd say that about the Irish."

"Say, Stanley, are you being a wise guy?"

"Yeah, Patrick, what are you going to do about it?"

Before a punch could be thrown, I ordered a round for everyone. And when drinks were in hand, I proposed a toast:

"Here is for freedom for everyone."

"I'll drink to that," Stanley and Patrick said in unison. "Freedom for everybody—who's like us."

Punt This Marriage

September 12, 1982

I've known the two of them for years, and it used to be a good marriage. And sometimes it still is. But starting today, and lasting for the next four months, there will be stress, tension, and conflict that could send the marriage into the courts.

"I love her," the husband told me, "but I don't know if I can take it. After all these years, we might be headed toward Splitsville." (For those who are not followers of gossip columns, Splitsville is where estranged couples are always heading.)

You used to be so happy, I pointed out. What went wrong?

"You won't believe this. Or maybe you will. But the problem is pro football. Sunday football."

I wasn't surprised. Sunday football is a common cause of marital conflict. You want to watch the game. But your wife doesn't want to.

"No, that's not it. That used to be a problem. We quarreled a little over that. But it was nothing real serious."

Then what is the problem?

"The problem is that last year, she decided that as

long as I was going to watch football every Sunday, she'd watch it with me. She said: 'If you can't beat 'em, join 'em.'

"So now, when the game starts, she's right there in front of the TV with me. If there's more than one game on, she'll watch both of them with me. And she watches Monday night football with me, too."

But that's wonderful. It's togetherness. It shows a laudable willingness on her part to learn to share your interests. She's a fine woman.

"It's awful. I can't stand it. I might move out."

But why? Does she eat too much of the pizza?

"No. It's the things she says. You see, she just doesn't understand the game. Even worse, she thinks it's *funny*. Can you imagine—thinking that professional football is funny?"

No, I can't imagine that. What does she think is so funny?

"I'll give you some examples. Let's say a linebacker really goes after the quarterback, but a back blocks him, so the announcer says: 'He picked up the blitz.'

"And she says: 'He picked up the blitz? Is that something like getting herpes?'

"Then there's a pass play, and the announcer says: 'He ran a down-and-out.' And she says: 'Oh, the poor man is down and out. I feel so sorry for the truly destitute.' "

Oh, a few wry remarks can't be that bad.

"A few? Every play. The announcer says: 'They're going into their nickel defense,' and she'll say: 'What tightwads. You'd think they could afford a fifty-cent defense or even one for a dollar. I mean, you get what you pay for, right?'

"And every time the announcer says that they're going into the 'pro set,' you know what she does? She holds up her beer and yells: 'Prosit to you!' That's German for 'cheers.' Then she belts down the beer and the next time he says they're in the pro set, she does it again: 'Prosit, prosit, cheerio, down the hatch!' "

That could be a bit distracting.

"Every time the announcer says that they threw to the

tight end, she says: 'Is that fellow tight again? My goodness, he was tight last week, and the week before. He's
been tight all season. Why can't they get him into an AA
program. I mean, he's still young and could be rehabili-
tated. Tsk, tsk, such a fine-looking boy, too.'

"And if the tight end drops the ball, she'll say: 'See?
They should throw it to one of their sober people.'

"Then if they throw it to the wide receiver, she'll say:
'You know, that announcer must be blind or there's
something wrong with our picture, because he's not
wide at all—why, he's very slender. Don't you think
he's slender? I think he's slender. Why, if they think
he's wide, what would they think of Mrs. Johnson down
the street, with her hips. Now there's somebody who's
really wide.'

"If the strong safety is in on a play, or gets mentioned
for anything, she'll say: 'Those announcers are so
biased. I don't think that he's any stronger than that
safety, but they never mention that the other fellow is
strong. And even if he is stronger, why do they have to
keep talking about it? The other safety must get very
discouraged.'

"Then they'll say something about the nose guard.
And she'll always say something like: 'That must be
such a dull job. I could see being a bank guard, or a
prison guard, but who would want to be a nose guard?
Besides, why would anybody want to steal a nose in the
first place? I think they are just paranoid, if you ask
me.' "

I don't know how you stand it.

"I don't think I can take another season of it. You
know what she said during the last exhibition game?
The announcer identified one of the linemen as a pulling
guard, and she said: 'I really think that is a terrible invasion of his privacy. I mean, a man's sex habits are nobody's business but his own.' No, I can't take it. I might
just pack up and move out."

Look, maybe for the sake of your marriage you
should give some thought to not watching football. I
know it's a lot to ask, but why don't you turn on some
other sport.

"I tried it. I watched tennis."

What happened?

"The announcer said: 'Love-three.'"

"She said: 'How promiscuous. Digusting.'"

Bran New Diet

October 13, 1982

An old friend stopped by recently and went to the refrigerator to get himself a beer.

He took the beer but stood looking inside the refrigerator for several seconds. Then he opened the freezer section and looked at that for awhile.

And he began opening kitchen cabinets and looking inside. Finally he shook his head and said:

"Are you moving or something?"

"No. Why do you ask?"

He looked in a couple of more cabinets, then said:

"You don't have any food in this place. I mean, absolutely *nothing.*"

I nodded. He was right. There wasn't a thing to eat in the entire kitchen. Not a morsel. Not a crust of stale bread. Not one can of tomato soup or a spoonful of peanut butter to be scraped out of the bottom of a jar. Nothing.

He shook his head. "You don't even have a can of stewed tomatoes or things like that. Everybody's got an old can of something or other in their kitchen. But you don't have a single thing. Don't you ever eat?"

Of course I eat. I eat too much.

"Ah, then you eat all your meals in restaurants."

No, only lunch. And dinner out maybe once a week. The rest of my meals I have at home.

"But there's nothing here to eat. I don't understand."

Most people don't. So I explained the Royko System of Food Shopping for the Single Man.

It works on a very simple principle: I buy groceries once in awhile. And in large quantities, too. But then I don't buy another thing until everything is gone.

My friend happened to come along the day after I had eaten the last food in the kitchen—a can of tuna and a frozen waffle.

"What is the advantage of your system?" he asked.

There are several advantages, and they go this way:

First, you don't have to go shopping very often. At most I make one shopping trip a month. I've gone as long as two months between trips.

Second, you don't accumulate things that begin piling up in most kitchens—those extra cans of stewed tomatoes and soup gathering dust in a cabinet; the smoked Korean oysters; the packages of frozen chicken in the back of the freezer; the half-filled jars of Welch's grape jelly, side by side in the refrigerator door.

Under my system, you cannot accumulate cans of stewed tomatoes because you have to eat them before you can shop again.

"You must have some peculiar meals," he said.

There have been a few unusual meals, yes. One evening, I found that the last edible items in the kitchen were three eggs, a half-stick of margarine, an onion, and some flour.

I could have taken the easy way out and had three fried eggs. But I was more creative than that.

It seemed to me that if I mixed a cup of flour with an egg, some margarine and water and chopped onion, I would have a form of dough. So I did.

I spread the dough on a pan and put it in the oven, hoping it would become some kind of bread.

As it turned out, my creation became something that resembled onion pancakes. Sort of dried out, slab-like, onion pancakes. Then I fried the other two eggs and put them on top of the sort-of pancakes.

"It sounds awful," my friend said.

Well, Julia Child wouldn't recommend it for a dinner party, but it did get me through the night.

The advantages to this system are obvious. It's economical, because you never buy anything you don't eventually eat. And it forces you to be innovative. I remember the night I had nothing left but two pouches of frozen creamed spinach, three small potatoes, and a frozen chicken leg. I made a stew. I don't remember how it turned out, but it was surely high in some kind of vitamin.

"But what about your children," my friend said. "Isn't this rough on them?"

Actually, my sons were partly responsible for my approach to food shopping.

I discovered a law of eating, which I call Royko's Law. It goes this way: Young people will always eat anything that is convenient, then wait until you buy some more convenient foods, and they will eat them, too.

In other words, if I went out every week and bought five pounds of chicken pieces, five packages of spaghetti, five jars of Ragu sauce, and ten frozen pizzas, they would eat the ten frozen pizzas and leave the rest. And the next week, they would do the same. Eventually I would have stacks of chicken pieces, bales of spaghetti, and cases of Ragu sauce, and they'd still be eating the frozen pizza.

So under my system, when the frozen pizzas are gone, they either eat what is left, or they don't eat.

"That's kind of sadistic, isn't it?" my friend said.

Yes, but then, what else are young people good for? I am particularly fond of the memory of the evening my youngest son came home and found me in front of the TV set with a bowl in my lap.

"What are you having for supper?" he asked, looking hungry.

"Raisin Bran," I said. "There's still some left in the kitchen."

He looked in my bowl and said: "Jeez, there's no milk. It's just dry Raisin Bran."

"It's not bad," I said, scooping some of it into my mouth with my fingers. "But some does tend to fall on your shirt."

My friend shook his head and said: "Your sons must be getting skinny as hell."

No, that's not so. My system just encourages them to make the acquaintance of young ladies who have more substantial qualities than mere pretty faces. When they meet girls, they don't ask questions like: "What's your astrological sign?" or "Say, do you come here very often?" They're more likely to say: "Hi! You don't happen to know how to make a good pot roast and dumplings, do you?"

My friend went back to the refrigerator and said: "I notice there's no shortage of beer, so you must do some extra shopping for that."

"As an ancient wise man once said," I told him, "man does not live by Raisin Bran alone."

Royally Flushed

October 15, 1982

A young guy should be good to his mother. He should phone her, be attentive, treat her with respect and try to eat the second helpings she heaps on his plate.

But there are limits to everything. And no young man should allow his mother to turn him into a wimp. Especially with most of the world watching.

I'm referring, of course, to Prince Andrew and his mother, the Queen of England.

By now, most people know what has happened.

After taking part in the Falkland Islands war as a helicopter pilot, Andrew, twenty-two, returned to Britain as something of a hero.

He didn't do anything really outstanding, but the fact that he was in the war was remarkable in itself. In this country, any kid whose parents had even a tiny fraction as much political clout as Andrew's parents would have been in the National Guard, graduate school, or declared to be 4-F.

When he returned from the Falklands, Andrew had the same thing on his mind that any normal, handsome, twenty-two-year-old would.

In his case, what was on his mind was a beautiful young actress named Koo Stark.

Recently, Andrew and Koo quietly flew off for a vacation on a secluded island in the Caribbean. They were discreet, traveling under the assumed names of Mr. and Mrs. Cambridge.

But there are members of the British press who go in for peeping in keyholes, peering through transoms, and snooping through other people's laundry hampers.

Back in the old days of Henry VIII and other nononsense rulers, such reporters would have had their malicious heads taken off.

With no such restraints, they galloped into print with headlines and stories about the secret journey of Andrew and Koo.

Even worse, they dug up the fact that Koo once appeared in a nude scene in what was described as a "soft porn" film. I'm not sure what a soft porn film is these days, since there are now shows on prime-time TV that would have once caused Chicago cops to close down a movie theater.

The story became a sensation in Britain. But with typical good sense and restraint, most Englishmen remained calm—if the man-on-the-street TV interviews accurately reflected their attitudes.

One middle-aged man, when asked how he felt about Andrew and Koo slipping off to the island, said, "I feel a sense of envy."

A cheery-faced woman said something like, "Oh, he's a handsome young fellow and that's what handsome young fellows do, isn't it?"

Ah, but the Queen's reaction was something else.

According to the British press, she was outraged by what her boy Andy had done. Or at least by what she suspected he was doing. And what I assume he was doing. I mean, that's a long way to go just to get a suntan.

She was said to be even angrier than when Princess Margaret, her kid sister, who is no longer a kid, went off to the same island with a young rock star.

And the queen reportedly sent word to Andrew that he should say goodbye to Koo and return to England immediately.

Much to the dismay of most of the world's envious twenty-two-year-old males (as well as the thirty-two-, forty-two-, fifty-two- and sixty-two-year-old males), Andrew did as his mother said.

I was deeply saddened when I picked up my newspaper today and saw a picture of Andrew with a caption that said:

"Britain's Prince Andrew, twenty-two, manages a wan smile upon arrival Wednesday at London's Heathrow Airport after a flight from the Caribbean. He departed alone after an eight-day vacation with erotic movie actress Koo Stark."

Andrew did, indeed, look "wan" in the photograph. However, there could be a number of reasons why he looked wan. After eight days with Koo, it's possible that any young man would look wan regardless of how his mother felt. I'm sure that there are twenty-two-year-old men who would not only look wan after a vacation with Koo, they might look seventy-two years old.

But let us assume that Andrew looked wan because of the embarrassment of being told by his mother to drop what (or whom) he was doing and come home *right this minute.*

What a humiliating experience.

I'm aware that being a member of the royal family imposes special rules of conduct on a person. But Andrew, while a prince, is still a twenty-two-year-old who has just returned from a war. And this might shock mothers everywhere, but any twenty-two-year-old returning from a war has more on his mind than baseball, apple pie, and Chevrolet.

I have trouble imagining any young American GI,

after being told by his mother to *stop doing that terrible thing,* saying something like, "You're absolutely right, mom. G'by, Koo."

Instead, he'd probably say, "We have a bad connection, ma, I can't hear you. I'll call you back in a month."

I don't know what Prince Andrew said to his mum, the Queen, when she ordered him to stop messing around, but what he should have said was:

"What do you think I was over there fighting for, mum? Cricket, kidney pie, and Rolls-Royce?"

Well, the Queen got her way, as queens usually do. But if poor Andy has to go into therapy, it will be his mum's fault.

And I hope it makes the history books and Alistair Cooke tells everybody about it on public TV.

Ole Saint (Hic!)

December 21, 1982

The woman was very upset. She had taken her small son to see Santa Claus at a department store in one of the nearby, blue-collar suburbs. The boy had waited his turn in line, climbed on Santa's knee and had gone through the ritual of saying he had been good and describing the gifts he wanted.

The boy's mother had stood nearby. Close enough, she said, so that she could sniff the air and notice the definite odor of whiskey.

"The man was half stewed," she said. "I got close enough to get a look at his eyes. They were glassy and he reeked of liquor. His speech was kind of slurred and his face was flushed. Very red.

"When my boy finished, I asked the man if he had

been drinking. I told him that I didn't think he should expose children to that kind of thing. He said: 'Don't worry, lady, I haven't dropped a kid yet.'

"So I went to the manager of the store and told him that I thought he had a drunken Santa Claus. He just shrugged and said that they hadn't had any other complaints about him and that he was the best Santa Claus they could find.

"My son heard all this, and in the car on the way home, he asked me: 'Mom, was Santa Claus drunk?' I didn't know what to tell him. How do you explain something like that to an impressionable child.''

The woman then suggested that I call the manager of the store and chide him for exposing children to a half-stewed Santa Claus.

But I can't bring myself to do it.

For one thing, there is something of a tradition in department store Santas being a bit juiced.

The first Santa I ever saw was in a store in Milwaukee and Division. As I was in the middle of telling him about the sled and pirate pistols I wanted, his eyes rolled up in his head and he appeared to pass out.

My mother, an understanding and quick-thinking woman said: "It is a long ride from the North Pole to Chicago. He must be very tired.''

Slats Grobnik, who was next in line, said: "Yeah, my fodder gets tired like that every Friday and Saturday night, and at weddings, too.''

Jon Hahn, a former Chicago newspaperman, once told me about a traumatic experience he had with a neighborhood department store Santa.

"We went to see him on Christmas Eve, in the afternoon,'' Hahn recalled. "I thought something was kind of strange about him because his leg kept collapsing and the kids would slide off onto the floor.

"Then later, when we got home, my mother told me to run down to the corner tavern and tell my father to come home for dinner before he spent his Christmas bonus.

"When I walked into the tavern, there was my father and Santa Claus—the one from that department store—

in the middle of the barroom throwing punches at each other.

"I don't remember what caused the argument, but I'll bet not many kids ever saw their father and Santa Claus duking it out on Christmas Eve."

There are probably reasons for the tendency among some store Santas to be drinking men.

It might have something to do with being exposed to so many children. Any school teacher can tell you what being in the same room with thirty or forty little kids all day can do to your stomach lining. And if you've ever had to run a birthday party for a couple of dozen of them, you know what a terrible experience that can be.

So I would think that the experience of sitting for hours, with dozens and dozens of the little buggers, climbing on your knee, would be enough to frazzle the nerves.

Even worse is the whole atmosphere of deceit, lying, greed, and materialism that permeates the ritual.

Tradition requires that the Santa ask the child if he or she has been good all year.

They always say, yes, of course they've been good, which is usually an outright lie. The kid knows it and the store Santa knows it. Most kids are not good. They are nasty little creatures who try to make life miserable for adults and one another.

Then, after the kids lie about their behavior, the store Santa has to ask them what they want in their stockings. And they make their greedy, outrageous demands. I want this, I want that, bring me this and bring me that.

He, in turn, has to lie right back and say he will bring them just about everything they ask for. If you think about it, no politician—not even an alderman—has to tell as many lies about what promises he can deliver on.

And then they have to top it off with a jolly ho-ho. During the Christmas season, in a busy store, some of these guys probably have to say ho-ho 5,000 times. What a way to make a buck, saying ho-ho to thousands of kids with runny noses.

So I think that suburban woman, and everybody else, should be tolerant of an occasional bleary-eyed Santa.

After all, nobody ever asks him what *he* wants in his stocking. And if he wants it with an olive or a lemon twist.

Continuing Education

December 26, 1982

For ten years I've been writing out those monthly tuition checks and—like many parents—sometimes wondering if it's really worth the cost.

First it was the private high school. Small classes. A lot of personal attention. Part of the American dream—giving the kid some of the advantages you didn't have.

Then the good, small, liberal arts college, with a campus that looks like an old *Saturday Evening Post* cover, and dedicated professors who know almost every student by his or her first name.

Then the checks for the master's degree. And now the checks for the Ph.D. Only a couple more years to go, but it seems as if it will never end.

But at last I've stopped asking myself whether it is really worth the cost.

The answer came to me a few days ago when my son the scholar and a few pals returned from a between-quarters vacation.

They had driven down to New Orleans to spend a few days looking at the French Quarter, eating gumbo, listening to old-timers blow jazz trumpets.

It's a good city for young men to knock around in. I did it myself at about the same age. Of course, my father didn't send me there. My bearded Uncle Sam picked up the tab.

Anyway, he came home the other day, and we sat around talking about his trip.

After expressing his admiration for the French

Quarter's wonderfully preserved old buildings, the
music, the food, he said:

"You know, one of the most interesting things to
happen to me down there was meeting this young
shoeshine boy."

And he told this story:

He had been walking along Bourbon Street when a
black kid, about fourteen, asked him if he wanted his
shoes shined.

He pointed down at his tattered gym shoes, the preferred footwear of many young men, and said:

"I don't think you can shine these."

The boy looked at the shoes. Then he furrowed his
brow and looked at them closer.

"Hold on, mister," the boy said, dropping to his
knees and studying the old gym shoes with the intensity
of Sherlock Holmes looking at a clue.

Then he stood and said: "You're right, mister, I can't
shine those ol' shoes. But I got a deal for you."

"What kind of deal?" asked my son the scholar.

"I'll make a bet with you," said the shoeshine boy.

"What kind of bet?" asked my son the scholar.

"I will bet you five dollars that I can tell you where
you got them shoes," said the shoeshine boy.

"Where I got them?" asked my son the scholar.
"These old shoes?"

"That's right," said the shoeshine boy. "I will tell
you where you got them shoes."

My son the scholar shook his head and said: "I don't
think you can do it—unless you have guessed the city I
live in by my accent."

The shoeshine boy shook his head and said, "OK, I'll
even tell you what street you got 'em on."

"That's impossible," said my son, the scholar.

"You 'fraid to bet me," said the shoeshine boy, with
a sneer.

"OK," said my son the scholar. "It's a bet."

"It's a five dollar bet?" asked the shoeshine boy.
"Five dollars—right?"

"Right," said my son the scholar.

"OK, mister, I am goin' to teach you a lesson," said the shoeshine boy.

"What kind of lesson?" asked my son the scholar.

"The lesson is: Never play the other man's game," said the shoeshine boy.

"What do you mean?" asked my son the scholar.

"I mean that I didn't say I would tell you where you bought them shoes, I said I would tell you where you got them and what street you got them on."

"Uh," said my son the scholar.

"And where you got them," said the shoeshine boy in a triumphant voice, "is on your feet."

"Uh," said my son the scholar.

"And the street you got them on," crowed the shoeshine boy, "is *Bourbon Street.*"

"Uh," said my son the scholar.

"So you owes me five dollars," said the shoeshine boy, sticking out his hand.

My son the scholar looked at his companions.

"I think he's right," they said. "You lose."

My son the scholar handed the shoeshine boy five dollars.

"Remember," the shoeshine boy said, "never play the other man's game."

"Uh-huh," said my son the scholar.

So to return to the subject of all that tuition I've been paying all these years.

I demand a refund!!!

Watt Is Buggy!

December 30, 1982

I have a theory about James G. Watt, the controversial secretary of the interior.

And it was further reinforced this week when he weakened the potential federal protection of hundreds of thousands of acres of wilderness lands.

My theory is not nearly as complicated as those of most of Watt's critics, who include most of the nation's nature lovers and environmental groups.

Some of them say Watt is nothing but an errand boy for the big oil companies, strip-mining interests, lumber companies, and all the other big-bucks corporations that want to take a bite out of the federal wilderness and parks system.

After all, they say, that's what Watt did for a living before he joined the Reagan Cabinet—he headed an alleged "public interest" law group that was bankrolled by right-wingers and oil, mining, agri-business, and power companies.

He's still in their pocket, they say, which is why he is always coming up with new ideas that would let them go in and dig, bulldoze, saw, and chew up the millions of acres of protected federal lands.

Others say that isn't Watt's motive. His problem, they say, is political philosophy. He believes that anybody who likes trees, grass, and clean water and air is a liberal. And since he despises liberals, he assumes that trying to conserve and protect the environment is a sinister liberal plot.

Then there are those who think Watt is just kind of
. . . well, kind of strange. They point at the wild gleam
that never leaves his eyes, and at some of his balmier
ideas—such as unleashing dune buggies, snowmobiles,
and motor boats on federal beaches, wilderness areas,
and rivers that have traditionally been protected against
such nuisances.

And they wonder about his proposal to turn some of
the federal park operations over to private conces-
sionaires. Does he really want to see a giant McDonald
golden arch spanning the Grand Canyon?

There might be something in all of these theories. But
I've analyzed Watt's record, and I believe that the
answer is much simpler.

I think Watt is afraid of snakes and bugs.

Basically, there are two kinds of people. Those who
are afraid of snakes and bugs and those who aren't.

Those who have this fear let it shape much of their
leisure activity.

They won't go to the woods in Minnesota because
there are black flies.

They don't like walking in a flowery meadow because
there are bees.

They won't sit on a beach in Florida because there
might be tiny chiggers in the sand.

They don't want to spend a weekend in a cottage in
Wisconsin or Michigan because there might be a spider
in the bathroom.

So they're always waving their arms at the flies. If one
bee is in the vicinity, they wrap their arms around their
necks and twirl or run in circles. If one tiny spider creeps
down the shower wall, they act as if they're being at-
tacked by vampire bats.

The thought of snakes drives them even crazier. They
can't walk through any kind of grass that isn't perfectly
mowed without looking down to make sure they aren't
going to be bitten by a copperhead. Even in a Chicago
forest preserve.

If they have to travel in the South, and stay at a motel
along an interstate, they shake their shoes out in the

morning for fear that an asp is hiding inside.

I know people who refuse to ever take vacations anywhere but in a city because they are afraid that they
might meet a bug or a garter snake.

One of the worst was my friend, Slats Grobnik, who
wouldn't even go into Humboldt Park, because it had
so much grass. "Worms live in that stuff," he would
say with disgust.

These people don't fear muggers, stickup men, peeping toms, purse snatchers, aldermanic candidates, or
other urban menaces, as much as they do a ladybug or a
nightcrawler.

And to such people, all the wilderness areas represent
are bugs, snakes, lizards, flies, bees, spiders, creepy,
crawly things that hide in trees, grass, and might even
fly up their nostrils.

Now, I can't be 100 percent certain that Watt feels
this way. We don't know, because during his confirma-
tion hearing before Congress for his present job, all the
more liberal congressmen asked him about were the corporations that had financed his alleged public service
law group.

None of them thought to ask: "Mr. Watt, are you
afraid of bugs and snakes?"

But it seems obvious to me that no sensible person—
not even a conservative such as Watt—would be so opposed to conserving some of this country's most pre-
cious natural beauty.

There has to be something more deeply rooted in his
psychology driving him to turn forests into fields of
stumps, rivers into sewers and rolling hills into strip-
mined scars.

Maybe, and this is only a theory, at an early age a bug
got in his ear.

If so, it's probably still there, since there's so much
empty space in which to fly around.

Jane Ads It Up

January 26, 1983

It's not easy to impress a New Yorker. But when I casually mentioned a fact about Chicago politics to a friend from that city, his jaw dropped.

I simply told him that Mayor Byrne had raised more than $9 million for her political campaign fund since taking office.

"Good God, that must be a new national record," the New Yorker said.

Probably. The former governor of Texas raised about $13 million for his race, but that was in an entire state that's bigger than many nations. And since Byrne's contributions are still rolling in, before this election is over, her political bundle might even exceed the Texas figure.

But no other city or state officeholder has ever piled up that kind of money mountain. Even when candidates for the United States Senate spend a couple of million dollars to win an election, there are cries of disgust about the menace of checkbook politics.

It's truly an awesome figure, especially if you play around with your pocket computer and break it down into more understandable terms.

For example, you might divide $9,214,827.90—the amount she raised—by 3½ years, the time it took her to raise it.

That comes to $2,632,807 a year.

If you break it down further, it comes to $50,630 a week.

And you can take that one more step to see how much

she has raised an hour—based on the standard 40-hour workweek. That comes to $1,265 an hour since she took office.

What a remarkable thought. Every hour, day after day, week after week, year after year, somebody is stuffing $1,265 into her purse. She must have a purse the size of a Streets and Sanitation truck.

And some naive people still wonder why she was so staunch in her defense of Charlie "Mr. Sleaze" Swibel.

Swibel is her chief money raiser. It is Swibel who gets on the phone and persuades those who have money that it is their civic duty to share it with Mayor Bossy.

Swibel has a genius for knowing the people who have a strong sense of civic duty—which in Chicago means they think they have something to gain from City Hall or fear that they have something to lose.

And after a phone call from Swibel, they are either overwhelmed by dread that they will suddenly become poor, or filled with the greedy hope that they will become rich.

Fear or greed. It doesn't matter. You can lose sleep from either emotion. It's results that count. And most of them grab for their checkbooks, write out a few zeroes for Charlie, and they immediately sleep better.

So it would take a real ingrate not to feel a deep sense of loyalty and affection for somebody who could twist enough arms to raise $9.2 million in 3½ years. Why, if the Creature from the Black Lagoon raised that kind of dough for me, I'd fix him up with my sister.

The New Yorker shook his head and said, "But what can she possibly do with that much money in a local election?"

The answer is that she can use the money to perform political miracles.

And if you turn on your TV set for more than a few minutes a day, you will see the biggest of these miracles.

She has been completely transformed by the expensive process of hiring a New York image-maker and flooding the airwaves with her TV commercials.

Gone are the goofy clothes we saw for three years.

Gone is the hard-eyed look, the brassy manner, the flippant whiplash retorts.

What we now see is the soul of sweet reason, the dignified, compassionate, forgiving lady with the well tailored wardrobe and the well tailored responses. Sometimes I'm not sure if I'm seeing Jane Byrne or the old *Mrs. Miniver* movie.

Gone, too, is Jay McMullen, the bombastic husband. The image-makers have stashed the poor guy away somewhere, almost like Heathcliff's wacky wife in *Wuthering Heights*. Somebody ought to check the attic in City Hall for strange sounds in the night.

We're being sold the "all-new!" Jane Byrne, just the way we're regularly sold an "all-new!" detergent, the "all-new!" light beer and the "all-new!" toilet paper—through the mind-numbing drip, drip, drip of the thirty-second commercial.

We're being sold the message that Chicago is now one of the happiest spots on Earth. By the time the ad campaign is over, muggers and their victims will be hugging and kissing and dancing a soft-shoe to "My Kind of Town."

So, yes, there is much that can be done with millions of dollars in a local election. You can buy yourself another term.

The only problem is that after the money is spent and the election has been bought, we will find that life is not a TV commercial. The same dubious characters will still be hanging around—the Swibels, D'Arcos, Griffins, and Bradys.

And all those people who have kicked in the biggest chunks of that $9 million-plus—all the contractors, consultants, and LaSalle Street money boys—will be asking the traditional Chicago question, "Where's mine?"

When the bills come due from this crowd, the rest of us will be lucky to keep the gold in our teeth.

Ban It, Please

February 13, 1983

The reporter sounded very grave. Obviously he considered it a serious matter.

He called me from a newspaper in Syracuse, New York, to tell me that one of my books was in danger of being banned.

Some parents in a town near Syracuse had found that seniors were reading a book I wrote twelve years ago called *Boss*. It was about Mayor Daley and Chicago's Machine politics.

"They want the book banned," the reporter said. "They say it contains obscene language and they don't want their kids exposed to such language.

"They have contacted the school administration and have begun circulating a petition among other parents, demanding that the book be removed from the class reading list and from the school library.

"So I'm preparing a story and I'm calling to get your reaction to their efforts at censorship. Is there anything you'd like to say?"

"Yes," I said. "There is something I'd like to say. I think it's terrific. I would like to encourage those parents to keep going and get that book banned."

There was silence for several seconds. Then in an incredulous voice the reporter said: "Wait a minute. You want them to get your book banned?"

"Hell yes," I said. "I offer them my wholehearted support. Tell them if there's anything I can do to help them, I'll be glad to do it. Ban it! Ban it!"

"But why?" the reporter asked.

I explained it to him.

Most people don't realize how difficult it is to get a book banned in this country today. Consider a typical Harold Robbins novel. Men do it with women. Men do it with men. Women do it with women. Men and women do it with anything else that's handy.

Is the Robbins book banned? No, it becomes a best seller.

So I feel fortunate that a book of mine, that has absolutely no sex, and only a few quotations containing swear words, should have a chance to be banned anywhere.

The reporter still didn't understand. "Why do you want it banned? Don't you want people to read it?"

Of course I do. That's why I want it banned. There's nothing that can stimulate interest in a book as quickly as when somebody tries to ban it. The wire services might write stories about the ban. Then network TV might pick it up.

If a writer is really lucky, the TV cameras go out to a meeting and the network news shows people expressing their disgust that somebody is trying to corrupt their children's morals with a filthy book.

Oh, what that can do for sales. Even a hint that a book is filthy is enough to send thousands of people rushing to their bookstores to buy it.

And I'll be frank—I'm greedy. I'd gladly see a few dozen high school seniors do without my book if I thought we could sell thousands of copies to people gullible enough to believe a book about Chicago politics might tickle their libidos.

"But what about the broad issue of censorship?" the reporter asked.

"Let the American Civil Liberties Union worry about that," I said. "I'll take the cash."

After I spoke to him, I phoned Bill and Barbara Younis, in Hannibal, New York, who are leading the drive to ban my book.

Mrs. Younis, thirty-nine, expressed her disgust. "It's

the language. The vulgarity. These are words no child
should read."

(I agree that some of the words are vulgar, but that's
the way Chicago politicians talk. It's also the way many
teen-agers in Chicago talk. Apparently they don't talk
that way in Hannibal, New York.)

Then I spoke to Mr. Younis, forty-four, who proudly
said that he and his wife are born-again Christians.

Mr. Younis said that he was getting so many names
on his petitions that he was sure he would succeed in getting my book banned.

I told him: "I hope you do. I'm totally behind you."

"You are?" he said.

"Definitely. I'll do anything I can to help you in your
efforts, 100 percent."

There was a long pause and he said: "You're with us?
And it's your book?"

"That's right. I think your efforts to ban my book are
terrific and if I was there, I would sign your petition."

Mr. Younis sounded delighted and said: "Would you
be willing to send me a letter saying that?"

I assured him that I would.

"Why, thank you," Mr. Younis said.

"Glad to help," I said.

And the letter is now in the mail. It says:

"Dear Mr. and Mrs. Younis: I wish you great success
in banning the book *Boss* from your local high school.
And I offer my support.

"It is a filthy, sex perverted book, filled with shocking language and scenes too horrible to mention. Why,
it would probably make Harold Robbins blush.

"I hope that erotic, unspeakable book is banned
before the birthrate in your town soars.

"By the way—I have another book on the market
right now. If there's anything you can do about getting
that one banned, too, I'd really appreciate it."

Now I know how the one hundred-year-old man felt
when he was hit with a paternity suit. He said: "I didn't
do it, but I'll be downright proud to plead guilty."

Give Washington a Break

February 24, 1983

So I told Uncle Chester—don't worry, Harold Washington doesn't want to marry your sister.

That might seem like a strange thing to have to tell somebody about the man who will be the next mayor of Chicago. I never had to tell Uncle Chester that Mayor Daley or Mayor Bilandic wouldn't marry his sister.

On the other hand, no other mayor, in the long and wild-eyed history of Chicago, has had one attribute of Washington.

He's black. It appears to be a waste of space to bother pointing that out, since every Chicagoan knows it.

But you can't write about Harold Washington's victory without taking note of his skin color.

Yes, he is black. And that fact is going to create a deep psychological depression in many of the white, ethnic, neighborhood people who read this paper this morning.

Eeek! The next mayor of Chicago is going to be a black man!

Let's all quiver and quake.

Oh, come on. Let's all act like sensible, adult human beings.

Let us take note of a few facts about Harold Washington.

First, Washington was born in an era when they still lynched people in some parts of the United States. By "lynched," I mean they took a black man out of his home, put a rope around his neck and murdered him by hanging. Then they went home to bed knowing they were untouchable because the sheriff helped pull the rope.

Washington suffered through it. God knows how he did that. I think that most of us—white, privileged, the success road wide open to us—might have turned into haters.

Washington didn't turn into a hater. Instead he developed a capacity for living with his tormenters and understanding that in the flow of history there are deep valleys and heady peaks.

He fought in World War II. Yes, blacks did that, although you don't see them in many John Wayne movies. He went to college and got a degree. Then he went to Northwestern University's law school, at a time when blacks were as common as alligators there.

Had Washington been white, he would have tied in with a good law firm, sat behind his desk, made a good buck, and today would be playing golf at a private country club.

But for a black man—even one as bright as Washington—an NU law degree meant that he was just about smart enough to handle divorce cases for impoverished blacks.

Being no dummy, he gravitated toward politics. And the Democratic party. It may have been pseudo-liberal, but the Democratic party did offer a black lawyer a chance, meager and piddling as it might be.

And he went somewhere. Come on, admit that, at least, even while you brood about a black man becoming your next mayor.

He became a state legislator. Then a United States congressman.

I'm still enough of an idealist to think that most people who become members of Congress are at least a cut or two above the rest of us.

And even his critics say that as a state legislator and as a U.S. congressman, he was pretty good.

So I ask you: If Jane Byrne is qualified to be mayor of Chicago after holding no higher office than city consumer affairs commissioner, what is the rap on Harold Washington?

And I also ask you? If Richard J. Daley is qualified to be mayor after being a state legislator and state's attorney of Cook County, what is so unthinkable about a man holding the mayor's office after being a state legislator and a U.S. congressman?

The fact is, Washington's credentials for this office exceed those of Byrne, Bilandic, Richard J. Daley, Martin Kennelly, Ed Kelly, Anton Cermak, and most of those who have held the office of mayor of Chicago.

Byrne was a minor bureaucrat. Bilandic's highest office was alderman. Richard J. Daley was the county clerk. Kennelly was a moving company executive. Kelly was a Sanitary District payroller. Cermak was a barely literate, but street-smart, hustler.

All become mayor. And nobody was horrified.

But this morning, the majority of Chicagoans—since this city's majority is white—are gape-jawed at the prospect of Representative Washington becoming mayor.

Relax, please. At least for the moment. There is time to become tense and angry when he fouls up as mayor— as anybody in that miserable job inevitably will do.

Until he fouls up, though, give him a chance. The man is a United States citizen, with roots deeper than most of us have in this country. He is a sixty-year-old Chicagoan who has been in politics and government most of his life.

He is a smart, witty, politically savvy old pro. He is far more understanding of the fears and fantasies of Chicago whites, than we are of the frustrations of Chicago blacks.

The city isn't going to slide into the river. The sun will come up today and tomorrow, and your real estate values won't collapse. History shows that real estate values in a town like Chicago go up and up, over the long haul, no matter who is mayor.

He'll fire a police superintendent, hire a new one, and the earth won't shake under us.

He might hire some jerks. I haven't seen a mayor who

hasn't. They don't learn. Two days before Lady Jane was first elected, I wrote: "How she does will depend on the kind of people she surrounds herself with."

She surrounded herself with Charlie Swibel and other bums, and got what she deserved.

If Washington is smart, which I think he is, he'll surround himself with the very best talents and minds available. And they're available.

If not, we'll survive and we'll throw him out.

Meanwhile, don't get hysterical. As I wrote four years ago, if we survived Bilandic, we can survive Jane Byrne.

And if we survived Janie, we easily can survive Harold Washington.

Who knows, we might even wind up liking him.

Atta Boy, Hersch

March 1, 1983

The sports world, which is easily frustrated, has been in an uproar lately because a large young man named Herschel Walker has decided to accept money for stomping on other large young men.

Most of the sports experts seem to agree that Walker did a terrible thing when he signed a contract to play professional football after finishing only three years of college.

I have to assume that most of these sports experts don't have any sons who are Walker's age.

But I happen to have a couple of them. And I know how I'd react if one of them came home and announced:

"I have been offered a job that will pay me $5 million for three years of work, so I've decided to accept the offer. I can always finish college later.''

I would burst into tears. Tears of joy. I'd say: "I always knew you were a good boy. Do you think you could see your way clear to slip your old dad a couple of hundred thou' to see him through his old age?''

And if anybody tried to talk him out of taking the money, I'd call the Cook County sheriff's office and hire a process server as a hit man.

The thing that puzzles me most about the attitude of the sports experts is why they expect football players to spend four years in college.

They don't ask that of other professional athletes. Teen-age girls make fortunes playing tennis even before they finish high school. Baseball players begin their careers right out of high school. Hockey players start even earlier.

Did anyone get upset because Muhammad Ali didn't finish college before he began punching people in the face for money?

One of this year's top college basketball teams is the University of Nevada at Las Vegas. The last time somebody did a survey at that school, they discovered that in twelve years, only about nine basketball players received degrees. Some left the school without being able to spell its name.

Most people watch football. So I ask you—of what use is four years of college to a football player?

Football is a barroom brawl with rules. The purpose of the game is to knock the other person down and/or avoid being knocked down yourself.

To do this, you try to tear up your opponent's knee, give him a concussion, dislocate his shoulder, rearrange his spine, and cause him to bleed from the nose and mouth.

You don't need four years of college to learn to do these things. You don't need one day of college. There are young men on the streets of Chicago who maul people every day and they haven't finished high school.

One of the most famous sports action-photos showed Dick Butkus of the Bears tackling a player with one hand, while trying to insert the forefinger of his other hand into his victim's eye socket.

Did Butkus really need 120 hours of college credits to insert a forefinger into somebody's eye socket?

Of course not. Butkus was a natural and was capable of plucking out somebody's eye the day he finished high school. It is said that the day he was born, when the delivering physician slapped him across the bottom, Butkus responded with a forearm to the doc's jaw.

So why did Butkus and Bubba and Bobby Joe and Billy Bob and all the other hulks have to spend four years hurting people in college before they could begin receiving a paycheck for hurting people?

The answer is that the colleges have a good racket going.

They kidnap some big, simple-minded kid right out of high school and walk him around the campus so he can see all the pretty coeds.

Then when his tongue is hanging out, they get him to sign a paper in which he agrees, in effect, to work for them for four years.

They pay him with a scholarship and room and board, worth a few thousand dollars, and maybe slip him a few bucks under the table.

In return, he plays football and the school packs hundreds of thousands of paying customers into the stadium, and gets a cut of millions of dollars in TV revenue.

Considering how much money they generate for the schools, and how little they get in return, this arrangement probably makes college football players the lowest paid hired thugs in the world. Even a bouncer on Rush Street is paid more. And the people he belts around are usually much smaller than he is.

Herschel Walker did the right thing. Three years is more than enough college education to learn how to step on somebody's chest, knee them in the groin, or run like hell when somebody large is chasing you.

Right after Walker signed his contract, he handed his

old mom a check for more than $1 million and told her: "Put it in the bank."

Maybe Herschel is a dropout, but Mrs. Walker is the envy of the parents of every liberal arts major in the country.

Watergate's Big Loser

March 3, 1983

Frank Wills, the Watergate guard who shook the knob that shook the world, always had trouble figuring things out. He just couldn't understand why he wasn't a rich hero.

We talked a few years ago and he didn't hide his bitterness. He was out of work, nobody was interested in his story anymore, and others involved in Watergate were becoming famous. Or at least notorious.

"If it wasn't for me," he complained, "there wouldn't have been no Woodward, no Bernstein, no Sirica, no Watergate. None of it. I made it all happen."

For those who have forgotten, Wills came along on his regular rounds at the Watergate office complex, found tape on the doors of the Democratic Party headquarters, phoned the cops who caught the White House's burglars, and the great scandal was off and running.

Wills had a brief fling at being a celebrity. He made a few paid speeches, but the audiences became bored. How much can you say about finding some tape on a door and dialing the police number?

He played himself in the movie *All the President's Men*, but there isn't much demand in Hollywood for actors who are limited to shaking doorknobs.

For a while, we had a lawyer-agent who put grand ideas in Wills's head by saying things like:

"There are books to be written, possible movie contracts in Hollywood, the possibility of starting up a Frank Wills detective agency.

"What we have here is the possibility of another Mark Spitz [the Olympic swimming hero]."

He was almost right. When was the last time you heard about Mark Spitz?

By the time I met Wills, he no longer expected to be the star of publishing, movies, or run his own detective agency.

But he still couldn't figure out why.

"I've been out of work. I've been suffering. But all these other people—they been doing real good."

Some of them went to prison, I pointed out, which they probably don't consider to be real good.

"Well, it's better than being out of work like I am," Wills said. "None of it would have happened without me."

I tried to explain, gently, to Wills that he was just a fringe character in the Watergate drama. That he was like the nail that was lost, causing the horseshoe to be lost, causing the battle to be lost, and all that.

The nail might have been important to the battle, but the history books only mention the generals.

But he wouldn't have any of it. He was a classic victim of hype. He was an obscure person who had become an instant celebrity and he expected it to make him an instant fortune. It's the American way.

"People don't appreciate what I did," he said. "It's not right."

Wills dropped out of sight for a few years. But now he's back in the news. Unfortunately, his luck isn't running any better.

Wills was recently sentenced by a judge in Augusta, Georgia, to serve one year in jail.

He was found guilty of trying to shoplift a pair of twelve-dollar gym shoes from a discount store.

I know what your question is—so I'll give you the answers:

John Dean, the White House aide who fawned over Nixon before squealing on him, served four months in prison for obstruction of justice. He cleared more than $1 million from a Watergate book and TV movie. He now gets $2,000 for a Watergate speech.

John Ehrlichman, one of the creators of the coverup, did eighteen months in prison. He now lives comfortably in New Mexico, where he writes lucrative books about politics and his Watergate experience.

H. R. Haldeman, Nixon's top aide, served eighteen months, has written one Watergate book that did very well, and is now vice president of a California real estate firm.

G. Gordon Liddy, the aspiring superman who organized the break-in, did fifty-two months in prison. He has since written a best-selling autobiography that was made into a TV movie, and he gets $4,000 a lecture.

Spiro Agnew wasn't involved in Watergate while vice president. He was too busy grabbing bribes in his White House office. After resigning in disgrace, he paid a $10,000 fine for tax evasion, and has been ordered to repay some of his kickbacks. He didn't serve a day in prison and now lives well in Palm Springs.

Richard Nixon was not prosecuted for his role in the Watergate coverup because President Ford thought that would give the country a nervous twitch. So Nixon has gone on to make a fortune from his writings and TV interviews.

And there was Frank Wills, sentenced to a year in a Georgia jail for stealing a twelve-dollar pair of gym shoes.

The least the rest of the Watergate crowd should do is take up a collection for him.

He helped make most of them rich.

A Flashy Springtime

March 15, 1983

With the arrival of spring-like weather, we're seeing more and more of the outdoor recreation people—the joggers, skaters, bicyclists, softball players, golfers, heel-and-toe walkers, and casual strollers.

Also, the muggers, purse-snatchers, package-grabbers, and window-peepers, who also look to warm weather for greater comfort in their endeavors.

And finally, the flasher.

Flashers are not as well known as other outdoor recreationalists, but they, too, come out just as soon as the temperatures become high enough for them to avoid frostbite while doing what they do.

And flashers are not all alike. True, most of them are traditionalists who believe that the only correct way to flash is to fling open their topcoat at some unwary female, causing her to say "eek."

But just as joggers have different, subtle variations in their running styles, many flashers take their own, unique approach.

This early flashing season has already brought out one of the more imaginative approaches to flashing that has been seen in many years.

He's a suburban man who decided to take advantage of the popularity of jogging in order to pursue his own favorite activity.

If you saw him at a distance, or just gave him a passing glance, he appeared to be nothing more than another ordinary jogger—sweat shirt, running, shoes, and dark shorts with a white stripe at the hips.

However, a closer examination—which some policemen eventually made—showed that he was not wearing conventional jogging clothes.

The sweat shirt was genuine. So were his socks and shoes.

But his shorts were unusual. Actually, they weren't shorts at all.

He had carefully painted his body so that it looked like he had on dark shorts. He even painted in the white stripes. But it was just paint.

And that's all he was wearing from the waist down—just a few ounces of paint—when the police showed up near a schoolyard and took him away for a long talk with a shrink.

Whether this will become a trend, I don't know, although just about everything has a chance of becoming a trend today. Once summer arrives, and the parks are jammed with people, a flasher could probably paint on an entire wardrobe and not attract much attention.

I asked a couple of veteran policemen if they could remember any similarly painted flashers.

"No, I don't," one said. "I suppose that would be a difficult thing to do. Sort of like scratching your own back. You'd have to use mirrors and have a long paint brush to really do it right, if you know what I mean.

"One of the most unusual jogger-flashers I've run across was a guy who'd sit on a bench in the park with a newspaper across his lap, like he was resting and reading.

"Then when a lady would walk by, he'd smile, say hello, and pick up the newspaper. Well, you can imagine what she saw there under the newspaper.

"And we pulled in a guy one day who used to flash from his car. He'd be wearing a shirt and tie. But when he stopped at a light next to a woman in a car, he'd toot his horn and point at her tire, as if he was telling her she had a flat. Then if the woman got out to look at it, he'd open his car door, too. Except he wouldn't have anything on except the shirt. He was caught when he was stopped for a routine traffic violation. My partner asked him why he didn't have no pants on and he said: "My air conditioner is broke and I'm cooling off."

Both policemen agreed that the most memorable Chicago flasher was a man who used to indulge himself on CTA elevated train platforms.

He used to stroll onto a platform during rush hour, and he appeared to be just another commuter—topcoat, shirt, tie, trousers, fedora.

He would appear to be boarding, but at the last moment he wouldn't get on the train. Instead, he would stand near the front of the platform and wait.

Then when the train began slowly pulling out, he would fling open his coat.

The passengers who looked in his direction would discover that there was less to his clothes than it appeared.

The shirt was one of those phonies. Just the collar, the front and the tie.

"And he didn't have on a complete set of pants. Just enough of the pants legs to go from the cuffs to his knees. He held them up with some kind of long suspenders.

"When we pinched him, I asked him why he went to all that trouble.

"He told me: 'Well, I'd look pretty stupid if I was walking around in a topcoat with bare legs, wouldn't I? I couldn't go in any restaurants or anything dressed that way.'

"I remember asking him: 'You go in restaurants in that outfit?'

"And he said: 'Of course. Do you think I spend my whole life on CTA platforms? That wouldn't be normal.'"

Life Under the Lens

June 1, 1983

Should you walk into the lobby of the CBS building in Chicago, you would be met by one or two uniformed guards who would look you over and ask what you want.

If you had an appointment with somebody, they wouldn't point you in the direction of his office. You would be told to wait in the lobby while they checked with that person. Then you would be asked to wait until somebody came down and got you and took you there.

You would also be asked by the guard to sign a register, putting down the time you entered and the time you left, and who you were there to see.

If you showed up without an appointment and just said you wanted to walk around, and maybe pop in to say hello to little Walter or Harry or Johnny and Jeannie, you'd be turned away. Of course, Channel 2 and the rest of the CBS operation here can't have people wandering into their offices and surprising the anchor-creatures as they are spraying their hair, powdering their cheeks, and otherwise preparing to deliver the news of the day.

I point this out because of the way Channel 2 reacted Monday when one of their cameramen was shoved by Lee Elia, the manager of the Cubs.

Elia, depressed by still another Cubs failure, apparently didn't want TV cameras in his office. He told the cameraman to leave. The cameraman didn't leave. Elia says he again told the cameraman to leave. And again and again and again. And the camerman still didn't leave.

So Elia tried to shove him out the door, causing the camera to bang against the camerman's jaw and resulting in a minor wound that could best be described as a boo-boo.

Now, if you listen to Channel 2, the incident sounds like a major atrocity.

Their sports broadcaster immediately raised the question of whether Elia would be fired from his job because he pushed that cameraman.

When the day ended without Elia being fired, the broadcaster said something to the effect that Elia just can't go on doing things like that and keep his job.

I disagree. There might be other reasons to fire a man from his job, but shoving a TV cameraman who won't leave your office shouldn't be one of them.

TV people in general are under the impression that the rest of the human race exists for one reason only—to provide twenty-second snippets for the ten o'clock news.

In pursuit of these snippets, they will barge in anywhere, anytime, on anyone, shoving their cameras and microphones in the faces of their intended victims.

"Madam," they shout as they chase some suburban housewife down the hallway of a courthouse, "how do you feel about being accused of plotting the murder of your husband?"

"Sir," they shout as they chase somebody from his car and into his place of business, "how do you feel about the rumor that your company is being acquired in a takeover and that you face ruin and personal disgrace?"

"Young man," they ask the hysterical child, "how did you feel when you saw the floodwaters sweep away your mommy, daddy, and your new puppy?"

If you don't want to talk to them, they keep the cameras on you and keep shouting the questions. Then you are shown not wanting to talk to them and appear guilty of something.

If you don't want your face on the news show, and cover it with a hat or handkerchief, they keep the cameras going and show you covering your face, and you again appear guilty of something.

If you get fed up with having a camera and microphone in your face, and give them a shove, they show that. And with the joggling camera and the lurching figures, a minor shoving incident appears to be an act of brutality.

In other words, you can't win. You can't just say, "Look, I don't want to talk to you, so please go away." Because they'll just go on peppering you with questions and recording the embarrassed expression on your face.

And you will appear to be guilty of being embarrassed.

Some time back, most TV newspeople in Chicago became angry with me because I praised a group of people who beat hell out of a TV newsman.

These people had been at the funeral of a relative, who was a minor mob figure. The TV news crew showed up at the funeral home in pursuit of a twenty-second snippet.

The family of the deceased—believing that even the relatives of a mobster have the right to privacy while mourning their dead—told the crew to leave. When they didn't, the mourners took appropriate steps. Such as punching them.

In Elia's case, it doesn't seem unreasonable for a man to say he doesn't want a TV camera in his office. And when the cameraman didn't leave, what was Elia to do?

He had to draw the line. If he did nothing, then the next step would be for the TV crew to follow him into the shower. And after the shower, the crew would follow him into the men's room.

And how would you like to be in that situation, with somebody shoving a microphone in your face and asking, "How do you *feel* about squeezing the Charmin?"

Thin Golfers and
Fat Harry's Dream

June 21, 1983

Everybody at the bar was staring at the TV set. Somebody on the screen was lining up a putt. An announcer
with a British accent was explaining the great import-
ance of the ball rolling in the hole.

Just then a gravelly voice from the end of the bar
said:

"Why don't you switch channels? Let's see what else
is on."

It was Fat Harry.

"What are you talking about, Harry?" somebody
protested. "That's the U.S. Open."

"I know it's the Open," Harry said. "But I'd still
rather watch something else. OK?"

A debate broke out, and the bartender stood near the
TV waiting for a consensus.

Then someone said: "Wait a minute, Harry. You're a
golfer, aren't you?"

"Yeah," Harry rasped. "So what?"

"Well, if you're a golfer, why don't you want to
watch the Open? I don't even play the game and I'm
watching. But you're always out on a golf course."

"Doesn't matter," said Harry. "Put on a ballgame or
something."

"But if you're a golfer, you ought to be interested. I
don't get it."

Harry stood up and said: "Look at me."

We all looked at him.

"What do you see? Describe me. Describe my physique."

We looked some more. Then somebody said: "Well, you're kind of chunky."

"Yeah," somebody else said: "Stocky."

Harry grimaced and shook his head. "Don't try to be kind. Be honest. I'm short, right? And I'm fat."

Everybody nodded. "That's right. You're short and fat."

Harry slid back on the stool and said: "OK, now you understand."

We thought about that statement for a while. Then somebody said: "Understand what?"

Harry pointed at the TV screen. "Look at those guys. Are any of them short and fat?"

We looked at the screen, and somebody said: "No. They're not short and fat. They're all lean and in good shape. But so what? They're professional athletes. They're not supposed to be short and fat."

"Oh, yeah?" said Harry. "That just shows how much you don't know. Well, I'll tell you something. There used to be great golfers who were short and fat.

"That's why I took up the game. I've been short and fat all my life. I was a short, fat baby. I was a short, fat kid. I was a short, fat young man. I think it was my glands. I had short, fat glands.

"I was never any good at sports so I didn't even try. Nobody wanted a short, fat shortstop or a short, fat quarterback.

"Then one day I looked in the sports pages and I saw a picture of a golfer who won a championship. It was Porky Oliver. Imagine that. A professional athlete they called Porky, because he was short and fat.

"So I started following golf and you know what I found out? There were other short, fat pro golfers. And I found out that there were other kinds, too. Skinny guys who looked like they had TB. There was one who was a hillbilly and had only three front teeth. There were guys with tattoos on their arms, and bald heads and little potbellies.

"In other words, the professional golfers didn't look

any different than the guys who play it on Sundays for fun.

"That's when I knew I had my sports heroes and my game, so I bought a set of clubs and started playing.

"I'd go watch the tournaments, and I'd see Billy Casper, who was short and fat, and Julius Boros, who was almost fat. And Nicklaus came along, and he looked like a baby whale.

"Then something happened. Maybe TV caused it. Or the youth culture. But the fat golfers either disappeared or they became skinny.

"Now you look at them and they all look the same. They're all lean. They all have the same hairstyle. There's not one short, fat guy out there. Not one guy with missing front teeth. Not one who looks like he's coughing himself to death. They're just a bunch of clones. They make me sick. Give me another bag of potato chips."

Somebody said: "But there are other sports, Harry. Maybe you can find other heroes."

"Where?" Harry said. "You ever see a short, fat basketball player? Or hockey player? Or football player? No; professional golf was the last of the games that had real people playing it. Porky Oliver. What a guy. He looked like he ate five bags of chips with every beer."

"Harry, what about bowling?" somebody said.

Harry shook his head. "You haven't seen bowling on TV lately. Same as golf except the bowlers look like they're wearing the ten-dollar polyester version of the golfers' thirty-dollar shirts. They have hairstyles that are sort of truck-driver chic, with their hair spray on their sideburns. But they're all lean, too. They're just imitation clones of the golf clones."

Harry resumed munching on his potato chips. And somebody said: "Harry, maybe you ought to go along with the times."

"What do you mean?"

"Go on a diet."

"What? And lose my identity?"

Let Inmates Hear
the Call of the Wild

July 4, 1983

The problem is simple enough. We have a huge surplus of criminals and an extreme shortage of prisons.

But the solution isn't simple.

The obvious answer would be to launch an emergency program to build enough new no-frills prisons to hold all of the criminals.

The trouble is, that costs money—money that would have to be raised through our taxes.

People might be willing to pay higher taxes to build prisons. But they might not. And few politicians are brave enough to risk angering the voters by calling for higher taxes.

Another possible solution would be to use some available facilities to house non-violent inmates. There are unused military bases, farms, and so on.

But people who live in those communities don't want convicted criminals dumped near them, and they'd scream their heads off to their local politicians who would collapse from fright at the thought of losing votes.

One of the more intriguing proposals I've heard came from an acquaintance who is not exactly your typical knee-jerk, bleeding-heart liberal.

He said: "Most people don't know it, but there is a large system of tunnels under the city. Miles and miles of them. There used to be trains of some kind down there for shipping things from one part of the downtown area to another.

"My idea is to convert these tunnels to dungeons. They wouldn't have to be anything elaborate. Just a bunch of cells. So the costs would be minimal. You wouldn't have to build walls or anything.

"I'm sure there would be room for thousands. Even tens of thousands. And you wouldn't need many guards, either. Just at the entrances and exits at ground level. How would somebody escape—by drilling their way out?

"And I think it would have the effect of discouraging people from a life of crime. I mean, some punk looks at TV and sees some cheap hood being dropped into a dark, dank hole in the ground, and he'll think twice about mugging some defenseless old lady."

I like the idea, but it will never come to be. There are too many tender-hearted judges who would rule that it is cruel and unusual punishment to sentence someone to ten years of living the life of a mole.

So that brings us to my proposal, which I think is practical and inexpensive.

First, we should remember that this is not merely a local problem. The prison explosion is happening all over the country.

So the surplus of criminals should be dealt with as a national problem.

All right, what does a country do when it has a surplus of anything?

That's right—you try to export it.

So I propose that we export our convicted criminals.

You ask: Who would want them?

I'm sure that a lot of countries would—if there was something in it for them.

A perfect choice would be Brazil, which is having all kinds of financial problems, and is about to default on the $90 million it owes us.

So we approach the leaders of Brazil with this deal:

"Look, we have a huge surplus of convicted criminals. You have a large surplus of jungle. So let's do business.

"We'll ship you ten or twenty thousand of our convicts. You put them in camps somewhere out there in the most impenetrable parts of your jungles. You know, places that are surrounded by thousands of square miles of snakes, bugs, alligators and things that creep and crawl in the night.

"You could put them to work chopping down trees or picking coconuts or whatever people do in jungles. That way they could learn a useful trade.

"They wouldn't try to escape because where is there to go? And if they did try, good luck. They'll probably be eaten by little fishes.

"In exchange, we will reduce your debt to us by so much per prisoner. Do we have a deal?"

This would be much cheaper than building new prisons. It wouldn't require raising taxes. And nobody can say it is cruel and inhumane. After all, American tourists spend millions of dollars a year traveling to exotic places that are sunny and warm in the winter.

And I'm sure there are a lot of nations besides Brazil that would like to get in on this kind of deal.

Consider all the emerging Third World nations that have discovered how expensive and difficult it is to emerge. All those new countries with strange names in Africa would be delighted to make a fast buck by setting up prison camps in their jungles and swamps and deserts.

Boy, that would be the last we'd hear about prisoners rioting and engaging in other unruly behavior.

If they messed around, the guards might eat them.

"California Burger"
Can Drive You Nuts

July 20, 1983

I should have become suspicious when I looked in the window and saw all the ferns hanging from the ceiling and walls in the bar section of the restaurant. Bars that have ferns everywhere are not part of the Chicago tradition of interior design.

More suitable Chicago barroom decor includes softball and bowling trophies, hand-printed signs that say: "No Checks Cashed," and somebody taking a nap on the shuffleboard.

But we were looking for a fast lunch and the sign outside said the place served food, so we went in and took a table.

"Hamburger," I said to the waitress.

"With our without pecans?" she said.

"With or without what?" I asked.

"Pecans," she said.

"Uh, maybe you misunderstood me. I asked for a hamburger."

"Yes, I heard you. With or without pecans?"

Well, I didn't know what to say. I had never heard of pecans with a hamburger.

So I asked: "How do you serve the pecans? As a side dish or what?"

"No, they're in the hamburger."

"Ah, of course," I said, trying not to appear unsophisticated. "Of course, I'll have it with the pecans."

"How do you want it done?"

Now she had me. I had stepped right into a trap. I always get hamburgers well done. As Slats Grobnik once told me: "Real hot grease kills all the germs."

But what about pecans? Should pecans be rare, medium, or well?

So I asked: "Could I get the pecans rare and the rest of the hamburger well done?"

She blinked at me. "The pecans are in the hamburger."

"OK, well done for both of them."

Then she asked if I wanted cheese, and I said yes. And she asked: "Swiss, cheddar, blue cheese?"

There is only one cheese for a hamburger—plain American cheese. The processed kind. My favorite is Velveeta. That's why I never go to Paris. You can't get real Velveeta from those barbarians.

"Do you have Velveeta?" I asked.

"Velveeta? No, but we have some American cheese."

"God bless America," I said. "I'll have it."

She returned in a while and put a plate in front of me. I gaped at it and asked: "What is this?"

"Your hamburger," she said.

"It is?"

"That's what you ordered."

I had ordered a hamburger. Everybody knows what a hamburger is. And this was not a hamburger.

It was the size and shape of a baseball. And it was wrapped in bacon and covered with the melted cheese.

It sat atop half a roll, and the other half was on the side. There was no onion. There was no mustard or ketchup.

I pointed this out and she said: "You didn't order onion. But I'll bring you mustard and ketchup."

The mustard she brought was that brown, French kind. I demanded honest, yellow American mustard, which is the only mustard you should put on hot dogs or hamburgers.

I doused it with the condiments and put the top half of the roll on it and picked it up.

It was impossible. It measured about eight inches

from bottom to top. There was no way a person with even a big mouth could take a bite out of it.

"How do you eat this thing?" I asked my companion.

"I don't know. Maybe you should sort of press down on it with your hand to flatten it out."

I tried. Mustard squirted out on my shirt.

I looked around to see what others were doing. They were eating hamburgers, too. With knives and forks. Knives and forks.

There are many gray areas in life. Some things can't be called right or wrong.

But it is *wrong* to eat certain foods with knives and forks. Ribs, hot dogs, fried chicken, egg rolls, and hamburgers—they should all be eaten with hands.

To eat a hamburger with a knife and fork is as unnatural as drinking a shot and beer through a straw.

"It's the California influence," my companion said. "That is a California-style burger."

Of course. The ferns should have told me that. And the pecans and foreign mustard.

And the fact that a wan young man at the next table was sipping white wine with his hamburger.

As we were leaving, the waitress said to me: "Was everything all right?"

"Everything was subversive and un-American," I said.

That evening, I stopped at the Billy Goat Tavern, where a hamburger is still a hombooger and a cheeseburger is still a chizbooger: flat circles of meat cooked on a greasy grill, with onions and yellow mustard and slices of pickle.

And I warned Sam Sianis, the owner, that times were changing and he should consider changing with them.

"Ferns, Sam, you had better think about ferns."

"How you cook dem?"

"You don't cook them. They're plants. You hang them from the walls and ceilings."

He shook his head. "No plants een dees place. Plants got bugs. I no like bugs."

"Well, then you should consider pecans in your burgers. It's the coming thing. It's already here."

"Pecans?" he said. "You mean knots?"

"Yeah, nuts."

He thought for a moment. Then he went and got a hamburger and put it in front of me. Next, he turned around and pulled a package of beer nuts from the nut rack on the back bar.

He lifted the top of the bun and put the package of beer nuts on the hamburger. Then he replaced the bun.

"OK, you got nuts in your chizbooger."

Ah, sanity prevails.

Buying Clout in Heaven

July 28, 1983

At this moment, heaven must be echoing with prayers for my sinful, wayward soul.

It happens every time I write about the Rev. Jerry Falwell, the Rev. Billy Bob, the Rev. Bobby Joe, the Rev. Joey Jack, and other TV and mail-order preachers.

I immediately hear from the devoted and gullible followers of the dollar-hustling hallelujah-peddlers, who think it is just the most terribly sinful thing for me to do.

Most of them sound like the lady from Memphis, who phoned me and said:

"Why are you helping the devil do his work?"

Huh?

"I want to know why you are in league with the devil."

Which league is that?

"You know very well what I mean. You are doing the

work of the devil with your godless, sinful columns
about Jerry Falwell. Do you want to burn in hell
through eternity?''

No, especially not after this summer in Chicago.

"Well, I think you are some kind of communist sym-
pathizer or even worse. But I'm going to pray for you
anyway."

Well, thank you.

"I don't think it will do any good, but I'm going to
try. I'll be praying for you every day this week. Goodbye."

Or the man in Dallas, who wrote:

"I grieve for you in your blindness. Don't you realize
that this country is being corrupted by the left-wingers
in TV, that crime and moral decay are running rampant,
that filth and pornography are everywhere, that nine
out of ten young people are addicted to drugs, and that
only spiritual leaders like Jerry Falwell and the others
can save us?

"Why have you chosen to fight this holy crusade?
Why do you try to obstruct the great and good work
that these men are doing?

"Can it be that you are part of the devil's conspiracy?
Are you one of his demons?

"I wouldn't be surprised. You even look evil in the
picture of you that they run in our local paper.

"I can only pray for you and hope that you see the
sins of your ways.

"May you rot in hell.

"Sincerely."

At last count, more than 2,000 people in various parts
of the nation have vowed to pray for me. This, of
course, was after they declared that I am a left-wing,
porno-loving, gay-encouraging, dope-dealing agent of
the prince of darkness.

Fortunately, they are widely scattered. If they all
gathered in one place to howl their prayers, I would
probably be subject to arrest for creating a public
nuisance.

Well, I'm grateful for their prayers, of course. But I

have to tell them that they won't do much good. They can pray, they can sing, they can shout hallelujah as much as they choose, but I'm still going to persist in my wicked ways.

These ways consist of my having a deep distrust of the countless TV and mail-order preachers who play upon fear and prejudice, while plucking the pockets and purses of the gullible.

Many in my volunteer prayer brigade are angry because I wrote about an elderly widow who died recently, leaving behind financial records showing that she had sent most of her life savings—more than $60,000—to the various Bible-thumpers she saw on her TV set.

"What better use for her money than to fight against sin and corruption?" is what one rustic said.

Hell, I can think of many better uses she could have put that money to than to give it to some long-side-burned, polyester-clad charlatan who claims to have the ear of God. She could have bought herself a new wardrobe, kicked up her heels and taken a trip on a luxury cruise ship. That's probably what the Rev. Billy Bob is going to do with her money anyway, as soon as nobody is looking.

"I'm sure that woman was seeking answers concerning her immortal soul," said another hallelujah-shouter. "Her life savings were a small price for her to pay for these answers."

Yes, if she had received such answers, it might be a small price to pay. But all her relatives found in her apartment were more computer-written requests for money. They're still pouring in, long after she and her soul are no longer subject to their TV pitches.

As far as I can tell, the only message these hustlers have to offer goes something like this: Send me cash and I'll put in the fix for you at heaven's gate.

Which is why I like the frankness of a guy in California, who calls himself "Michael, the New Improved Guru."

Michael, who doesn't use a last name and works out

of a P.O. Box number in Santa Rosa, sends out the following letters:

"Introducing, from the end of the rainbow, from the quake state: Michael, the New Improved Guru!

"Michael has absolutely nothing to offer you or anyone else. I won't call you a you-know-what. I won't tell you that you can't go to the bathroom. I won't ask you to sell flowers or dress up in sheets. I won't ask you to spend a weekend or a week in a hotel or a country retreat. I don't want to mess with your mind. I just want you to send money. Send $100 (more if you have it) to me, Michael, at P.O. Box——.

"This is not a cult, not a religion. It is not anything. Just send money.

"Look, if you've got a problem, you solve it. I don't have the answers.

"However, due to increasing demands that people want something for their money, the following products have reluctantly been made available:

"I Have No Answers: A book that contains nothing, as there is nothing to say.

"T-shirts that have no message, as Michael has nothing to say.

"Posters having nothing printed on them. You get the idea?"

I'm not encouraging anybody to send money to Michael. But if you do, you'll be getting from Michael what you will get from the others. With one difference.

Truth in packaging.

Beertown Wurst? Naw

August 4, 1983

I don't know how I get involved in these ridiculous controversies.

All week my phone has been bouncing off the hook with angry phone calls from Milwaukee.

It appears that the citizens of that fine city took offense at something I wrote about them last Sunday.

They thought I was being critical—even insulting—when I was actually making a friendly and affectionate observation.

While writing about some White Sox fans who claimed they were mistreated by police while attending a game at County Stadium, I noted that Milwaukee is a pleasant but unsophisticated city, and that people who live there take great pride in how loud they can burp.

Some morning radio personalities, who enjoy creating mischief and misunderstanding, grabbed this column and read it on the air.

And, to my amazement, their listeners were outraged. They called to shout and swear and even burp at me over the phone.

The radio personalities, who have a malicious nature, kept the controversy going by inviting me to attend a game at County Stadium, so I could see for myself what fine folk live in that city.

I declined because I have been to several games at County Stadium, and I had already seen what congenial people Brewers fans are.

They do tend to stuff great quantities of sausage in their mouths, and to burp and act rowdy and crude and

pour beer over themselves and everybody else in the
vicinity. But, in general, they are friendly rustics.

What surprises me about this situation is how easily
people misunderstand a well intentioned remark. And
how quick they are to take offense at what they mis-
takenly believe is an insult to their city or state.

Something similar happened to me only a few months
ago, when I wrote a column about the competition between Chicago and San Francisco for next year's Democratic National Convention.

Naturally, I argued that Chicago was the best place
for the convention, but I did concede that San Francisco
is a pleasant city.

And I noted that it is populated by many delicate
young men who eat quiche and sip white wine, while
rolling their eyes and hips.

I didn't say there was anything wrong with these attributes. Quiche is nourishing and white wine is a splen-
did accompaniment. As for the rolling of their eyes and
hips—well, any exercise is good.

But what an uproar it created. San Franciscans
shrieked and squealed and their lips trembled. They accused me of implying that they were just a bunch of
wimps.

Actually, I had never even said they were wimps,
although San Francisco probably has more wimps per
capita than any other city. But so what? We're in the
age of wimps. It is nothing to be ashamed of.

Before that tempest subsided, the mayor of San Francisco invited me out there to have dinner and see her
city. I declined because I've been there before. And I
just can't get used to football fans blowing kisses at the
players.

And before that, there was the misunderstanding
about Indiana and the city of Indianapolis.

Well, the way they reacted, you'd think I had said
something untrue or unfriendly. They fumed and
snorted and said things like "by cracky" and "goldang
it" and other popular Indiana expletives.

Before that, there was the misunderstanding about

my views on Los Angeles and the rest of southern California.

And a couple of years ago there was the misunderstanding by the residents of downstate Illinois—which includes everything south of 111th Street—about something I wrote during a controversy over state financial aid for our transit system.

I pointed out that most downstaters are bumpkins, rubes, rustics, stump-jumpers and clod-kickers. They became so angry that hundreds of them broke toes kicking clods and jumping over stumps.

Apparently they didn't realize that I was paying them a compliment. After all, Abe Lincoln was something of a rustic. Daniel Boone was a rube. Many of our greatest statesmen were bumpkins and yahoos at heart.

But I've learned my lesson. No more friendly observations about other cities and states. People just don't know a compliment when they hear one.

So I'm throwing away a column I wrote about Texans being the world's tallest midgets.

They'll just miss the point.

Punch Line for Lennie

August 21, 1983

A white-haired man wrote me a nice letter this week that I'd like to share.

He wrote that he had been at an amateur baseball tournament in Quincy, Massachusetts.

In the evening, he was sitting around with some of the sportswriters and baseball scouts who were swapping stories.

Then one of them brought out a copy of *Baseball Digest* and—with a grin—started reading an article.

Courtesy of Lennie Merullo

Cub quiz regular Lennie Merullo, a shortstop in the 1940s, catches a line drive.

It was my annual Cub quiz, which that magazine had reprinted. As Cub fans know, my quiz is about the futility of past Cub teams and players and is written strictly for laughs.

Most of the quizzes contain at least one question about a former Cub shortstop named Lennie Merullo.

Fans who go back to the 1940s will remember Merullo. He hit about .240 or so and usually led the league in errors. We Cub fans were not always kind to him with our boos and jeers.

This year's Merullo question went this way:

Q. Everyone used to laugh at the immortal Lennie Merullo because he made so many errors at shortstop. And they laughed at the way he hit. But in 1947, he led the Cubs in stolen bases. How many bases did he steal that year?

A: Four. They laughed at him for that, too.

Everyone at the gathering got a laugh out of it— except the white-haired man, who tried to grin, but couldn't.

After the evening broke up, the white-haired man sat down at his desk and wrote me this letter:

"Dear Mike:

"I suppose I should have laughed or smiled to cover my feelings when one of the baseball men at this tournament read your Cub quiz. Everyone enjoyed it thoroughly.

"But I'm writing because I thought you might like to know whatever became of your favorite Cub shortstop.

"I'm now 66 years old, the father of four wonderful grown sons, grandfather of three, and still married very happily to my girl-next-door sweetheart (nee: Jean Czametzki).

"And I've spent my entire years in baseball—a very much respected scout here in the New England area and on special assignments throughout the country.

"Mike, I never professed to have been a good major league shortstop with the Cubs. As you have put it, I was a no-hit, very erratic player. I've had to live with that.

"However, it was not from not working at it. I worked at it too hard. I was not relaxed. Too tense.

"I was a Cub fan since 16 years of age. Was a protege of theirs at 17, was sent to Villanova by Mr. Wrigley, signed in 1939, and lost all that season when I hurt my arm in spring training trying to impress everyone with my strong throwing.

"I'm still a Cub fan and appreciate the opportunity they gave me and like to remember my major league experience as having played with some very good Cubs players and against some great players who broke in about the same time. (Roomed with Phil Cavaretta for eight years.)

"I once read a column of yours in which you remembered how frustrating it was to be a Cub fan when you were a kid because of the way Lennie Merullo played. Or something like that. Well, at least I've given you something to write about and something that gives the readers a smile or even a good laugh.

"Perhaps my contribution to baseball can be described as being able to understand and have a feel for the player who is having a bad day—as I have had many, and know the feeling.

"I'm enclosing a photo of me that I think you'll get a kick out of because it's the way I hit and played short-stop for the Cubs—with my eyes closed.

"Yours truly,

"Lennie Merullo."

I suppose I'm a typical baseball fan. We boo and yell at the players and give little thought to the fact that those are human beings out there on the field.

I didn't consider that when I tossed off a few funny lines about Lennie Merullo and other Cub old-timers.

Nor do most of us fans consider that anybody who makes it to the major leagues—even a .235 hitter who makes too many errors—is a remarkable athlete.

Millions of us played sandlot or high school or college ball. But only a tiny percentage of us made it to the majors. It takes great athletic ability.

And, as Lennie Merullo said, his main problem was that he tried too hard. And that must have made the boos even more hurtful.

So, I now take a vow—no more wise-guy remarks about Lennie in future Cub quiz columns.

And I'm going to put his gracious and gentlemanly letter in one of my scrapbooks along with the picture of him closing his eyes at the camera's flash.

Wait, I have to amend that. There will be one final brief quiz about Lennie Merullo. Here goes:

Q: In about 1946, the Brooklyn Dodgers had a powerhouse team, loaded with top players. They really enjoyed bullying our hapless Cubs. One day, in Ebbets Field, a fight broke out and both teams poured out on the field. One of the most belligerent Dodgers was Dixie Walker, one of the top hitters in the league, and a very tough guy. When the fighting ended, a Cub player had a set of bruised knuckles on his right hand. And Dixie Walker had some gaps where his front teeth used to be. Quick, name the Cub player who separated Dixie Walker from his front teeth and made us Cub fans proud.

A: The immortal Lennie Merullo, of course.

So don't tell me you never gave us anything to cheer about, pal.

Woes by the Million

September 23, 1983

For a few moments, hardly anybody in Billy Goat Tavern noticed the night bartender when he went on duty. He came out from the storage room behind the bar, tied on an apron and began drawing beers.

Then someone focused a red-tinted eye on him and said: "Holy cow, look—it's him."

"What in the hell is he doing here?" someone else asked. "I can't believe it."

"The guy's a millionaire and he's tending bar. A millionaire."

Strictly speaking, that wasn't accurate. The man who caused the amazement—Dimitrios "Jimmy" Nicolopoulos, fifty-four—isn't really a millionaire.

A millionaire is somebody who has a net worth of a million dollars.

What Jimmy did was win a big state lottery about six months ago. So he'll receive more than $1 million spread out over 20 years.

Still, $55,000 a year for 20 years is more than most of the regular customers in Billy Goat Tavern will receive in the mail.

"I don't understand it," one of the regulars said. "Why would he want to come in here to wait on a bunch of stewbums like us?"

"I am not a stewbum," a short fellow said, lifting his head from the bar and opening his eyes. "I'm just taking a catnap. Executives take catnaps, so why can't I?"

"I apologize. But I'm really curious about Jimmy."

"Then why don't you ask him?"

"A waste of time. He doesn't speak enough English to explain."

That was true. Jimmy was probably the most difficult million-dollar lottery winner the press has ever interviewed. He didn't have the slightest idea what they were talking about, so he just shrugged and smiled.

"Then let's ask Sam," somebody said, referring to Sam Sianis, the bull-necked tavern owner, who has an excellent command of broken, short-order-grill Greek-English.

"Sam," someone asked, "what is Jimmy doing here? He's a millionaire now. I thought he quit this job for a life of leisure."

"He deed. He queet dees job and he queet job in factory. Dees was jost part-time job anyway. But he want to stay in factory. But he figure out eencome tax and government take so much of his pay, he can't afford to work in factory no more. Hees in too big bracket to work in factory."

But what is he doing here?

"He come here once in a while to work, when I'm short. He like to do these. It geev him somebody to talk to."

But he never talks. He can't speak English.

"He talks to me."

Ah. What does he say about his wealth? Has he found that money can buy happiness?

Sam shrugged. "I don't think so. You see, what happen is that the day after he win lottery, he get all excited and his blood pressure go up.

"I go over hees house to see heem and he's laying down and I ask him what's wrong. He say he feeling no good. I tell to go see doctor. He goes and doctor takes his blood pressure and eet's 220. Dat's high. His eyes could pop out, you know?

"Doctor says to him: 'Jimmy, blood pressure too high. I don't want you to have no more drinks until it is down.'

"Jimmy gets mad. He likes to have a few drinks. Now

he's got all thees money, he has time to have a few drinks.

"But the doctor say, no. Not one drink.

"So, Jimmy has to stop drinking.

"Then he goes back to Greece and veesits relatives. Oh, boy, in Greece he's like a king. You know what $50,000 a year is in drachmas? Eet's 1 million drachmas. You got 1 million drachmas, you have a chauffeur.

"So hees brother cooks a ninety-pound pig on grill. Ninety pounds! And every day Jimmy and brother eat pig meat. They eat so much pig that in one week, pig gone. And they drink wine and drink ouzo.

"Jimmy, he's there three months, eating pig, drinking wine, drinking ouzo.

"When he come back, he go see doctor and doctor tell him now he has high blood pressure and high blood sugar or something like that, and now he can't drink and he can't eat no more pig or anything he likes to eat. He can only eat what doctor says he should eat, and none of it is good.

"So he say: 'When can I have glass of wine?' The doctor says, 'When your blood pressure and blood sugar go down.' So the next day he has glass of wine. His blood pressure had go from 210 to 220. So the doctor tell him to stop. Not even one glass of wine.

"So now he can't work much because hees income tax too high if he work. And he got high blood pressure because he got too excited from winning. And he can't drink because his blood pressure too high and he can't eat nothing but healthy food like hippies used to eat.

"Before he win, he used to work, have a few drinks, eat some lamb, and have a good time. No more. No more having good time."

The crowd at the bar thought about that for a while, then the man with the red-tinted eyes said, "Gee, and the lottery did all that to him."

And the little fellow lifted his head from the bar long enough to say, "See? That's why you'll never catch me gambling. It is the road to ruin."

An Electrifying Guitar Act

September 30, 1983

In an effort to be a well-rounded person, I've always tried to develop an appreciation for the more unusual forms of rock music.

I reasoned that if this many people enjoy something, there must be some worthwhile qualities there. All I had to do was pay attention and give it a chance to grow on me.

It didn't work. The earlier, simpler forms of rock were understandable. I could even understand a few of the more articulately mumbled lyrics.

But I just wasn't able to cultivate a taste for such performers as Wendy O. Williams, the lady who wears a Mohawk haircut and punches people, or Van Halen, the scantily clad group, or Ozzy Osbourne, who bites bats and chickens, and all the others who smash or burn instruments, wriggle, convulse, stick pins in their ears and otherwise bring joy to their many admirers.

And that failure to appreciate them bothered me. It made me wonder if my ear for music and eye for the creative was lacking. Was I a fuddy-duddy? Even a nerd?

But I'm not concerned anymore. Not after hearing about a recent performance by John Teasley, a California guitarist, who plays under the name of John T. of the McDowell County Line Band.

Teasley and his group were recently playing in a popular place called the Blarney Stone Bar, in Huntington Beach, California.

Suddenly, during a vigorous song, Teasley seemed to stiffen up. He began writhing and shaking.

Then he sort of whirled and went flying off the stage into the audience, guitar and all.

Witnesses say he flew about thirty feet, which might be a world's record in the category of leaps by a rock guitarist.

He landed with a loud crash and remained on the floor, quivering and wriggling, strange sounds coming out of his mouth.

The audience, of course, went wild with delight and cheered and applauded. They said things like "Wow ... far out ... dig that. . . .''

The owner of the bar delightedly said, "Hey, this guy is really putting on a great show."

Finally Teasley's eyes rolled up into his head and he seemed to go into a trance.

Many people in the audience thought that he had simply been overcome by his creative efforts.

After a few moments the cheering and applause ended and somebody said, "Hey, man, you OK?"

When he didn't respond, paramedics were called and they finally revived him.

It turned out that Teasley was OK. But it also turned out that his remarkable performance was caused by something other than his creative juices.

What happened was this:

Some drunk accidentally spilled a beer into his guitar amplifier. That caused a short circuit and sent hundreds of volts of electricity coursing through his body.

He was, in effect, being electrocuted.

Teasley later said, "I felt like I was in some giant washing machine or maybe in the eye of a hurricane or like some hulk was shaking me to death.

"I guess I must have looked like that chick in *The Exorcist*.

"I tried to call out for help but my voice came out like I was under water.

"So I tried to get myself free from my guitar. I turned myself backwards and flung off the stage, and the plugs worked themselves loose.

"I've done some wild things on stage before but nothing that can top that."

I find the entire affair reassuring because it means that my earlier worries are unfounded: There's nothing wrong with my ear for music. But there is something odd about many rock audiences.

Here you have a man who is in the process of being electrocuted, and is acting accordingly.

Now, if Sir George Solti was conducting the Chicago Symphony, and he suddenly began writhing, whirling and went sailing thirty feet from the stage into the seats, landing with a crash, I doubt if the audience would shout "Bravo."

If Frank Sinatra were in the middle of "My Kind of Town," and suddenly his eyes crossed and he twirled and sailed through the air into the fifth row, nobody would shout "My kind of guy, Frankie is."

But a rock audience not only thinks there is nothing peculiar about a performer who acts that way—they think it's terrific and give him a standing ovation and shout for an encore.

Well, despite the enthusiastic response of the audience, it was lucky for Mr. Teasley that he shook loose his guitar. A few more minutes, and there would have been smoke curling from his ears.

On the other hand, if he had hung on and smoke had curled from his ears, and maybe a few sparks popped out of his eyes, who knows what the result might have been.

Maybe an agent would have signed him for an appearance on "Friday Night Videos."

To Win an Island

October 27, 1983

"Mr. President, may we come in?"

"Yes, gentlemen, come in. I was just sitting here rereading the screenplay of *The Green Berets*. There is much to be learned from history."

"Mr. President, we are now receiving reports on Grenada. Do you wish to be briefed?"

"Well, yes, gentlemen. How does it look?"

"Sir, the marines have landed and the mission appears to be a complete success."

"Well, that's terrific, wonderful. Of course, I knew it would be. I recently reread the screenplay of *Sands of Iwo Jima*. Do you remember the scene where they planted the flag on that hill?"

"Of course, sir."

"Well, do we have any pictures yet of our boys planting the flag on a hill in Grenada?"

"Uh, we aren't planning to plant our flag there, sir."

"Why not? That was the best part of *Sands of Iwo Jima*."

"If we planted the flag, sir, it would appear that we were conquering the island."

"Well, so what?"

"But that isn't why we went there, sir."

"It isn't?"

"No, sir. Don't you remember? We went there to protect Americans on the island. From the leftist thugs who had seized the government."

"Oh, that's right. Oh, well then, I guess we can't have a flag-raising there, can we? Well, have we saved the Americans on Grenada?"

"Yes sir, the reports are that they're just fine."

"Wonderful. You know, I was recently rereading the screenplay from *Red River*. Do you remember the scene in which Montgomery Clift and his men galloped in to save the Americans in the wagon train who were surrounded by Indians? That girl was struck on the shoulder by an arrow and Clift pulled it out and she fainted. What was her name?"

"I believe it was Joanne Dru, sir."

"Ah, yes, and they fell in love. Fascinating subject, history. Tell me, were any of the Americans we saved on Grenada struck by Indian arrows?"

"Uh, no sir. They don't use arrows on Grenada. They were armed with guns."

"Well, that doesn't surprise me. There's always somebody who will sell them guns. I recently reread a screenplay—the name slips my mind—in which Jimmy Stewart caught someone selling guns to Apaches. And whiskey, too. Was there any whiskey found on Grenada?"

"Rum, sir. They drink rum on Grenada. Daiquiris and various fruit drinks."

"Same thing. It's all firewater. Makes them act crazy. Taking scalps. Tying people to stakes."

"There wasn't anything like that, sir."

"Good. Then we got there in time to prevent it. Well, gentlemen, what has been the reaction of the people we rescued? I imagine they are delighted. I recall that in *Red River*, the folks in the wagon train had a hoedown for Monty Clift's boys."

"It's rather mixed, sir. The head of that American medical school on Grenada says they were in no danger. They say that you had no business trying to rescue them because they didn't need rescuing."

"What?"

"They said that they had been dealing with the government there and that conditions were improving and that their main fear was that you would do something stupid, like invading the island, and that you just wanted to use them as an excuse."

"Well, I'm not surprised. It's happened before. I remember reading a screenplay in which settlers who were captured by the Indians went native. Took on their ways. Identities were confused. Obviously, that's what happened to those poor souls on Grenada. We'll just have to be patient with them."

"Yes sir."

"Then there was the thing that happened in *Invasion of the Body Snatchers*. Pod people took on the identities of decent, law-abiding Americans. Couldn't tell them from the real thing. I recently reread that screenplay. Fascinating thing, science. Have there been any reports of strange pods found on Grenada?"

"None that we know of, sir."

"Well, tell them to keep their eyes peeled. Now, what is the reaction of Congress?"

"It's kind of mixed, sir. Quite a bit of criticism."

"What?"

"Yes, I'm afraid so. A lot of them are saying we shouldn't have done this. They are using phrases like 'trigger-happy,' 'gunboat diplomacy,' 'cowboy mentality.' "

"Well, I'm not surprised. I was recently rereading the screenplay of *High Noon*, and that's exactly what happened to Gary Cooper when Frank Miller got out of prison and came gunning for him with his gang. None of the leading citizens of the town would back up old Gary. Ingrates. Too timid. So Gary made his stand alone. And he won. Grace Kelly helped. Fine girl, Grace. I wish our congressmen would study more history. We will repeat the mistakes of the past if we forget to look at the future. Right?"

"Right, Mr. President. Is there anything else?"

"No. Thanks for the report. Oh, there's one thing."

"Yes?"

"On your way out, would you send in my horse?"

A Happy Ending
for the Hereafter

November 17, 1983

A friend called with an urgent request. His TV set had broken down and he wanted to come over and watch mine on Sunday night.

"I won't be home," I told him. "Going out to dinner."

"Not home?" he said, sounding amazed. "You're going to miss it?"

"Miss what?"

"The movie about nuclear war. You know, *The Day After*. It shows what happens in Lawrence, Kansas, when bombs start falling. Everybody in the country is going to be watching it."

"Not me."

"Ah, then you must be one of those people who are against a nuclear freeze and are boycotting the movie."

"No, that's not it. I'm more or less in favor of nuclear freezes, disarmament, love and kisses, and all the peace stuff."

"Then why aren't you going to watch it?"

"Simple. It doesn't have a happy ending."

"A what?"

"A happy ending."

"What does that have to do with it? It's an important film. It forcefully and realistically shows the horrors of nuclear war. It . . ."

"I know all that. But I have a rule. Never watch a movie that doesn't have a happy ending."

"I can't believe that."

"It's true."

"But what kind of critical standards are those? You

miss many important films, great drama, and fine act-ing.''

"Nonsense. The only thing I miss is being de-pressed.''

And that's true. I've never seen any point in sitting in a movie theater or in front of my TV set for two or three hours just to wind up depressed when the hero lies crumpled in the dust or the heroine coughs her fragile life away.

That's why I never watch Bears games anymore. The average Bears fan doesn't realize it, but he's reducing his life expectancy by the stress and depression brought on by watching these weekly tragedies.

With movies, I never rely on the critics and their reviews because they conceal the most important in-formation: how the film ends.

They tell you whether the movie is rated G, R, or X. They tell you if it is a one-, two-, three-, or four-star movie. They tell you the actors, the producer, the direc-tor—sometimes even the chief gaffer.

But they withhold the most important information of all—whether it has a happy ending.

As a result, I used to be tricked into going to see movies that I should have avoided. But now I just wait until somebody I know sees a movie. Then I ask them if the ending is happy.

I think my attitude developed many years ago when I went to see *Casablanca*.

When the movie was over, I was stunned. I couldn't believe they would end it that way.

I've since had countless arguments about *Casa-blanca*'s ending with film buffs.

They say: "But Bogart did the heroic, unselfish thing. He went off to fight the war with Claude Rains, and gave up the beautiful Ingrid so she could remain with her noble husband.''

I respond: "Nonsense. Ingrid's husband was a self-righteous stiff. I'm sure that for the rest of her life, when Ingrid wanted to slip into something comfortable and mess around a little, he'd make a boring speech about the brotherhood of man. And Bogie would never

go off to fight the war with somebody like Claude
Rains. Why would he want to team up with a French-
man? Bogie would spend the rest of the war talking him
out of surrendering.''

Another downer was the movie *Frankenstein*. I was
just a kid when I saw it, but I'll never forget my disap-
pointment.

As you might remember, it ends with the alleged
monster being engulfed in a burning building.

Actually, the monster was the only decent person in
the movie. The townspeople were small-minded bigots.
Igor was an obsequious bumbler. The scientist was a
workaholic.

A much better ending for that movie would have been
to have the monster wind up as the first pick in the NFL
draft, and go on to stardom with the Dallas Cowboys.

After I explained all this to my friend, he said:

''But I know you violate your own rule because you
told me how much you liked *The Godfather*.''

''Yes, I thought it was great. Because it had a happy
ending.''

''Happy ending? What are you talking about? When
it ends, Michael Corleone's father and mother have
died; so has his brother, Sonny; he's had another
brother bumped off; his wife has left him and his step-
brother is ready to turn tail and run.''

''Yeah, but he still has his friends.''

''Well, I think your standards are unrealistic.''

''Not at all. Every movie should have a happy ending.
And they all could. It would just take a little more imagination on the director's part.''

''That's ridiculous. How could they make a movie
about nuclear war, such as *The Day After*, and give it a
happy ending?''

''Easy. It could be set in New York.''

IV.

1984–
THE TRIBUNE

New Address Sits Fine,
Thank You

January 11, 1984

I was born in the wrong generation. If I'd had any choice in the matter, I would have arrived years later so that I would have been growing up during the 1960s.

Say what you will about the youths of that era—dope heads, flower chompers, mantra chanters—they had an attitude toward work that appealed to me. They tried their best to avoid it.

My old pal Slats Grobnik, also born before his time, summed up our attitude this way:

"Everybody says that work is so good for ya. Well, if work is supposed to be so great, how come they got to pay ya to do it?"

That's always made sense to me. I've known a few people who were born rich and never had to work, and they always struck me as being a little dumb, but very happy.

Oh, those born rich will try to con you into believing

that with all their money they're still capable of being miserable. Occasionally, one of them will fake a nervous breakdown and blubber to *People* magazine about how his or her wealth has brought nothing but sadness, tension, and blotchy skin.

But don't believe a word of it. They only say that because they're afraid that if the rest of us knew what a good time they're having, we'd storm their estates, drink their wines, ravish the maid, and eat their polo ponies.

Consider that Onassis girl, the one with the bowling ball thighs. Every so often, we read about how her inherited millions have not made her happy. But every time I see a picture of her, what is she doing? She's on the deck of her yacht, wolfing down figs, baklava, snifters of Metaxa, ordering around a crew of handsome beach boy types.

If she's miserable, then the night scrub lady in this office would gladly trade in her mop and pail for that type of torment.

On the other hand, just go stand outside Union Station or a Loop "L" stop or a factory gate in the morning and study the faces. Grim, grim, grim. You can almost hear the stomach acid eating away at the lining.

Why? Because they're going to work, that's why.

So why do we do it if it is so depressing? The obvious answer is that we have to eat, pay the rent, clothe the kids, feed the cat, cover the bar tab, and put something aside for a good hairpiece in our old age.

But beyond that, we have been taught that it is good to work. Every generation, except that of the flower children, believed it. The Depression generation feared the soup lines. Today's generations fear Sony and Honda.

And we were taught that anybody who didn't work was a bum. (Many Republicans still believe that. Except those who are unemployed.)

It's this dread of being considered a bum that has motivated me to work, without missing a payday, since my fifteenth birthday.

My first job was setting pins in the old Congress

Bowling Alleys on Milwaukee Avenue. I was amazed to find that many of my fellow pinsetters were bums. That's when I discovered that life can be so tough, even bums have to hustle a living.

Later I tried other occupations: working in a screw machine shop, on a loading dock, in a lamp factory, a department store, and behind the bar of a tavern.

These jobs taught me a lesson that I still live by, in work or physical fitness: Don't run if you can walk; don't walk if you can just stand there; don't stand there if you can sit down.

That philosophy led me to my present line of work. It's not that I particularly enjoy chasing news stories, although it can be fun watching a frightened alderman crouch behind his wallet. And it's not that I enjoy writing opinions, since it is much easier to lean on a bar and mumble them instead. The true appeal of this job is that I can do it while I'm sitting. The only thing that would be better would be to find a job I could do while lying down. But hardly anybody, except Hefner, has that kind of luck.

So that's what I've been doing for the past twenty years or so—sitting and avoiding being a bum. To be truthful, I'd rather be doing nothing, leading the life of a boulevardier or a playboy, but that costs a lot.

Until today, I've been doing my sitting at another place about a block from here.

And I was content until this fellow came into town with a large sack of money and decided to buy that place.

As sometimes can happen between boss and employee, we didn't see eye to eye on a few things, so I decided to do my sitting over here.

That doesn't strike me as being any big deal. I would think that any self-respecting, international tycoon would be delighted to get rid of somebody who sits as much as I do.

And if he wants somebody for a sitting job, heck, I know people who are much better at it than I am. My friend Slats once tried for a world record in sitting. And he would have made it, too, if he hadn't become so fatigued that he had to lie down.

Anyway, that's how I landed on this page.

But now this international tycoon's aide says they are going into court to prevent me from doing my daily sitting here.

What a problem. I don't want to do my sitting there. But he doesn't want me to do it here. Can you imagine a guy coming all the way from Australia just to tell me where to sit?

So what option will that leave me? Sitting on a park bench, I suppose. And I wouldn't mind it, but it doesn't pay much, unless you work for Ed Kelly.

Life is strange. All those lousy jobs loading trucks, working in factories, slinging hash, digging holes, and running a punch press—nobody ever said they'd sue to make me stop.

Ah, Rupert, where the hell were you when I needed you?

Pasta's Not Just for the Poor Anymore

January 16, 1984

An invitation from an old friend arrived in the mail.

It said, "You are invited to a pasta party."

I immediately phoned him and said, "Look, I don't know what's going on, but I want to help."

He said: "Good. You can bring some Parmesan or a bottle of red wine."

"I'm serious," I said. "I'm right here. What can I do?"

"OK, you can make the garlic bread," he said.

I said: "Don't be proud. What do you need? A loan? Food? A cosigner? Just name it and you got it. Believe me, the kids will be all right."

He said, "What are you talking about?"

"This," I said. "This pasta thing."

"What about it?" he said. "I just bought a pasta machine. I want to try it out. What do you like? Fettuccine?"

"Level with me," I said. "Have you been fired?"

"I've just been promoted," he said.

"Then you're getting squeezed by your bookie," I said. "Don't panic."

"I don't gamble," he said.

"Look, you can confide in me. What's wrong?"

"I told you. I bought a pasta machine. What do you like? It makes great linguini."

I could tell he was serious. "You bought a pasta machine?"

"Sure. It's the latest thing. Electric. That's why I'm having the party. To try it out."

"But you're not Italian," I said.

"Of course not. If I was Italian, my mother would make pasta for me."

"You really have a pasta machine?"

"Sure. It's right next to my Cuisinart."

"But you don't even live in Lincoln Park. You're from the Southwest Side."

"What has that to do with it?"

Obviously, he was another victim of pasta chic, a craze that has gripped this city and nation.

When Slats Grobnik was a kid, he always knew the old man was having a losing streak at the race track.

"We ate spaghetti every day," he said. "Or macaroni. Or some of those other damned noodles."

If the streak was prolonged—and old man Grobnik had a fondness for horses that ran backward—Slats would start moaning: "The only fresh meat in the house is our dog. And I'm too weak to chase 'im."

It was that way all over the neighborhood. You knew when the paycheck was running out: The noodle appeared. There was no cheaper way to feed a family.

Poverty meant starch. Prosperity meant meat. That's why so many poor people are fat.

But now that has been reversed. Pasta is in. Meat is out. (At least red meat. You are still fashionable if you eat the flesh of a dead fish or chicken.)

It probably began along the lakefront, where most strange trends take root.

Maybe it was a broker who had bet on the wrong pork belly and went broke, causing his wife to face the anguish of canceling a dinner party because she couldn't afford to buy a sirloin tip.

"Let them eat pasta," the broker may have said.

Or maybe it was a jogger, seeking the ultimate carbohydrate high and faced with the rising cost of Adidas shoes.

It might have been an offshoot of Italian chic, which preceded pasta chic. Italian chic happened when Stallone, Pacino, and DeNiro unveiled their pectorals.

Whatever caused it, you can't escape the noodle.

Restaurant owners recognize a good thing when they see it. There was a time when no one except Italians ate pasta. People ate spaghetti. You could get a huge plate of it for about a buck and a half, including meatballs.

No more. Now you go into almost any greasy spoon and they offer a pasta course. Toss forty cents' worth of vegetables into sixty cents' worth of spaghetti, add ten cents' worth of cheese, and somebody puts an eight dollar tag on it.

Worse, it has invaded the home.

There was a time when people invited you over and you ate pot roast, baked chicken, roast beef, or meat loaf—which made the trip worth the price of the gas.

Now you get noodles, covered with olive oil, and powdered garlic.

A friend of Italian ancestry told me:

"I never accept invitations to dinner anymore. I can't stand it. Last week I went to a pal's house. And his wife, who is of Norwegian-Irish ancestry, served linguini with a sauce made of herrings and potatoes."

Incidentally, I did accept the invitation to the pasta party that my friend threw.

But his machine broke down and we sent out for Chinese food.

If There's a Will,
There's a Wimp

January 26, 1984

Because of the growing shortage of docile, obedient, old-fashioned females in this country, a booming import industry is developing.

About eighty firms are now in the business of finding foreign brides for feminist-weary American men, according to the *Wall Street Journal*.

The majority of the mail-order wives are from the Philippines and other Asian countries, where women have not been exposed to the preachings of Gloria Steinem.

Most of the men quoted in the *Journal* story sound pleased to have found wives who are content to be stay-at-homes without charge plates of their very own.

This isn't a surprising development, since many American males have never recovered from the shock of the feminist movement. As a bewildered male friend of mine says, "Gee, most of the women I meet swear a lot more than I do."

But the *Journal* story left unanswered—or even unasked—an intriguing question: What about the modern American woman who might want a docile, obedient mate? After all, that is one of the tenets of feminist thinking: Whatever a man can have, they want, too.

I sought the answer to that question from a strong-willed, independent-minded, liberated, career-oriented female acquaintance.

"That's an interesting question," she said. "To what country would a woman go to find a man who has the same qualities, if you can call them qualities, as those foreign brides? A man who could accept being ordered about, being dependent, and accepting a woman as the stronger, more dominant figure. A man who could not only accept all that, but would consider it to be natural, even desirable. Is that what you're asking?''

Yes, that's it.

"In other words, a wimp."

A cruel word, but probably appropriate.

She thought a while and said: "Well, I'm sure we couldn't get any from the Asiatic countries where these mail-order wives are coming from, because the men in those cultures are accustomed to dominating the women. That's why the women are the way they are.

"And I can't think of any European countries where they would have a large supply of docile men. Certainly not from the Mediterranean countries—Italy, Greece, Spain—where the men are very macho and like to strut about.

"German men are obsessed with giving orders, and Frenchmen all think they should always have at least three women doting on them.

"No, Europe is out, except for the possibility of England. And that only applies to the fops in London.

"We can also forget about the Middle East. The men in some of those countries believe in cutting off a woman's head if she gets out of line.

"And, of course, Latin America is the home of the supermacho man. I think that if they were taller, they might be a little more secure. So, I guess the answer is no. I can't think of any foreign country where we could get men who are the equivalent of those Asiatic brides.''

Ah, then women like you are out of luck.

"No, not at all. We have no need to turn to the import market for that kind of man. American women are very fortunate when it comes to wimps, because we are presently the most richly endowed nation on earth.''

Aren't you being unfair to American men?

"I'm just stating the facts as I find them. And I'm sure we have more wimps per capita than any other country, especially among younger men. Most of the men I meet are wimps.''

But who made them that way? Women like you did,

with your insistence that modern men be sensitive and sharing and caring and that they be willing to cry. No, not willing. Eager to cry. And to talk about their feelings and discuss their problems ad nauseam, to admit that down deep they are weak and fragile creatures. It's women like you who have turned them against John Wayne, the Duke, and made them try to be more like Alan Alda, the wimp.

"That may be true," she said, ending our conversation. "But they didn't have to make it so easy."

I've been thinking about what she said and it occurs to me that those international marriage brokers are missing an obvious business opportunity.

If we do have a surplus of docile, obedient, dependent young men, there might be a market for them overseas among women who are looking for someone with just those attributes.

It might be in countries where women are tired of being pushed around by macho men, just as those American men who seek Asian brides are tired of being pushed around by the new macho American women.

Or it might be in a country like Israel, where the women are tough and serve in the military. Who knows, an Israeli woman might like the idea of importing some sweet young lad from America who would want nothing more than to tidy up around the kibbutz while she's up at the front lines.

If somebody tries this, I'm certain that it will be highly successful.

And it could help this country's economy. It's always good to balance imports and exports.

It could happen—a buy-a-wife, sell-a-wimp program.

If it does, I'm just glad the Duke won't be around to see it.

The City of "Sourful" Souls

February 8, 1984

When I go to New York, I'm always struck by how grim the natives are.

They scowl, they snarl, they seldom smile. Their eyes glare or dart with suspicion. When they aren't scowling or snarling, they are moaning about their troubles.

I've always wondered why they're so miserable. Sure, I realize that living in New York isn't easy. But living in any big city isn't easy. Yet, people in other cities smile. Why, I once heard a man in Detroit actually laugh.

Now I think I have found a clue to the sour personalities of New Yorkers. They are miserable because they prefer being miserable, just as Californians prefer being crazy. It's a conscious choice.

I came to that conclusion as a result of having gone to see a new movie the other night.

It had been a hard day and I didn't want to be depressed. So that left out many of the more popular movies that have to do with broken relationships, teenage ax murderers, and the frustrations of the modern feminist.

The answer seemed to be the new Woody Allen movie, *Broadway Danny Rose,* which Chicago critics said was funny.

And it was funny. The guy on my left spent most of the movie doubled up with laughter. The woman on my right laughed at one gag for so long that she missed the next three gags. The guy in front of me bounced so hard at a joke that he spilled his popcorn.

When the movie ended, most of the audience was grinning. And as they walked out, they were repeating some of the lines and laughing all over again.

The last few days, I mentioned to several friends that I had seen *Broadway Danny Rose*. Those who had seen it agreed that it was hilarious.

But one of them—a former New York person—said: "I hear it isn't very good."

Says who? I asked.

He returned in a few minutes with the current issue of *New Yorker* magazine, which is the favorite magazine of the most sophisticated New Yorkers, and bumpkins who wish they were sophisticated New Yorkers.

"Read Pauline Kael," he said rather smugly, referring to the magazine's film critic, whom many people consider to be the most profound critic in her field. I'm sure she is profound because I almost never understand anything she says.

But I think I understood her this time. She didn't like the movie. She called it "cloying."

Why? Because Woody Allen was trying to make us laugh, that's why. As Kael explained it (the italics are mine):

"In the 1970s, Woody Allen, the first post-Freudian movie comedian, channeled his own anxieties into his clowning. He was the first to use his awareness of his own sexual insecurities as the basis for his humor, and when he turned psychodrama into comedy, he seemed to speak—to joke—for all of us. Moviegoers felt themselves on insiders' terms with the neurotic Woody Allen hero, who reflected their defenses, their feelings of insignificance, their embarrassing aspirations. But the culture has changed: *Woody Allen no longer tells us what we think about ourselves.* A wall has come down between him and us: in *Broadway Danny Rose* . . . he's on the other side, with the rest of the comedy specialists, beating against it, *trying to make us laugh.*"

See what I mean about the grimness of New Yorkers? Here's a comedian who makes a movie with the intention of *trying to make us laugh.* Which is what comedians are supposed to do. If a comedian doesn't make us laugh, he might soon be earning his living slicing corned beef.

But from the perspective of a New York person, he has failed because he *no longer tells us what we think about ourselves.*

No wonder the people in that city are so strange —they have been depending on a neurotic comedian to tell them what they think about themselves.

I don't understand that. How could Woody Allen tell me what I think of myself when we don't even know each other?

And during all these years of watching his movies, I never even realized that I was supposed to learn from him what I think about myself. If I was going to ask anybody what I think about myself, I'd ask myself. Or, if it was late at night, I might ask the bartender.

To be truthful, I hadn't even realized that I was supposed to be on any "insiders' terms" with Allen's neurotic problems, his feelings of insignificance. I really thought he was joking about being goofed up. How could a guy who was Diane Keaton's real-life lover feel insignificant?

But now, if I can believe Kael, it turns out that New Yorkers went to his movies seeking sex therapy and psychological counseling.

If that's true, I'm glad it was Woody Allen who became one of New York's most popular stars and not somebody like Anthony Perkins. I'd hate to think of all those New Yorkers going to see a movie like *Psycho* for guidance on career fulfillment.

All That Money Down the Drain!

March 2, 1984

A fascinating tidbit about Washington high society caught my eye the other day.

It had to do with a spectacular weekend of fancy balls, black tie dinners, parties, and a fashion show luncheon that were attended by the Reagans, top people in government, and hundreds of wealthy industrialists, tycoons, and movie stars. Sort of a Republican rainbow coalition.

Some of them wore such heavy gold objects that they set the Secret Service's metal detectors to howling.

They paid $5,000 a person to attend all the events, less if they wanted to be choosy. But it went to a worthy cause—the Princess Grace Foundation, which will provide arts scholarships.

Actually, this is routine recreation for rich Washington Republicans. They don't go in much for Saturday Night Bingo.

But one fact struck me as unusual. It was tucked down in a story in the *Washington Post*.

It said that at the fashion-luncheon, carnations were sprinkled in the toilet bowls in the ladies room.

When the ladies came in and used the toilet bowls and flushed them, a maid (presumably a Democrat) would scatter more carnations in the bowl.

Naturally, this item set my social conscience to quivering with thoughts of poverty, the jobless, homeless, foodless, and cutbacks in social programs.

In the midst of this suffering, there were all these Republican ladies having flowers scattered, not at their feet as is traditional, but at their. . . . Well, you know.

And what Republican ladies. The guest list included Mr. and Mrs. James Baker, of the White House, Mrs. Alfred Bloomingdale of the New York store, Clare Booth Luce, Mr. and Mrs. Caspar Weinberger, Margaret Heckler, secretary of health and human services (flowers in the can are some human service), and about 120 others.

So I decided to track down the full story and find out why they put carnations in the toilets. I mean, I entertain, too, and I've always thought that Ty-D-Bol, that blue stuff, is pretty classy. And much cheaper. Carnations go for a buck each. And with that many people at the luncheon, if they had weak kidneys it could deplete an entire floral nursery.

Well, it turns out that things are not always as they appear.

A call to the Princess Grace Foundation brought a response from a spokeswoman who was almost trembling with indignation.

She said: "Neither the foundation nor the White House had anything to do with the carnations being put in the toilet bowls."

Then who did it? A volunteer?

"No. It was the hotel's idea. They thought it was a gracious thing to do. But the *Washington Post* didn't mention that. Oh, I could kill the reporter who wrote about the carnations. But that's off the record, of course."

Of course. By the way, have you any idea how many carnations were used?

"How would I know that? You'll have to ask the hotel."

The manager of the Loew's L'Enfant Plaza Hotel, where the luncheon was held, was also oozing indignation.

When he was asked about the flowers, he said:

"You mean my *overkill?* Hmmmph. *That's* what the reporter for the *Washington Post* called it.

"They were also inaccurate. They said we put chopped carnations in the toilet bowls. They were not *chopped*. We used only the petals. We pulled the petals off and dropped them in."

Good grief, that really is irresponsible journalism. But what was the idea in the first place? What's wrong with Ty-D-Bol?

"It is not new. It is a practice we have used for VIPs long before this. We have been doing this for four years. We did it for a reception for the mayor of Washington and for many others."

He was also miffed that the *Post* mentioned that the hotel answered their phones by saying "bonjour" and "bonsoir."

"This hotel has been here for fourteen years, and we

have always answered the phones by saying *bonjour* before 5 P.M. and *bonsoir* after 5 P.M.''

Of course. Who doesn't? But to get back to flowers. How many carnations did you use?

''Oh, I doubt if we used any more than a dozen for that event.''

The luncheon lasted three hours, so those Republican ladies must have the bladders of camels.

''By the way,'' he added, ''we normally use roses. But carnations were Princess Grace's favorite, so we used them instead.''

What a beautiful tribute.

So that's the story. Flowers in toilet bowls are definitely not a regular part of gracious living among Washington Republicans.

But even at one hotel, it does raise a question about sexual discrimination.

If you are going to sprinkle carnation petals in the ladies' toilets, in the spirit of fairness and equality, should there also be something put in the men's urinals?

The trouble is, I can't think of anything appropriate for a man's urinal.

Well, maybe there is something. For all those rich Republicans, how about a five-dollar cigar?

Let Us Pray—Just One Way

March 7, 1984

The issue of school prayer seems to have aroused America's rustics more than its big-city dwellers.

So I called an old friend, Billy Bon Stumpjump, who lives in a town called Pigkick, and asked him why organized prayer in the public schools is so important to him.

''It's like that great patriot Pat Boone says. The

Godless Roosians don't pray in their schools, do they?''

No, I guess they don't.

"Well, just look at what happened to them. They dropped prayin' and first thing you know, they turned into a bunch of Godless communists.''

But Russia became a communist country before its people stopped praying.

"Well, whatever. It's still a dang funny coincidence. And I don't want that happenin' to my children.''

Of course not. But what I don't understand is why the children can't just pray silently in school whenever they feel the urge. Why do you want them all to pray out loud at the same time, when the teacher tells them to.

"Huh, any fool ought to know the answers to that. If the children don't pray out loud, then how do you know they're really prayin'?''

Ah, that makes sense.

"Sure. They might be sittin' there thinkin' about doin' somethin' bad.''

That wouldn't be good.

"Nope, and besides, if they don't pray out loud so we can hear 'em, how'll we know what they're prayin' for?''

Yes, but as long as they're praying, what difference does it make what they're praying for?

"Are you foolin'? It makes a lot of difference. Why, a boy might be sittin' there prayin' that he has his nasty ol' way with the pretty girl sittin' across the aisle.''

But you don't really think that a prayer like that would be granted, do you?

"I hope not, especially if she happens to be prayin' for the same thing.''

I see what you mean.

"Sure. And how do you know some of them might not be prayin' that somebody sells them some of that marijuana. Or that the fellow at the liquor store will think they're old enough to sell 'em a pint of hootch on Saturday night.''

Well, if they pray out loud, what would you want them to pray for?

"Nothin' special. Just one of them general sorts of

prayers. You know, where they just ask that everybody be blessed nice and that they're grateful for everythin' they got, whatever that is.''

That's all?

"Oh, I guess they might throw in somethin' about how they want the school basketball team to beat Turnipville High next week. And that they want everybody blessed, but that maybe conservatives could be blessed a little more than liberals. And that Christians should be blessed more than all of them off-brand religions. And that maybe our kinds of Christians should be blessed a little more than those foreign kinds of Christians. You know, the ones who put garlic in their foods.''

But wouldn't that offend some people.

"Not around here it wouldn't. And, you know, there's another reason for prayin' out loud.''

What's that?

"You ever hear forty kids all talkin' and sayin' different things at the same time, like when the teacher goes out of the room?''

Sure.

"You can't make head nor tail out of what any of them is sayin', ain't that right?''

Absolutely. Just a terrible din.

"So what do you think will happen if you let a whole classroom or a whole school cafeteria or a whole school pray silently and make any kind of prayer they want?''

What would happen?

"Heck, the good Lord wouldn't be able to make sense out of anything any of them were sayin'. It would be just a lot of awful noise, and He wouldn't pay any attention to any of them, and I wouldn't blame Him one bit. With kids prayin' in every school in the whole country, it's gonna be hard enough for Him to sort out one school from another. But if you start lettin' every little bugger pray any way he wants, it'll be nigh impossible to sort them out.''

A very practical consideration. But tell me, why don't you just have your children pray when they get home from school and you can tell them what kind of prayer to use?

"How can I do that? What if I'm bowling or stopping with the boys after work? And after school, there's football practice, or they're goin' to work at the hamburger stand, they're goin' somewhere and doin' somethin'."

What about at dinner.

"You mean at Christmas or Thanksgivin'?"

No, every night.

"Uh, well, we don't always sit down and eat all at the same time."

Then how about when they all finally get home.

"Can't pray then. The TV makes too much noise."

Kind of busy, I guess.

"Sure. That's why the teacher should do it. I mean, she's with 'em a lot more anyway."

I suppose it is convenient.

"That's right. And they'll listen to her. My oldest, he just won't pay any attention to me unless I yell or whop him. I guess I could yell and whop him to pray, but then his mother'll get mad at me. She always does. And then we'd start fightin' and forget about prayin' and that wouldn't do much good. Nope, the teacher should do it."

Maybe you're right.

"By the way, how do the folks up in Chicago feel about prayin' in the schools. Are they for it?"

Oh, we already have prayer in our public schools.

"You do? You mean the students up there pray?"

I don't know about that. But a lot of the teachers do.